Living Well

Living Well

Eight Fundamental Principles for Developing a Healthy Lifestyle

Dale and Kathy Martin

Wolgemuth & Hyatt, Publishers, Inc.
Brentwood, Tennessee

Wolgemuth & Hyatt, Publishers, Inc.
P.O. Box 1941, Brentwood, Tennessee 37027.

Printed in the United States of America.

Library of Congress Cataloging-in-Publication Data

Martin, Dale, 1945-
    Living well.

Bibliography: p.
    1. Health.   2. Health behavior.   3. Nutrition.   4. Cookery
    (Natural Foods)   I. Martin, Kathy, 1949-   II. Title.

RA776.M429   1988   613   88-10628
ISBN 0-943497-07-8

To our precious girls:
Brooklynn Dale and Blair Alexandra,
our most priceless gifts.
May the principles in this book
provide for you a legacy of health.

CONTENTS

ACKNOWLEDGMENTS

Even though only six months of our lives were spent actually writing *Living Well*, the roots of its creation span many years. Without the help and influence of countless friends, this book would have been an impossibility.

Thanks to our parents Lyndon and Lillian Davis, and Herschel and Thelma Martin, who provided warm, caring environments to nuture our inquiring minds.

Thanks to Warren Peters, M.D., Gayle Wilson, M.D., and John Goley, D.H.Sc. for the unselfish sharing of their resources and insights regarding principles of health.

Thanks to Kathy's brother, Greg Davis, M.D., who reviewed the manuscript and offered several valuable suggestions.

Thanks to Marcella Lynch, Preston and Jeanne Wallace, Janet Spickard, and Patty LaVanture for their friendship and countless creative ideas in the kitchen.

Thanks to friends Dick and Lorena Mayer for their friendship and support.

Thanks to Colin Standish, who for years encouraged Dale to write.

Thanks to a special friend, Peter Jenkins, for his editorial advice and suggestions, as well as for sharing his great knowledge of the publishing industry.

Thanks to Barbara Jenkins for her hospitality during the writing of this book and for her encouraging words about the benefits of this program in her own life.

Thanks to our talented editor, George Grant, who truly knows how to temper his toughness with compassion.

Thanks to our publishers, Robert Wolgemuth and Michael Hyatt, for their belief in us and our ideas. Their commitment to this work has been first-class, deluxe in every way. We would also like to mention their wives, Bobbie Wolgemuth and Gail Hyatt, whose friendship and support we will always remember.

Finally, and most importantly, we wish to thank our God for revealing His instruction for a lifestyle that not only optimizes our physical health but our spiritual worship as well.

INTRODUCTION

Do we really need another book on health and fitness? Do we really have the time to read another book on the subject? Do we really want to put ourselves through the mill one more time for another fad diet that probably won't work?

Probably not.

If you're like most Americans you've already got a stack of health and nutrition books scattered around the house—a couple spotted and stained back behind the cookbooks in the kitchen, a couple more gathering dust on the bookshelf in the den, and one or two others stashed away in the bedroom closet right next to the jogging suit and the tennis racket. You've probably tried countless times to prove to your family, your friends, and even yourself, that you can get control over your body and your health. You've probably tried to lower your cholesterol—whatever that is. You've probably tried to drop your extra pounds—and your extra inches. You've probably tried to increase your stamina, strengthen your resistance, and firm up your figure. And you've probably found that sticking to a healthy regimen of diet and exercise to accomplish all those goals is easy—just like quitting smoking: you've done it a hundred times. For a day or two.

So, what makes our book any different? Why should you expect any better results, any more consistency, or any higher satisfaction with our plan?

Well, first off, this book was born out of *our own* frustration with the confusing array of diets, programs, systems, and gimmicks that toss the American marketplace to and fro on alternate waves of doubt and guilt and despair. We began to search for a sound and sensible approach to good health and found that we had to first push aside mountains of advertising hype, medical bias, and thousands of off-the-wall fringe diets—more hocus pocus than even the witches of Macbeth were able to conjure up. We also discovered that although Americans spend almost a billion dollars every single day of the year for health care, only three percent of that is used for prevention. The other ninety-seven percent goes to cover the astronomical costs of treating the symptoms of a very sick nation. Too little too late.

Undeterred though, we pressed on. We were sure that there was a better way. And we were determined to find it. We read. We researched. We tried recipes. We went through several ups and downs.

Finally, we were able to hammer out a realistic plan. A plan that made us look better, feel better, and live better. A plan that helped us to discover the remarkable freedom and abounding blessing of genuine health. It is a plan based on our own real-life experiences. It isn't just theory. It isn't just ideas and concepts. It isn't just one more in the long line of fads and fancies. It is a livable, *do*able lifestyle. The plan that we have put together is a lifestyle that we ourselves have lived. It is a lifestyle that our children have lived. It is a lifestyle that hundreds of students from our classes, lectures, and seminars have lived. And now, it is a lifestyle that *you* can live. Because that is what this book helps you do. By implementing eight basic principles in just five weeks time you too can look better, feel better, and live better. You too can discover the joy of good health, nutritional balance, physical fitness, and spiritual satisfaction. You too can begin the wonderful adventure of *Living Well*.

That is why this book really is different. And that is why we firmly believe that this is *not* just another book on health and fitness.

The first section of the book will give you a glimpse of just what the problem is—both with the standard American diet (known in some circles as SAD), and with most of the proposals designed to remedy that diet. We'll cover the root causes of many of our most devastating health crises including heart disease, cancer, diabetes, and even immunological disorders like AIDS.

In the second section you'll walk through the eight basic principles of health that we've discovered—water, rest, fresh air, sunshine, exercise, nutrition, self-control, and personal faith.

And you'll see how to put those principles to work in your life in a simple and straightforward five-week plan.

In the last section you'll learn some fundamentals about food, nutrition, and cooking that have made our healthy lifestyle easier to live. And then you'll discover some of our favorite recipes.

By the time you turn to the last page of the book, we're quite confident that you will have launched yourself and your family on an exciting venture of *Living Well*.

PART ONE

UNDERSTANDING THE REAL PROBLEM

THE HEART OF
THE MATTER

Let's get one thing straight from the top. The book in your hands is not another diet book. If anything, it is one of the few "anti-diet" books to be found in the market.

Why "anti-diet?" Because the very word "dieting" implies a taking away or a withholding of something good from an unfortunate individual who must endure all these misfortunes for a pre-set time. By implication, the word "dieting" also implies that this unfortunate happening will occur many times in the course of this person's life, almost as though it were one of the months of the year, i.e., January, February, March, Diet, April, May, June, Diet, July, August, September, October, November, Diet, December, Diet, Diet, Diet, etc.

In direct contrast, *Living Well* presents a rationale for what is becoming known as a "lifestyle" change, implying first that an individual will actually re-focus his entire concept of what constitutes total health, and second, that the word "diet" is truly a four-letter word to be stricken from one's vocabulary and from one's life.

But in this complex day and age, how do we arrive at a simplistic view of health? Thanks to our computerized and frenetic all-American approach to living, life in the United States somehow generates complex solutions to what would often appear to be simple problems. In other words, all too often medical science attacks health problems with the reasoning of a NASA scientist attempting to solve the problems in the Challenger shuttle system by merely repairing what broke: namely, coronary bypass surgery.

Quite simply, the long term solution is not only to fix the problem but to ensure that quality control steps are implemented which would PREVENT the problems altogether, or at least maximize lowering the risk of future problems developing.

So, if this book were to have a title that might reflect such a scientific approach to problem solving, it would be captioned "How to Develop a Quality Control Plan for Your Health." The philosophy contained in *Living Well* is not just born of a need to prevent disease, but rather of a desire to enhance the most valuable of all our resources: our health.

A major problem facing many of us is that our health is held together by the bailing wire of what might be called "pop" health: prescriptions, operations, and promises. The "prescription" is the quick fix that most often treats the symptom while ignoring the common cause—the lifestyle. "Operations" are those often necessary invasive procedures which repair damaged body parts or replace them with less than original equipment. And finally, "promises" are continually headlined throughout the media that a cure for the result of our poor choices is just over the next horizon.

But Americans will never be able to circumvent the cause-and-effect principle of "you reap what you sow." That is a law as sure as gravity.

Getting America's Health Into Focus

Summers are scorchers in Texas. And so can be the falls, especially when the days are filled with twenty-five to thirty sweaty little bodies, jockeying among themselves to be first in line for the water fountain following a hard work-out on the school playground. And particularly when twenty-five to thirty pairs of eyes focus on a male teacher for the first time in their four years of school.

Calling the roll, I can remember that special smile, even though fifteen summers have since steamed past my memory. Sweet beyond description. And her honey-brown hair lofted delicately by a wide red ribbon. Yes, and the hands, folded neatly on her desk. A teacher's pride and joy.

But it was something in her eyes, those mirrors to the heart. Tahoe-blue they were, and deep reflections of the naturally uninhibited nature of a child. Yet looking into her upturned face, I discovered another dimension, a reflection that belied the beauty and innocence of childhood, a reflection often well-hidden by adults but rarely so by children, a reflection of pain.

Pain is never a welcome guest, but especially do we resent its intrusion into the lives of our children. In Julie's case, this uninvited intruder had settled in the form of rheumatoid arthritis, forcing her youthful nine years to assume the maturity of an adult in order to cope with this ever-present boarder.

When we compare America with other first-world countries, she, like Julie, is truly a reflection of the innocent school-age child, possessed of unbounded idealism, lovely to behold, and filled to the brim with enthusiasm and talent. Yet when we focus on the soul spirit of America, the "can do" attitude that appears so appealing, we begin to see a new inner dimension of pain and suffering that conflicts dramatically with the brilliant exterior we so often view.

Rightfully so, we applauded the entrepreneurial spirit (not the product, please) of a Ray Kroc that parlays a small investment in a fast food restaurant in San Bernardino, California, into a multi-billion dollar enterprise. But along the way we have failed to ask the question of the fast food industry, "What is your marketing of convenience going to cost us in terms of health?"

Surely there must be a strong correlation between the exponential rise of fast "junk" food consumption over the past twenty years and a 50 percent increase in the number of overweight and obese children. Of course there are other factors involved, including more sedentary time in front of television and a growing number of latch-key kids. Nevertheless, Americans seem slow, if not paralyzed, in asking questions regarding factors which negatively impact their health. Why is this?

One of the more logical answers to this question is unquestionably America's idealistic "can do" attitude that places an unreasonable trust in the ability of medical science to bail us out of our dilemmas of pain and suffering. Therefore, the challenging objective of this book is to convince the reader to gain control of his health by making intelligent, educated choices that will result in a quality of lifestyle heretofore experienced by too few Americans. In addition, the *Living Well* program is designed to help America live up to her image as a health conscious nation, as opposed to one whose health consciousness is skewed to the

side of restoring health primarily through patchwork efforts
rather than preventing disease and enhancing good health
through thoughtful, educated choices.

What You'll Discover

For example, you will discover why the average American
only absorbs 20 to 30 percent of his intake of dietary calcium
while in other cultures people absorb as much as 70 to 80 percent
of their daily ingestion of calcium. Consequently, you will see
why our calcium deficiency problem in this country is actually
based on faulty reasoning rather than too little calcium intake.

Using research as a basis, we will show you that the average
American is eating more than twice his daily need of protein
and is consequently damaging his body with these excess
amounts of protein.

The role that adequate pure water plays in promoting good
health and higher energy levels will undoubtedly surprise you,
especially in light of the simplicity and effectiveness of the suggested program. You will also learn from both example and
research exactly what your "Americanized" habits of daily living
are doing to weaken your body's ability to fight off a whole host
of ailments, including the "famous four" lifestyle diseases (as well
as many others) that are so prevalent in the 80's: heart disease,
cancer, diabetes, and immune system disorders.

But most important, you'll discover how simple it can be to
implement the health habits outlined in this book. Good health,
according to the *Living Well* program, is a simple yet comprehensive lifestyle that emphasizes a balanced philosophy that is
lifelong in its impact.

Good Health Witnesses

The question that every thinking reader will ask is "Will the
Living Well lifestyle work for me?" Based on our personal experience and our knowledge of hundreds of others, the answer is an
unequivocal yes!

We have been growing into the *Living Well* lifestyle for several years now. Dale has replaced some twenty-five pounds with
a higher degree of fitness. While never having had a weight
problem, Kathy has found her problem with allergies much

more manageable since becoming an active participant in the *Living Well* lifestyle. For both of us, our level of energy and fitness has given us an increased vitality that is no match for the way we felt ten and even fifteen years ago.

To be sure, there are days that we miss our exercise or find ourselves making less than ideal nutritional choices. But remember, like character, a lifestyle is developed, not by the occasional good deed or the occasional misdeed, but rather by the direction in which we are headed. Without question *Living Well* will point you in the right direction. Literally thousands of individuals have learned to live these principles at health conditioning centers such as Hartland Health Center in Rapidan, Virginia, and the Weimar Newstart Program in Weimar, California. You, too, can begin to experience the same benefits at your own pace both at home and in the work place.

And don't forget the children. As we are, to a large degree, products of our environment, so are our children. Our daughters, Brooklyn and Blair have been two excellent motivators for us to live our lives according to principle rather than inclination. Good health habits bequeathed to our children will significantly assist their ability to have a positive impact on society.

Remember, *Living Well* is not just another health book. It's an invitation to live well. Forever.

THE REAL
BIG MAC ATTACK

"Susan! SUSAN! My arm! Someone is stabbing my arm!"

Instantly awake in the somber-black of the night, Susan shook her husband, trying to calm him. "Carlton, are you dreaming? Wake up! Please wake up!"

"No! Susan! This pain is . . . is alive . . . It's ripping down my left arm! I can't move my arm!" Carlton's screams of pain were mixed with crying. "I'm only thirty-eight! It can't be a heart attack!"

Frigid with fright, Susan fumbled in the crushing darkness. Horrifying images pounded her temples and competed with Carlton's cries as she knocked over the lamp in a desperate attempt to stop the confusion of screams and shadowy forms invading the black room. Grasping the phone as a drowning victim grasps a buoy, she pressed the digits . . . 9 . . . 1 . . . 1 . . . . Her fingers moved, it seemed, in slow motion. She couldn't make a mistake. There wasn't time to make a mistake.

"Emergency operator. May I help you?"

A voice in the darkness. A voice able to help. Susan's words were breathless. Relief at reaching someone almost made her pass out.

Suddenly the room was seared with light. Carrie, still clutching her pillow, had located the wall switch.

"Daddy! Daddy!" Their nine-year-old daughter's screams mixed with Carlton's anguished cries as she ran to him in helplessness.

"Carrie, I . . . I'm going to be okay. I'm . . ." Another round of pain creased Carlton's face, thrusting his head back and suffocating his efforts to talk. Carrie fell beside the bed on her knees, her face buried in her pillow.

Susan, throwing on a robe and calling for Evan, their seven-year old son, was resolute with activity. "Quick, Carrie, get dressed. Get Evan. Get ready!"

In less than ten minutes the house was alive with activity. EMTs hooked a pale Carlton to an oxygen supply. In a blur of motion, someone relayed vital signs: "Pulse, weak and irregular; blood pressure, 70/50; patient complaining of dizziness."

The neon blue of the emergency room sign was like the welcoming marquee of a hotel for the weary. As the sirens slowly unwound, their death-defying shrieks growing silent, white coated attendants pried open the doors and glided an unrecognizable Carlton into a pristine room, fitted with tanks, hoses, and enough instrumentation to delay death itself.

Sometimes.

Carlton Samms happened to be one of the lucky ones. Millions over the next few years won't remember the sirens and the suffering, the needles and the nausea, the antiseptic and the anguish. Remembering is the job assigned to their loved ones and friends.

At the current rate, over fifty percent of all American men will die of cardiovascular disease. Each calendar year, a total of 540,000 deaths result from coronary heart disease alone.[1] And that doesn't take into account additional damage done in the form of strokes, kidney disease, and other arterial diseases.

Seventy-five percent of all American men aged twenty-two to forty-five have coronary atherosclerosis, while some sixty-five percent of women have cholesterol levels that put them into the higher risk category.[2] Dr. Bogdenoff of Cornell University has stated that "probably no other disease in the history of humanity has affected so many individuals in any one calendar year, including the peak years of the black death in the fourteenth and seventeenth centuries."[3]

Costs for this plague upon humanity are phenomenal. Some sixty million patient visits a year yield a total medical bill of more than sixty billion dollars. That doesn't reflect either the lost earnings—more than 100 billion dollars for 1986 alone[4]—or the lost productivity of future years for those who are stricken in the prime of life.

Toying with heart disease is more dangerous than trying to cross the Santa Monica freeway on foot at 5:00 P.M.

Could it happen to you? Are you kidding? Do you live in America? Preventable heart and blood diseases kill more in one year than the combined number of American victims from World War I (116,000), World War II (405,000), the Korean War (54,000) and the Vietnam War (57,000).[5] One in every two people will become the forgotten POW's of this massive and debilitating conflict. One and a half million will be taken hostage this year alone in the form of a heart attack. An incredible 350,000 will never even make it alive to the hospital to warn others of the absolute agony of heart failure, while another 155,000 will forfeit their lives to an insidious revolutionary known as stroke.[6]

Intima Damage

According to the American Heart Association, the single biggest cause of heart and blood vessel diseases is atherosclerosis.[7] While most people would define "atherosclerosis" as "hardening of the arteries," this expression is only partially correct. "Athero" means "mushy," in contrast to "sclerosis," which means "hard." A good way to picture the progress of this disease is to imagine freshly poured cement. At first it is viscous and relatively easy to work with, but after setting over a period of time, the cement hardens, becoming impossible to reconstruct and difficult to move.

Visualizing the physiology of this killer disease makes the factors that cause it easier to understand.[8] The inner layer of the artery is called the intima. It is so smooth that if it were compared with the slickest teflon under an electron microscope, the teflon would resemble a chainsaw blade by contrast. It is when the cells which make up the surface of the intima begin to separate that problems first occur. There are approximately nine factors, most of which are a result of enjoying the "good life" in America, which may cause damage to these little cells, consequently setting the stage for atherosclerosis.

The first factor is decreased oxygen, primarily from smoking. As most of us are aware, smoking releases significant amounts of carbon monoxide into the blood which the body must expel. So the hemoglobin, the little red blood cells designated to carry oxygen, are recruited to remove the toxic cells. As a result, they can't carry as much oxygen. This lack of ready oxygen causes the fragile intima cells to begin to separate. It is interesting to note that there are some 4,000 other chemicals released by tobacco smoke which also cause damage.[9]

A second problem that damages the minuscule cells of the intima is high blood pressure.[10] We've all heard that almost everyone is eating too much salt—usually three, four, or even five times the recommended amount. Ingested salt must be suspended in water (a drop of water per grain of salt), thus when we overdose on this additive, our blood volume has to increase to accommodate all the extra water to hold the extra salt. The increased volume of our blood then puts more pressure on the inner lining of the artery, the intima, and causes the cells to begin to separate.[11]

Interestingly enough, a third cause is a high protein diet. The wastes, or by-products, of a diet high in protein include ammonia. This chemical wreaks havoc on the helpless little cells lining our arteries.[12] Those of us who frequent health food stores should not be taken in by articles written in "free handout issues" given at the check out stand advising highly active people to double their recommended daily allowance of protein. Especially when the adjacent page carries an ad for protein supplements. It is better to listen to the unbiased: the American Heart Association. Advice from its literature states that "the protein needs of both sedentary and active people are the same. A football player has about the same protein requirements as a clerk of the same size."[13]

Number four on the list is the use of caffeine. Regarding our passion for caffeinated drinks, few of us think beyond the fact that caffeine is a stimulant. But medical textbooks classify stimulants as drugs,[14] and caffeine is one drug that wreaks havoc on the intima.

Diabetes is a fifth condition that causes damage to the intima. This is attested by the fact that eighty percent of all diabetics die from atherosclerosis.[15]

In view of recent campaigns sponsored by the American Dairy Association to promote their fortified products, it is especially interesting to note that excess Vitamin D is another factor in causing damage to the lining of the arteries. Due to the love affair of most Americans with dairy products, the average person in this country has over six times the recommended dose of Vitamin D in his tissues. Much of this vitamin is already rendered inactive by processing and consequently ends up intensifying the atherosclerotic process. If we're concerned about our levels of Vitamin D in the body, a thirty minute walk in the sun can give us all we need for the day.[16]

The seventh factor responsible for intima damage is oxidized cholesterol. The word "oxidize" simply means that oxygen has been attached to something. When oxygen attaches itself to pure cholesterol, which it does fairly rapidly at room temperature, over one hundred products of this combination are produced, all of which cause damage to the arteries. Most of us would be surprised to learn that the worst culprit in hiding large amounts of oxidized cholesterol is pancake mix. The milk and eggs are dried in the presence of oxygen. Thus most of the cholesterol is oxidized, resulting in an almost lethal mixture.[17]

An eighth factor is frequent viral infections. This fact should help us realize that a healthy immune system is important for fighting off more than just the AIDS and cancer viruses.[18]

Finally, in the presence of a previous build-up of cholesterol in the arterial wall, casein and sugar are the worst known causes of atherosclerosis known. Casein is milk protein, and most of us would have little trouble guessing the foremost combination of milk and sugar: ice cream.[19]

If we examine the nine factors that most often damage the cell wall, it is encouraging to note that almost all of them are within the realm of our daily choices. However, in time, damage is not to blame for the statistics on heart disease. It is in the ensuing "sclerosis," or hardening, that Americans find themselves in trouble.

Decreasing Diameters

Our bodies are marvelous sustainers of life. When damage occurs to the intima from one of the multiple factors listed, there is an immediate response to try to heal that damage. We might say that cholesterol is the unwanted Florence Nightingale of the bloodstream. When the intima cells need repair, this waxy little friend floats along and covers the cells of the smooth intima which have separated, just like a bandage. In doing so, it also slips into the layer underneath called the muscularis.

Because this addition of cholesterol is an irritant to the cells below, they begin to bulge up into the artery. As this mass expands, it eventually outgrows its blood supply and undergoes necrosis. In other words, the tissue dies. Calcium is then brought in to harden this mass. From this picture the meaning of the prefix "athero" in atherosclerosis should be evident. The soft tissue is turned into calcified deposits.[20]

This process continues until there is little space for blood to circulate. The victim becomes a prime candidate for the agony of myocardial infarction that Carlton Samms suffered, or any of the other confederates of heart disease, including angina, strokes, kidney failure, and numerous other problems.

Interestingly enough, our bodies would actually repair the damage done to the arterial walls without the atherosclerotic buildup if our cholesterol levels were kept to a minimum. The 1984 National Institutes of Health Consensus Conference raised this issue: "Does deposit really make any difference in atherosclerosis?" The consensus was that cholesterol, or deposit, which includes saturated fat, is the bottom line.[21]

So what role do fats and cholesterol play in contributing to buildup, or atherosclerosis? A very interesting one, in fact. First, we should note that cholesterol comes exclusively from animal sources such as eggs, meat, cheese, and milk. So do saturated fats with the exclusion of avocados, coconut oil, and palm oil. (But these plant sources of saturated fat are at least more digestible than the animal sources because of their shorter fatty acid chains.) Next, we need to understand that about twenty percent of this cholesterol problem comes from saturated fats, or fats that remain solid at room temperature. Here's how.

When we eat the typical American high-fat diet, our digestive systems have a problem in dealing with these saturated fats. Because it is impossible for the body to dump these types of fats directly into the blood stream, they are moved through the intestinal wall into the lymph channels. Then the body actually makes its own cholesterol to keep the fat soluble — that is, to keep it floating and moving through the system. Eating saturated fat in any form actually forces our bodies to produce cholesterol. As we increase our total fat intake of all kinds, we program our bodies for the production of cholesterol.

Some years ago the average American consumed about 1,000 milligrams of cholesterol a day. But thanks to intensified media coverage of heart disease, that average is now down to about 600 milligrams of cholesterol a day. And fortunately, we absorb only about half that amount. But with our typical high fat diet, where about forty-five percent of the calories come from fat, our bodies are forced to manufacture another 900 milligrams of cholesterol just to process all the fat. This is too much for our bodies to handle. While we must have cholesterol for processing fat, we don't need one milligram from outside sources.[22] And because atherosclerosis and hypertension are often found to be co-conspirators within the body, a lower intake of dietary fat may be not only protective against atherosclerosis but also helpful in controlling blood pressure.[23]

Fixing the Dump Trucks

Many people are confused as to why two people can eat virtually the same diet and one succumb to coronary heart disease while the other doesn't. The reason is that other factors such as exercise and heredity play an important role in this life and death issue.

There are two particular by-products of cholesterol known as HDL and LDL. HDL, or high density lipoproteins, are the "good guys." LDL, or low density lipoproteins, are the "bad guys." Most of the cholesterol that is measured in the laboratory is LDL, which does the real damage.

An analogy in reference to these two types of cholesterol will perhaps help us to understand their role in this story of heart disease. Try to think of LDL as garbage to be dumped and HDL as little dump trucks. The HDL is eager to pick up the LDL refuse out of the blood and the artery walls as quickly as possible, then carry it to the liver to be unloaded there.

At this point things can get complicated. If the HDL is low while the LDL is high, that means that there are too few dump trucks to do the work. But exercise "builds" more dump trucks.

So it would seem reasonable to assume that we could basically eat what we want so long as we take up the slack with exercise.

Indeed, that is precisely what Jim Fixx thought. He was the author of *The Complete Book of Running*, and one of the gurus of running back in the 1970's. He ran an average of some ten miles a day and looked like a greyhound, yet he dropped dead in his early fifties from heart disease caused by atherosclerosis. No doubt his exercise habits had produced plenty of HDL to pick up the LDL. Unfortunately for him, there is a third critical factor involved: the efficiency of the liver at receiving the LDL cholesterol to be dumped.

The liver has little receptors which function like loading docks at a warehouse, but the high fat diet of Americans causes these loading docks to shut down. In fact, the average American has about fifty percent of these LDL warehouse trash receptacles closed by age forty. Simply put, that means that we can have an immense fleet of HDL dump trucks, which Jim Fixx undoubtedly had, and still not have sufficient receptor sites for the trucks to dump their load of LDL.

In spite of his exercise habits, Jim continued to eat a diet high in fat, thus contributing to the shut-down of the LDL liver receptor sites. In addition, he had a history of heart disease in his family. It's no wonder that people everywhere, both healthy and otherwise, were confused by his death.

Tests in laboratory animals have shown that once these liver receptor sites are closed by a diet high in saturated fats, they stay closed for the next two and three generations. Jim Fixx's father died of heart disease at a relatively young age. Jim himself was obese and a heavy smoker until his late thirties. Consequently, with his history, Jim's best hope was to carefully watch his diet (which he did not do) to enable his HDL dump trucks to pick up the excess LDL cholesterol which already had been deposited by his former lifestyle. Even though Jim may have extended his life by exercise, we must remember that what we eat is equally, if not more, important.[24]

However, recent studies related to human angiograms show that atherosclerosis is reversible. Three major factors that play a role in reversing this disease are stopping smoking, reducing cholesterol intake, and exercising.[25]

Fiber: The Tie That Binds

Dietary fiber also plays an important role in reducing the risk for heart disease. Our liver uses about seventy-five percent of the cholesterol in the body to manufacture bile to use in the digestive process. This bile is then stored in the gall bladder until the small intestine calls for it. When fat is present in the small intestine, it must be emulsified, or broken down into smaller particles, before it can be properly digested. This is the work of the bile.

The bad news is that after the bile has done its work, it is sent on to the large intestine. In the typical American diet, ninety-eight percent of the cholesterol that was used in the formation of that bile is reabsorbed into the body.

The good news, however, is that certain kinds of fibers greatly decrease the reabsorption of that cholesterol by binding it and carrying it out of the body in the elimination process. Oats and legumes (any pea or bean that comes from a pod) have a type of fiber that appears to be the most effective in helping the large intestine flush out the unwanted cholesterol.[26]

Damage Versus Deposit

The American Heart Association ranks smoking and high blood pressure as two of the top three risk factors for coronary heart disease. Yet if there is no deposit factor in the form of cholesterol, then a damaged artery will normally heal itself. According to research by Dr. Jeremiah Stamler, a world-renowned nutritionist at Northwestern University, "Data from both human and animal studies indicate that high blood pressure and cigarette smoking are minimally significant in the absence of the nutritional metabolic prerequisites for atherogenesis."[27]

In other words, high blood pressure and smoking both create damage as it relates to atherosclerosis, but there must be excessive levels of LDL for the bandage of cholesterol to be applied and for the deposits to continue to build over the years.

For all the millions of Americans suffering the ravages of heart disease — most of them through their own choices — the solution is obvious.

One of The Few

Al Thomas was dying. No one could deny that. Not when they watched him attempt a flight of stairs. Or walk across the street to the parking lot. Not when they saw the agony of endless pain beaded across his face. Especially not when they looked into his eyes for more than a moment.

Sally had known it first, as most women know when the men they love begin slipping away bit by bit. Through all the mysterious aching, breathlessness, incredible pain, and confusing medical reports, she had known. And pretending she knew nothing was beginning to take its toll.

Allison knew, too. Her mother's smile was different. Not alive, as before, but always framing her face, always ready to mask the glint of truth from her eyes as she looked into her daughter's.

All those best kept secrets whispering throughout the house pushed Al to the outer limits of prevention. He cut out salt, he reduced his protein intake to the minimum. Caffeine, dairy products, sugar, fat — what were those to him now?[28] He relished whole grains, fresh fruits, vegetables, all the good and necessary foods. Alcohol? Cigarettes? He hadn't touched them ever. But exercise. Why wouldn't his heart let him exercise? Why wouldn't his heart let him walk to the mailbox and back without gripping him with such intensity that even he told lies about the extent of his condition?

A virus, they called it, a virus that had attacked his heart. A virus was squeezing the very life out of him, making him reckless, making him despair of ever savoring another moment without pain. A most unusual occurrence in view of his conservative lifestyle to be sure, but it was a reality, nevertheless.

He didn't remember the first time "heart transplant" settled into his mind as an option. But he did remember the day, the very hour, when the full responsibility heaved itself upon him. At what point in time does one begin wishing for the death of another, he had wondered, to salvage a life and a family?

And so it was that a seventeen year-old boy with multiple head injuries removed Al from the top of the list it had taken him months to climb. A new heart. A new life, albeit a life filled with immuno-suppressant drugs. A new hope. Maybe time would, after all, start over again for Al Thomas at the age of thirty-five.

Healing Through Prevention

The story of Al Thomas' heart disease is tragic in light of millions who suffer needlessly from the more common spawnings of this killer disease. Unfortunately, a majority of the heart disease sufferers trust in their pills, wait for the latest pharmacological breakthrough, or simply, blindly, and confidently allow surgeons' knives to search their torn hearts in an effort of "bypass salvage."

But more and more compassionate and rational physicians seem to agree with Washington University Cardiologist Thomas Preston that surgery is not the best alternative for most severe heart disease cases. According to Preston, fully half of the bypass operations performed are unnecessary and the net effect of this surgery on the nation's health is "probably negative."[29] This is a strong indictment against a procedure that can lift as much as $25,000 from a victim's pocket.

Yet for those willing to take preventive steps, the future is brighter. We must keep in mind that this awesome killer disease can be seized and quarantined. For persons under sixty-five, heart attacks are ninety percent preventable.[30] Likewise, heart disease is preventable and/or reversible ninety percent of the time.[31] An editorial in the *Journal of the American Medical Association* states that a total plant diet can prevent ninety-seven percent of all coronary occlusions.[32] Probably the most forceful voice to urge prevention as the major means of controlling heart disease was the Consensus Conference on Lowering Blood Cholesterol. Its report asserted that the first step in prevention is diet therapy.[33]

If, in our mind's eye, we visualize some sort of radical vegetarian with all manner of vitamin deficiencies, then we should consider that the average American is no candidate for the "health hall of fame" either. Many of us don't really have a good concept of what constitutes a balanced diet, especially as a total vegetarian. But if the percentage of unhealthy vegetarians were as great as the percentage of unhealthy Americans on the average diet, there would be sweeping recommendations to educate those unhealthy vegetarians to pile on the meat and dairy products. If the opposite recommendations are becoming more common, it is because our "average" diet needs reforming.

What major habits are in need of reform? Consider the list below, which summarizes the factors which help prevent and heal atherosclerosis: (1) Decrease the damage factors to cell intimas; (2) Decrease the intake of saturated fat, which would cause less cholesterol to be made by the body; (3) Decrease the total intake of cholesterol to 100 milligrams per day or less; (4) Mobilize the HDL in the body to get rid of the LDL; that is, increase the presence of HDL primarily through exercise; (5) Decrease total fats to help open the liver receptor sites; and (6) Increase the intake of fiber to bind significant amounts of cholesterol and move it out of the body.

Over sixty-three million people suffer from some form of heart disease. That is one person in four.[34] It should be a pleasure and a privilege to do whatever we can to remove ourselves from this statistical suffering and death, whatever the cost of change. Carlton Samms would agree. And Al Thomas, if he lives, would too.

THE BIG SLOWDOWN
TO COLON CANCER

"This rice looks dirty," Michael Austin fretted, wrinkling his forehead as he helped himself, cautiously, from the serving dish. "What's on it anyway?"

"Nothing, honey. Just thought I'd try a whole grain for a change. It's simply called 'brown rice.'" His wife Karina was cheerful.

"What do you mean, 'whole grain'? The rice we've always eaten in the past seemed pretty whole to me. This stuff has pieces that look like thin shells in it." Michael eyed the food particles on his fork closely.

"Michael, that's the bran. It keeps you regular." Karina slid a forkful into her mouth.

"Mom," Their teenage daughter Shane objected loudly. "Do we have to talk about it at the table?"

"If you don't mind, I prefer my rice clean." Michael pushed the rice to a far corner, as if expecting it to contaminate the remainder of the contents on his dinner plate.

"Come on, Dad, you haven't even tried it," coaxed his son Jonathan, grinning. "Remember, you used to tell me how important it was to be a member of the 'clean plate club'?"

Karina explained. "I just saw it at the store and thought we'd give it a try. Anyway, you've got to think about your history, Michael, with your dad dying of cancer of the colon, and then your brother last year from the same thing."

"Aw, Karina, there's scant chance that those cancers could have been prevented by brown rice. I never dreamed such questionable logic could escape your gray matter!" Michael was determined to prove his point.

We Are What We Eat

Regardless of how popular this scene has become in American households, facts are now surfacing from nation- and worldwide studies that indicate we are, indeed, what we eat. A recent study from the National Academy of Sciences on diet, nutrition, and cancer states that, contrary to the fast-food mentality, what we eat does affect our health.[1]

Forty million ex-smokers in the United States today are a testimony that Americans can and will adjust their lifestyles based on evidence.[2] Cancer of the colon looms directly behind lung cancer as the second-ranking, up and coming, cancer in this country.[3] Yet Americans, for the most part, have been unable to recognize the cause and effect relationship between eating the typical American diet and suffering the all-American ailments, many of them terminal. Instead, thanks to heady advertising campaigns from the American Dairy Association, the American Beef Council, and the like, Americans are convinced that dietary choices really are not proven contributors. Consequently, the role of heredity in an individual's destiny is regarded as the unchangeable culprit. But the fact that sixty thousand deaths result from cancer of the colon every year—preceded by countless mutilating surgeries, debilitating chemotherapy treatments, and a host of side effects, not to mention astronomical medical fees—make a case for taking another look.[4]

Why is it that countries in Africa have little or no incidence of this insidious disease? In the seventies, Dr. Dennis Burkitt gave ample evidence of major dietary differences in those countries as contrasted to the United States, concluding that diet was a major contributing factor for our high incidence of colon cancer.[5] In other words, environment—our choices—can and do make a difference.

Your Food Dollar

Of the thousands of available packaged food items on the grocery shelves, as many as ninety percent have been refined to some degree. Restaurants are not much more help, either, in promoting healthy eating habits. What ordinary eating establishment will risk losing your business by placing a scoop of brown rice or mashed potatoes cooked in the jackets on your plate? When was the last time your dinner was accompanied by whole wheat rolls? How many ordinary Americans (not to mention restaurant chefs) have even the faintest conception of what "legumes" are? And isn't it fun trying to eat vegetarian and grease-free in a fast food restaurant these days (let's face it, salad bars have peaked)? Yet Americans, by their choices, are literally eating themselves to death.

What are the food choices of the average American? Consider a dietary day in the life of Michael Austin, our friend who suspiciously refused his wife's attempt at bettering his diet.

One Day in the Life . . .

"Where did I put that alarm clock?" moaned an incoherent Michael, as the insistent clanging dragged consciousness into the dark room.

"It's on the TV, and hold your breath when you reach for it," responded Karina in exhaustion.

"Well, I used your new mouthwash last night, don't blame me. All I can taste is recycled fajitas, and they certainly tasted better last night." Michael flipped the covers back and silenced the clock.

Shuffling to the kitchen, Michael fired up the coffee maker. "Tomorrow," he promised himself, "I'll bring out the decaf." He crammed the toaster oven full of doughnuts to be warmed for the family, then remembering that a normal pace would make him late for his appointment, he washed down the doughnut with a mouthful of hot coffee. His throat burning, Michael rushed upstairs to throw on his clothes, brush his teeth, and round up the kids.

Fifteen minutes late and breathless from the race, he unlocked the back door to his office and slid into his chair. He buzzed Casey; his appointment was going to be an hour late. Tension drained off of him, leaving him limp, like a squeezed dish rag.

"Might as well relax with a cup of coffee and the paper," he sighed, opening his desk drawer. The sight of peanut butter and cheese crackers stashed beside his paper clips caused Michael's mouth to water. Simultaneously, his empty stomach groaned. For lack of anything better, he pried open the wrapper, barely cleaning up the crumbs before his secretary beamed through the

door, bearing a platter heaped with thick, gooey squares. "Inter-
state 65 Cheesecake," Casey announced proudly. "I followed the
recipe from the radio last night. You've got to try it. It's heavenly."

Not being one to hurt anyone's feelings, Michael sampled
the riches. Two Tylenol and a coke later, he shuffled papers and
checked his watch. It was half an hour before his lunch appointment. Putting important papers into his suede briefcase,
Michael once more mentally rehearsed his presentation for what
he had come to call "diet and the deal." Because of time (he told
himself), he chose to ride with his secretary over walking the
four blocks to the restaurant.

Scanning the menu, he decided to eat "lite." "A bareburger
and oven fries for me." Michael barely noticed the waitress as he
tried ahead of time to ascertain the financial mood of his client.
"And iced tea with lemon." The cool leather of the seat beneath
him was reassuring. The indirect lighting and muted carpeting,
however, did not disguise the sounds and smells of frying that
slipped through the double swinging doors to their left.

Vigorously stirring a second packet of sugar into his second
iced tea, Michael smiled to himself as he heard his client agree to
the contractual details of his proposal. Snapping his pen shut,
Michael signaled the waitress. Success motivated a new hunger.

"We'll each have a slice of your double chocolate crème pie."
Michael felt ready to sign up the world.

Stuffed full of food and fulfillment, he caught a ride back to
work.

But two hours later, Michael discovered all the goodness of
his lunch had suddenly evaporated. He wondered where it had
hidden, why he felt like locking himself in the filing closet and
dozing off. So he served himself another cup of coffee with a few
bites of Casey's cheesecake to tide him over until dinner.

And dinner was the usual: white bread, meat, salad, and a
cooked frozen vegetable, preceded by an appetizer of potato
chips scrounged from the pantry. The raw broccoli in the salad
made it in one piece from the refrigerator to the disposal, resting
only momentarily on Michael's plate. Despite second helpings of
everything but the salad and vegetable, Michael managed to
find room for two big helpings of chocolate brownie ice cream.

"A great day!" Michael thought to himself as he polished off three oatmeal cookies and a giant glass of milk following the evening news. "I'll sleep like a baby."

Sleep he may, but while Michael is dreaming of new foods to celebrate success, his body will be trying to sort through the maze of fat (at least one hundred-fifty grams), sugar (over sixty teaspoons or almost one-and-a-half cups), and additives (found in over ten of his sixteen food items for the day). Most unfortunate of all, his body will despair of moving this mostly fiberless food through his digestive system. Hence Michael's reliance upon laxatives and hemorrhoid preparations. Aside from the meager helping of salad and vegetable, and the small amount of oats in the cookies, Michael's entire intake for the day was in the form of refined foods, which contain only a trace of fiber, and animal products, which contribute no fiber at all.

Fat for Life?

Ask any vegetarian who shies away from animal products and oils. He will tell you that well-meaning friends constantly hound him about his body's need for "a little oil, a little fat, to keep things moving smoothly." It's as if people picture the body as a system of internal gears, all of which turn more easily with a few shots of WD-40 at each meal. Yet consider a recent report on ingested fat:

> Of all the dietary factors that have been associated epidemiologically (the study of the sum causes and incidence of disease) with cancers of the various sites, fat has probably been studied most thoroughly and produced the greatest frequency of direct associations. However, since dietary fat is highly correlated with the consumption of other nutrients that are present in the same foods, especially protein in Western diets, it is not always possible to attribute these associations to fat intake per se with absolute certainty.[6]

According to this same report, the average American eats about forty-five percent of his calories in the form of fat. Some nutritional counselors have seen patients who get up to seventy to eighty percent of their calories from fat. Assuming that our friend Michael Austin eats an average of three thousand calories per day, and forty-five percent of those calories are in the form of fat, then Michael is eating 1,350 calories of fat alone.

Because of studies which tie fat into heart disease, the American Heart Association is now recommending we reduce our intake to thirty percent or less of our total calories from fat.[7] The Pritikin Diet encourages people who want to escape major lifestyle diseases such as cancer and heart disease to keep the percentage of calories from fat to around ten percent or less.[8]

Yet other research has suggested that reducing fat has little impact on the cancer rate. Based on research and statistics from the American Cancer Society, the media would have us believe that the war on cancer is being slowly won. An article published in a recent issue of the *New England Journal of Medicine* suggests otherwise. In fact, according to the age adjusted mortality rate that is associated with all cancers combined, the war is being lost. The article called for a reallocation of research funds from new treatments to better prevention.[9]

Other studies do show that colon cancer, which affects between twenty and thirty percent of the families in the United States, is thought to be caused by the foods we eat — in particular, our all-American diet of high-fat, high-cholesterol, and low-fiber.[10] The most sensible approach to fat intake, taking into consideration all the available information, seems to be to decrease the percentage of calories from fat to around fifteen to twenty percent for those who are healthy. For those already diagnosed as having cancer or other diseases caused by lifestyle, the prudent decision regarding fats, especially cholesterol-laden foods,[11] would seem to be to strive for the ten percent figure.

One other little known factor that should motivate us to reduce fat in our diet is that fat is the most likely storage facility of pollutants from our environment. As we eat upward on the food chain, from root vegetables to grains, fruits, leafy vegetables, vegetable oils, and fats, the concentration of pesticides and other chemical pollutants gradually increases. Dairy products give us a 250 percent increase of pollutant concentration over leafy vegetables and a 1,500 percent increase over eating root vegetables. With the consumption of red meat, fish, and poultry, the percentages already cited double again.[12] So fat adds more than what can be seen; it also carries unseen toxins.

The American Cancer Society also encourages us to consider making changes: "There is a growing indication that dietary patterns play a key role, with some scientists believing that a diet high in beef and/or deficient in high fiber content may be a significant causative factor. Research in both these areas is continuing."[13]

We must remember that people flooding the offices of the American Cancer Society are usually in some particular stage of cancer or else are wanting to know the warning symptoms for undetected cancers. They are not really people seeking some preventative plan for their lives. But why wait to get cancer to do something aggressive about it?

Sugar in the Morning, Sugar in the Evening . . .

In the May, 1985, issue of the *Tufts University Diet and Nutrition Letter*, an article entitled, "Why Sugar Continues to Concern Nutritionists," indicated that the average American consumes about 125 pounds of sugar annually. This refined product comes in various forms, many of which slip by an unsuspecting public. These forms include sucrose, fructose, corn syrup, dextrose, glucose, dextrins, and invert sugar.[14] Since almost all simple sugars yield the same number of calories—four per gram, or about 115 per ounce—the "average" person who consumes 125 pounds per year is eating and drinking more than six hundred calories per day in sugar alone. Our friend Michael, who eats 1,350 calories in fat and six hundred in sugar, is consuming sixty-five percent of his daily intake of calories in fat and sugar alone.

Taken in great quantities, simple sugars (which are normally found in sweet foods without fiber, such as candy bars) can crowd out food sources which provide the nutrients essential to good health.[15] One of these nutrients is thiamine, a vitamin which keeps the nervous system in balance.[16] A diet high in sugared junk food can inhibit self-control. So parents who give their children sugary snacks and then get upset over their behavior should realize that poor eating habits could be a stronger factor than lack of self-control or poor discipline.

Sugar is more often than not an accomplice of fats; their association plays a major role in the cancer issue. Let us examine Michael's sample diet. Of the thirteen food items he ate which were high in fat, six were also high in sugar. We should add that few people with a sweet tooth are conscientious about other dietary factors, such as fat and fiber. Finally, we should remember that sugar plays a direct combat role in killing off white blood cells, those little soldiers which fight off viruses, such as cancer and the common cold.[17]

Additives Add?

Because of our continual quest for time-saving devices, a deluge of worthless gimmicks has been flooding the market. Packaged and pre-processed foods have virtually taken over the food market, creating a demand for a home version of the "box-crusher." In his "Focus on the Family" film series, Dr. James Dobson commented that a trash compactor "takes thirty pounds of garbage and turns it into thirty pounds of garbage." Unfortunately, convenience foods are the stuff of which many of us are made.

How many consumers consider the effects of the nearly three thousand substances intentionally added to foods during processing? How many consider the effects of another twelve thousand chemicals (e.g. vinyl chloride and acrylonitrile, used in food-packaging materials) which are classified as indirect, or unintentional, additives, and which are occasionally detected in some foods? Even the ubiquitous salt and sugar are classified as additives.[18]

It is indeed chilling to learn that very few studies have even been conducted to assess the effects of these food additives on the incidence of cancer, except those done on non-nutritive sweeteners like saccharin and aspartame.[19]

The Fiber Factor

Since its reintroduction into the postwar dietary world of white flour, white rice, white potatoes, and white sugar, fiber has reappeared on the table and has even become a current cause of concern in much of the health-related studies and literature. Everyone has heard of fiber, but few can define it if asked. Actually, fiber is simply the non-digestible part of plant material. Like the simple Vitamin B of the past, fiber has now been broken down into several elements or complexes.[20]

Basically, there are two types of fiber. Type I is comprised of three forms: cellulose, hemicellulose, and lignin. These fibers increase the size of the stool so that elimination time is reduced. Increasing intake of Type I fiber can relieve symptoms of constipation and other intestinal disorders. It may also help to prevent colon cancer. Predictably, sources of Type I fiber may be found in food items brown in color: wheat bran, whole grain breads, and cereals.[21]

Type II fiber is comprised of three forms also, one of which—lignin—overlaps with Type I fibers. The other two forms are pectin and gums. A diet containing these fibers lowers cholesterol and help to manage blood sugar. Food sources are oats, fruits, vegetables, brown rice, barley, and nuts.[22]

A recent issue of the *University of California, Berkeley, Wellness Letter* states: "Colon cancer, the second most common form of cancer in the U.S., is rare among people with a diet low in meat and rich in high-fiber foods. The evidence is not yet conclusive that fiber is protective, but fiber may reduce the bacteria that interact with fat and bile acids to create carcinogens (cancer causing chemicals), as well as reduce the level of bile acids. In addition, by moving stools quickly through the digestive tract, fiber lessens the contact of carcinogens with the intestine."[23]

People who eat high-fiber diets are seldom obese, and for good reason: fiber fills us up without adding calories. One study showed that subjects who ate a high fiber diet reached satiety (a feeling of fullness) on significantly fewer calories than those who ate the typical low fiber diet.[24] Fibrous foods also take longer to chew, which slows us down at the table.

Many people who know they should be eating fiber purchase bran by the jar, and "sprinkle" it here and there, while continuing to eat the standard diet of high fat, high sugar, and low fiber. What few people realize is that fiber, in addition to soaking up moisture, will also seize vitamins from the digestive system. The score comes out even if the fiber is eaten in the whole grain form. Concentrated bran added to other foods can actually rob us of vitamins.

The food packaging industry has become very cognizant of the new emphasis on dietary fiber. Consequently, as consumers, we need to beware. Just because a food item is brown in color is no indication that its contents are whole grain in nature. The package must be marked 100 percent whole grain or whole wheat; a label that indicates the ingredients are "100 percent wheat" simply means the product is made from refined "wheat" (white) flour. We discovered this one day by reading the fine print on a package of unbleached white flour. Instead of being identified as "white flour," it was classified as "wheat flour." By using white flour and a little bit of caramel coloring plus a few sprinkles of cracked wheat, the food industry tricks its customers into believing that the bread or crackers they are buying is a whole grain product. Consumers are left to puzzle over the fact that store-bought bread products are so light while their attempts at making one hundred percent whole wheat bread usually result in a disastrous loaf of "lead bread" that few family members will touch once it has cooled down.

If we look back at Michael Austin's diet for the day, it's easy to see why his use of laxatives and hemorrhoid preparations is also part of the all-American habit. Actually, television ads alone should convince us that elimination has become a major problem in this country. Add to this the evidence showing the advantages of a high fiber diet for reducing the time that wastes reside in the colon, as well as lowering the production of irritating bile acids, and we can more readily see the significance of what we eat.[25]

It makes sense to rid the body of waste products as quickly as possible, once the small intestine has done its work of absorption of all the available nutrients in any four to five hour period. But the average transit time (the time between eating and eliminating any given food) for Americans is about seventy-two hours, or three days. This is a long time for poisons and toxins to sit around in the large bowel. But without the fiber necessary to produce a soft stool, Americans find themselves in need of hemorrhoidal medications, laxatives, and other drugs to counteract lower bowel discomfort. Yet Dr. Burkitt's study done on African groups with little or no incidence of colon cancer showed their transit time to be twenty-four hours or less.[26]

One final word on dietary fiber: it is not to be found in animal products of any kind. Fiber passes virtually intact through the digestive system, soaking up moisture and keeping things on the move. An examination of the sources of fiber reveals that the original diet of fruits, grains, nuts, and vegetables given man on this planet includes both Types I and II fiber.[27]

Some health professionals, frustrated by the conventional treatment of symptoms (i.e., medication, tests, hospitalization, and/or surgery), are beginning to examine the causes for so many of the diseases that plague Americans. As a result, a whole new branch of "preventive medicine" has taken root in this country. Many people with few, if any, ailments, have begun making slow but significant changes in their diets. But unfortunately, the vast majority of people in this country continue to enjoy the typical American diet. They look smugly at the statistics, poke fun at the fanatics buying tofu in the produce department, and dare fate to prove them wrong.

Doctor's Story

Dr. John Benton wasn't always the perfect picture of health—tanned, spare, healthy. But after years of a frustrating surgical practice, he decided to start taking his own advice. He had never felt better physically. Or worse, professionally.

Even the palpable cool of the golf greens and stirring laziness of trees and clouds could not remove his thoughts from his calling. He wished the constant drama of life and death could stay where it belonged, locked in the sterile halls and rooms, barely masked by the taint of alcohol.

His thoughts flashed back to three surgeries that had taken place that very week. And to the follow-ups. He had told one patient his days were numbered. And then the family. "Sorry kids, your daddy won't be around after Christmas." Sometimes he felt more like an undertaker than a doctor. It was impossible to paint a portrait of sickness and present it as a gift to people who weren't sick. If they weren't in the portrait, they wouldn't accept the picture.

His eyes rested on Michael, his corpulent golfing partner, who was reaching for a club. Here was a good example of someone who'd be sitting for a portrait soon, he thought, recalling his friend's eating habits. Momentarily, John's thoughts took in a picture of Michael, on the wall at home, after the Navy had worked him over. He wondered what it would take to get Michael back to Navy size. Probably joining the Navy again, he thought. Another picture of his friend flashed through his mind. He forced it out. Planting his feet, he took a reckless swing.

John shielded the sun from his eyes as he watched his drive soar into the sapphire sky, disappear momentarily in the sun's brilliance, then arc out against the powdery clouds and drop right onto the green.

A fortuitous longshot, he thought. About all most of my patients have.

He sighed. With a shot like that, a day like this, and a friend like Michael, he should basking in positive feelings.

But he was tired. Tired of tediously tinting and shading the portrait with his scalpel. Even the pen and ink of his prescription pad rarely changed the pallor of sickness reflected in the eyes. There must be some way to remix the shades of death and dying. But who would allow the brush of prevention into the artist's hand? And who would buy the picture?

With his club, John knocked a clod of dirt off his shoe.

The picture everyone had bought, he reflected, is the one that heredity sold. It was selling them out, too.

The balance between heredity and environment is a delicate one, he knew, not so much for what is predisposed in the genes, but rather for what sort of environmental habits a person has acquired and continues to perpetuate in his daily choices.

Exploding sand crystals etched an image of his friend, wedging out of a trap.

John took a long, clinical look at Michael. If he were betting, he'd put money on Michael's lifestyle being one big Polaroid picture of the same factors that contributed to his father's and brother's deaths.

But he had quit betting long ago. The stakes were too high.

The Decision Is Ours

While no one knowingly stops to pick up a dangerous hitchhiker, all of us have had at least two encounters by the age of fifty with a cancer virus of one type or another trying to get on board.[28] Besides keeping the engine of our immune system running at an optimal level, we should do our best to watch for the red warning flags along the highway. From the information available in current studies, diet seems to be a major contributing factor in our body's ability to ward of these undesirable interlopers.

It would seem prudent to cut down drastically on fats. Since the use of free fats contributes considerably to our Americanized taste of food, we need to reeducate our dietary inclinations over a period of time. And it is better to do it on our own than to wish we had done so when it is too late.

The use of simple sugars in our diets is a difficult area for many of us to address. But the rule of thumb for cutting back on sweets is to replace them with fresh fruits. Many families cease to cry for dessert when tantalized by an attractive bowl of Nature's confections.

Additives speak for themselves. Never mind that healthfully prepared and packaged foods cost more. Prevention always costs less in the long run. And buying fresh food in its natural state saves even more money.

Finally, we don't have to look far to see the benefits of fiber which are being touted everywhere. Surely most of us can enjoy the challenge of preparing and eating higher quality foods. We can even demand them in restaurants and grocery stores.

If the local fast food franchise doesn't appeal to you after you've cut out the white bun, the fat and cholesterol-laden meat, the catsup, the mayo, and the greasy, salty fries (is there anything left?), why not drive by the window, head for a supermarket, and brown-bag it? You'll save more than money.

All of us need to take a long, hard look at the shadows of our past. What sort of habits are we perpetuating and passing on to our children? Even if we can find no history of disease lurking in our family tree, at the current rate of illness in America, our children or grandchildren may not be able to make such confident statements.

Pain from the Past

Come to think of it, Michael never could recall his father feeling well. In the small home built by his father, sickness was hard to hide. At first it was asthma, perhaps intensified by the piney woods of East Texas. Later the picture that indelibly etched itself in Michael's mind was of the hot water bottle with a tube attached to it hanging over the shower curtain.

"What's this, Mom?" nine year-old Michael had wanted to know.

"That's to give your dad enemas, Michael," his mother had responded.

Nine year-olds are not supposed to worry, but as a boy, Michael had to crowd the picture of that strange contrivance wrapped around the shower curtain rod from his mind every night before he could sleep. Weren't enemas for sick people? He hated to go into the bathroom by himself at night.

Meals had been a lot simpler then, Michael recalled, visualizing the little drop-leaf table covered with one of his mother's starched white cloths. Just meat and potatoes and gravy. Lots of gravy. In summer time, when the garden had provided, or friends shared, there were greens, snap peas, corn on the cob, and tomatoes. He had never cared much for tomatoes, but he couldn't get enough of his mother's homemade bread or biscuits. And no one minded if you wiped up the last bit of gravy on your plate with another slice of white bread. After all, people in India were starving.

He recalled scalding summer days that would take the skin off his feet if he stood in one place too long. But he never once remembered getting into trouble for dallying on an errand to the store. It was barely possible to get the half-gallon of ice cream home before the Texas sun made liquid of it. After the heat and the watermelons were long gone, the fellowship of ice cream shared around their little table had always warmed him.

He must have gotten his taste for eggs back then. It was true, he recalled, that Texas summers were so hot that an egg could be fried right on the pavement. But no one could beat his mom's version: light and fluffy and scrambled with bits of bacon, crammed between two thick slices of homemade bread. He could still remember the mess he had always made when the mayonnaise dropped out the bottom.

But somehow, he couldn't seem to place his father in many of the good memories. Sickness had always been a wall between them.

Then came the surgery and Michael learned the meaning of a new word: cancer. Wouldn't this visitor ever leave them alone? He had sometimes tried to imagine life without his father, but he had never tried very hard. Surely the winds of happiness and good health would sweep through their little home one day and life would get back to normal.

One surgery followed another. Then came a colostomy. He remembered hating to witness a bowel movement through that opening. How embarrassing for his father, he thought.

His older brother Paul's visit late that summer, just six months before the death of their father, was forever seared in Michael's memory. Having just finished a residency in radiology, Paul had wanted to view the films that were a silent narrative of a killing disease. Yet what strange irony life deals its performers. How was Paul to know, as he viewed the twisted remains of his father's colon, that he was looking at his own colon just twenty-five years later?

And how was Michael to know why death chose Paul instead of him? Perhaps it was not a matter of choice, but of time.

Or was it a matter of choices?

FOUR

THE RUSH TO DIABETES

Mary Ellen Vincent winced as the needle on the bathroom scales crept past the mark of last month's weigh-in. Another pound this month. Her eyes flashed sideways to find her husband, Patrick, watching her intently.

"Maybe it's just water," she commented lamely.

"Good try, dear," laughed Patrick. "But I wouldn't worry about it. Didn't you know that age and weight are directly related? As one goes up, so does the other."

"Listen honey." Mary Ellen stepped off the offending scales. "Just because we've added a pound a year in the twenty-five years of our marriage is no reason to conclude that it's inevitable. Misery loves company, but when it comes to fat, I'd rather not have the company, thank you."

Patrick straightened his tie in the mirror.

"Mary Ellen, we've been on every diet known to mankind—from grapefruit to cookies. Bar none, we've always gained back what we lost plus a little extra for the effort. The only skinny people I know run fifty miles a week, don't like to eat, or take pleasure in starving themselves." So saying, he stuffed a handkerchief in his pocket.

"So what's your solution?" Mary Ellen turned and faced her husband.

"Since none of those conditions fit me, my philosophy is to enjoy life and face the music as it is played." Patrick studied his physique in the mirror.

"Sorry dear, but I haven't given up. I'm still game for another diet." Mary Ellen reached into the closet for something to wear. "I think I'll shoot for around 1,500 calories a day plus some vitamins and see what happens." She struggled into her dress, glad for the elastic waistband, hoping Patrick wouldn't see her move the notch on the belt forward another hole.

41

"Wait a minute, Mary Ellen." Patrick's hand was on the door. "Whoever heard of dieting on 1,500 calories a day? Every diet we've ever been on has had us at a thousand calories or less. Just how do you propose to lose?" His tone was skeptical.

"I've already thought of that." Mary Ellen smiled at her husband. "You see, the average person going on a diet wants immediate results. You and I didn't get fat overnight, so my plan is to lose weight slowly while eating the foods I enjoy, like those Godiva chocolates you gave me for Valentines." She brushed and sprayed her hair. "Besides, you're bound to find me attractive if you're in the same shape, right?" Mary Ellen winked at her husband.

"Well, for one thing, I don't consider myself 'fat.'" Patrick smiled at his wife. "But go ahead and try. If it works, and more importantly, if you enjoy it, then maybe I'll give it a try." He sounded noncommittal.

Dieters and Diabetes: On the Increase

"Oh no, not another pound" is a universal ritual replayed in countless homes on a daily basis. But what most Americans fail to realize is that diabetes mellitus, which runs third behind heart disease and cancer as the most prevalent disease in this country, is closely tied in with another all-American problem, obesity.[1] Diabetes statistics for obese women over forty-five years of age are certainly not in Mary Ellen's favor.[2]

Approximately one in twenty-five people over the age of twenty has diabetes. The risks are twenty percent greater for women than for men. People who are ten and fifteen percent overweight have nearly twice the risk of developing this disease, and for those twenty-five to thirty-five percent over their ideal weight, the chances increase threefold.[3]

All in all, about six million people in the United States have been diagnosed with diabetes, but with another four to five million undiagnosed sufferers, the total adds up to five percent of the entire population of the United States.[4]

Basically, people with diabetes have a problem with insulin. Insulin is the vehicle that moves glucose from the blood stream into the cells for energy production or to the liver for storage. For some, people with diabetes, the pancreas doesn't do its job of producing the necessary insulin. For others, there is a problem with absorbing the insulin into the cells.[5] Either way, without glucose in the cells to fuel our energy needs, our bodies can suffer severe complications, many of which result in death if not treated aggressively. Regardless of whether a person has a problem with insulin production or absorption, he is classified as diabetic if his blood sugar levels hit the two hundred milligrams per deciliter mark after a given fast. Normal blood sugar levels, by contrast, peak out at around one hundred-forty milligrams per deciliter of blood.[6]

Type I and Type II

Because of the two distinct diabetic categories related to insulin, diabetes has been divided into two types: Type I, or "insulin-dependent diabetes mellitus" (referred to as IDDM), and Type II, or "non-insulin dependent diabetes mellitus" (referred to as NDDM).[7]

Type I is often called "juvenile onset" diabetes. As the name implies, it often afflicts children around the age of puberty, although the majority of the cases occur in adults. It is by far the more serious type because the pancreas is unable to produce adequate insulin, hence the IDDM. No one is exactly sure what causes the shut-down of the pancreas, but viruses of the Coxsackie B group are possible culprits.[8] Only about ten percent of the total diagnosed diabetic population of six million fall into this category. Probably millions more remain undiagnosed. This year, there will be about thirteen thousand new cases of insulin-dependent diabetes in people under the age of twenty. Four times as many children develop Type I diabetes as get cystic fibrosis or multiple sclerosis. Actually, a child's chances of getting diabetes run about even with getting cancer.[9]

With Type II diabetes, the pancreas produces insulin for the body's needs. The problem in Type II appears to occur with the receptors which lie on the surface of each body cell. Insulin, we must remember, is critical for transporting glucose from the bloodstream into the cell. But it must reach the cell to do its job.[10] We might liken this situation to someone trying to put a nickel into a parking meter that refuses to accept it. The person has plenty of nickels, and the sign on the meter says "nickels only," but something in the meter is out of sync.

Type II diabetics comprise ninety to ninety-five percent of the entire diabetic population. Blacks, Hispanics and Native Americans are more likely than Caucasians to have this form of diabetes. At least eighty percent of all Type II's are obese, meaning they weigh more than twenty percent over their ideal body weight.[11]

Type II diabetes is a disease which arises, primarily, from hereditary patterns that predispose us toward the same eating habits as our parents. At least that's the way it was for Mary Ellen Vincent.

Mother Knows Best

The lunch crowd at Parisienne's was thinning. Mary Ellen's mother, Marilyn, sat across from her daughter, her well-manicured hands encircling a cup of hot herbal tea.

From behind her cup of coffee, Mary Ellen contemplated her mother, trim and vibrant for sixty-two, and at least twenty pounds lighter than the last time they had met for lunch. The soft rose tint of her stylish pullover highlighted her sparkling eyes and delicately blushed cheekbones. Mary Ellen couldn't help thinking that her mother looked like she could run a marathon . . . and win.

"It's never as easy as it sounds, honey." Mary Ellen's mother shook her head to her daughter's offer of a bite of chocolate croissant, delicately laced with rows of whipped cream. Mary Ellen's impending diet was the focus of conversation. Marilyn continued. "I've probably tried as many diets as I've had birthdays, and I can assure you that taste buds never beg for anything healthy." She took a sip of her tea. "What's going to happen to your body when you splurge on a chocolate sundae and leave yourself only six hundred calories to eat on for the remainder of the day?" Her eyes rested on the croissant.

Mary Ellen ignored the question. "Since when did you develop such an interest in healthful living? I don't recall this attitude when I was growing up." Another bite of the flaky croissant disappeared.

"I just got filled to the limit of being sick. It seemed I was sleeping in a hospital bed more than my own. You know, diabetics fall into that category two and a half times as much as the general population."[12] Marilyn leaned back in her chair.

"Well, I'm envious of anyone with so much control over their life." Mary Ellen glanced down at the croissant momentarily, then looked up. "Hasn't this change been difficult for you after sixty years?"

"Yes." Marilyn leaned over to retrieve her napkin from the floor. "And no. Actually, the possibility of going blind and losing a leg didn't leave me much of a choice. Unfortunately, that's the American way." She continued. "The hardest part was accepting the fact that the lifestyle I grew up with and raised our family on was the very basis for my problems."

"But it's been worth it, obviously." Mary Ellen couldn't help contrasting her mother's slenderness and vitality with her own. The chocolate confection was barely appealing in its antithesis.

"Any sacrifice would have been worth it, especially considering the sickness I've battled. I feel like I've dropped twenty years off my age. And I haven't minded saying goodbye to insulin, either." Marilyn signaled the waiter for more tea.

"Mom! You're off insulin?" Mary Ellen could hardly believe it. No more needles or alcohol swabs, unending blood and urine tests, frantic searches for bottles of insulin. "Mother?" The look on Mary Ellen's face was serious. "How would you raise me differently, if you knew then what you know now?"

Marilyn leaned forward, earnestly resting her arms on the table, hands folded, as she contemplated her daughter. "The answer to that question is simple: I'd raise you and your brothers to be as far removed from the possibility of becoming diabetic or dying of a heart attack as is humanly possible."

The two women were quiet, but their thoughts reverberated off the walls of the silent restaurant. Mary Ellen knew her mother was reliving that ill-fated vacation three years before where she had lost a husband and Mary Ellen a father.

Marilyn continued. "We don't have a pretty medical history, Mary Ellen. You probably remember my mother died of a stroke at sixty-nine. Not too many of us knew she was diabetic. Now we know that diabetes worsened her arterial disease which in turn dealt the killing stroke.[13] "And then you remember my sister, Faye. She died of diabetic complications at age thirty-two."

Mary Ellen remembered. The trip to the hospital. The doctor at the door. The cloth-draped body in the background. And the eyes. They had been taped shut to hide the expression no one could bear to see over her bloated body.

". . . Renal failure," Marilyn was saying. "Diabetes worked over her kidneys.[14] "But to answer your question, I wouldn't have gained forty-five pounds while I was carrying you. A healthy baby is one thing, but babies over nine pounds are predisposed to diabetes.[15] I wouldn't have let the nurses push sugar-water in the nursery, either. Why start a baby out with a taste for something sweet the day it's born? And I wouldn't have let my doctor talk me into feeding you formula."

Mary Ellen's eyes were on her mother, but her thoughts were recalling the similarities of her own daughter, Lindsay's, birth.

"If I were to characterize our diet while you were growing up, I'd say we ate too many refined foods, too much fat, too much protein, and too much sugar." Marilyn glanced at the remnants of the croissant, then at her daughter. "Oh Mom," Mary Ellen was slightly defensive. "We weren't that bad! The only things I can remember overdosing on were Baby-Ruth's and Slo-Poke suckers. I knew even then those things weren't helping me stay away from the dentist." Her mind drifted back to her childhood. Life seemed a lot less complicated then.

"But Mary Ellen," Marilyn was adamant. "Surely you can see the effects that our all-American diet of high sugar and high fat plays in heredity. I mean, my mother died of diabetes. She fed my sister and me basically what I fed you. I developed diabetes. Faye died from it."

Her eyes met Mary Ellen's.

She continued. "Are you feeding your family any differently now than the way you were raised?"

Mary Ellen was silent.

"If not, where's it all going to end?"

Welcome to the World

What sort of choices do we make that predispose us towards the world of Type II diabetes? What is it that causes those little cells to reject the ready insulin?

Research shows that excess calories over what our bodies' actual need—even those from good food—can cause our cells to reduce the availability of receptors.[16] The term is gluttony. And it's first on the list of our choices. Obviously, though, it's much harder to overeat good nutriments than it is to overdose on harmful food.

Second on the list is a diet high in fat. High means the average American intake with forty to fifty percent of the calories coming from fat. Our high intake of fat seems to play a major role in crowding out the availability of insulin to the cells.[17]

Following gluttony and high fat in the diet, the third offender is a high intake of sugar, especially simple sugar. Simple sugars may be found in candy bars, and in most prepackaged breakfast cereals and desserts, as well as in many hidden forms, such as corn syrup and corn sweeteners.[18] Fruit, when eaten whole, contains a complex sugar along with corresponding fiber. It takes three pounds of apples to get the same amount of sugar that's in a Hershey Bar.[19] The really deleterious foods are those highly concentrated in fats and sugars.

Fourth comes a lack of dietary fiber in the diet. By definition, dietary fiber comes only from plant sources, never animal.[20]

Fifth, and last, is lack of exercise. Exercise promotes good circulation by lowering blood fats and actually increasing the number of small blood vessels going to the muscles. And it also increases the effectiveness of insulin and the rate at which glucose is used in the body.[21]

Taking Yourself Out of Circulation

The old saying that "Perfect health requires perfect circulation"[22] is absolutely true. Of course, most all of us know that heart attacks are the result of arrested circulation. Even cancer cells seem to grow best in an anaerobic environment — one that has been deprived of circulating oxygen.

Unfortunately, when an individual becomes diabetic, circulatory problems, with all the attendant complications, begin to manifest themselves much faster than they do in the general population. It is becoming increasingly well known that atherosclerosis is virtually a certainty when the all-American diet of high fat and high sugar is faithfully followed. And the onset of diabetes intensifies, or speeds up, this degenerative disease of clogged arteries.[23]

This primary problem of circulation is identified as peripheral arterial disease. The high glucose levels of the diabetic, if not strictly controlled by diet and exercise, accelerate the narrowing of the arteries, primarily the ones which service the legs and feet.[24]

Miraculously, this clogging of the arteries apparently doesn't affect blood flow until the artery is about seventy-five percent occluded. However, when blockage reaches ninety percent, painful symptoms emerge. When an individual walks or exercises, aches and pains begin to appear in the feet, calf muscles, thighs, or buttocks. Then the symptoms will disappear, usually, with a period of rest, only to recur with more movement.[25]

Untreated diabetics often fall prey to a host of complications arising from this most serious problem of peripheral arterial disease. These include infections, gangrene, and amputations. Indeed, approximately fifty percent of all amputations performed annually in America are the result of diabetic complications.[26]

When diagnosed with diabetes, only eight percent of adults exhibit symptoms of peripheral arterial disease. But after twenty years of living with the disease, forty-five percent are reporting symptoms of this insidious killer. A comparison of diabetics with the general population reveals that diabetics are from four to seven times more likely to develop peripheral arterial disease than are the rest of us.[27]

Diabetics are also four times more likely to experience blindness because of capillary damage in the retina, and more than twice as likely to develop a hearing impairment. None of these figures take into account a diabetic's increased risk of heart attacks, strokes, and kidney failure.[28] Though not yet fully supported by data, there is a general concern that diabetes, and the consequent decreased efficiency of circulation of the blood, are prime factors in providing an optimum low oxygen environment for cancer cells to multiply.

Even though, as one article from a 1986 issue of *Diabetes Forecast* stated, "nobody likes to think about complications," it is the complications of diabetes that most often cause premature death, not the disease itself.[29]

One study which should raise the ire of any serious researcher or layman suggests that modest amounts of ice cream may be included in the diet of insulin-dependent (IDDM) diabetic patients.

The reason given is that the high fat of the ice cream causes less of an acute blood glucose rise than other concentrated sweets.[30]

But in the realm of diabetic complications, there is more to the story. The combination of milk and sugar will greatly aid in the development of all types of circulatory ailments. Hence we can see the wisdom in looking at the total picture when any study is presented as a rationale for maintaining habits that perpetuate our dietary lifestyle. In this case, the complications from diabetes more than double the likelihood of patients needing hospitalization.

Responsible diabetic research must focus on not only those procedures that help control the primary disease, but, more importantly, on the relation of cause to effect. After all, if health is the goal, as far as diabetes is concerned, only that lifestyle should be recommended that will also insure optimum circulation and consequently the best possible health.

Unfortunately, changing a lifetime of habits is no easy feat in a country such as the United States where food is both abundant and readily available. But fortunately, for those six million or more people suffering from Type II diabetes, research tells us that weight loss, increasing physical activity, and eating a diet high in fiber and low in sugar and fats will, in many cases, reverse the effects of this lifestyle disease.

Like Marilyn, Mary Ellen's mother, many diabetics are taking more responsibility for their own health, and in doing so, have a better than ninety percent chance of removing insulin from their daily needs.[31]

And many of the four to five million undiagnosed diabetics are heeding warning symptoms and finding out the truth about themselves.

Blood Sugar Blues

Mary Ellen rested in the slate blue chair with her legs crossed and foot bobbing up and down. She pushed a strand of hair back with one hand. As she did, her eyes focused on the bandage adhered to the underside of her forearm. She wondered how so much of one's future could be determined by the stick of one tiny needle.

Absentmindedly, she pictured Patrick's reaction. "You have what?" he would ask, incredulously. "That's for old ladies and fat people."

She tried to imagine the kids' response.

Her mind created a picture of the look in her mother's eyes.

She wondered how many people had waited in this very chair before her. People waiting to have their futures read from the palms of a physician, chart in hand. She wondered if they knew the answers before the questions were asked. But then, maybe they had never experienced the same frightful symptoms.

She had been shopping. Hoping to beat the rush hour traffic, she had skipped her usual snack. In her weakness she knew better. And she couldn't afford the extra thirty minutes an accident on the highway had delayed her. Such a minor thing. To sit in a car and wait for traffic to clear. But it was not so minor when weakness and then dizziness turned to confusion. The fog that had settled behind her eyes had clouded her ability to reason. To see with her eyes, but to be unable to know what she was seeing— nothing in her previous experience had ever been so terrifying. It had taken every effort of concentration to pilot the car, to re-member the turns, to remind herself who she was.

But it hadn't taken much effort to call Dr. Stephens. She had done it before the real terror had worn off.

There was her weight. And her craving for water. And the frequent urinating.[32] Plus her fantastic appetite for chocolate of any description. And her family history of diabetes. She knew why she was here. What she didn't know was what changes she would have to make. Changes. She was almost more afraid of that word than the diagnosis.

The door creaked open. Mary Ellen didn't turn around. Footprints padded on the soft gray carpet behind her, moving around to her left side. Dr. Stephens sat down beside her, leaving his massive desk an island in the sunlight splayed from the win-dows. His smile veiled whatever message the lab technician might have forwarded.

"Mary Ellen." He looked across the space between them. "I'm glad you've come in for this test." He opened the folder that would change her life forever. "Can you believe this printout from one little vial of blood?"

She was disarmed by the warmth in his voice. Her eyes took in his salt and pepper hair, curling softly over his forehead, the oxford shirt and sportive tie half hidden by his white lab coat, and the corduroy slacks, creased over his polished loafers. She noticed his legs were crossed and his foot was swinging. "He looks like an athlete," she thought to herself. She wondered what direction he would point her to in this matter of change.

She heard her voice answering his polite question. "Yes, a little spilled blood can change our lives, can't it?"

Pause.

"Dr. Stephens, is anything wrong?"

He repositioned his glasses. "Yes, Mary Ellen. I'm afraid there is a problem with your body's ability to properly handle glucose." His eyes looked to hers for a reaction.

"You mean I am a diabetic, Dr. Stephens?" Mary Ellen's detachment didn't surprise her.

"Your glucose tolerance test indicated a classic diabetic reaction by the body." He glanced back to the report. Leaning toward Mary Ellen, he rested his chin on his hand. "You don't act surprised. Have you diagnosed yourself?"

"Well, sort of. Actually, my mother is diabetic and I'm pretty familiar with the symptoms." Mary Ellen was comfortable with the friendliness of his eyes behind his glasses.

She was silent as he outlined her disease, the symptoms and the predispositions.

"Well, Mary Ellen," Dr. Stephens closed the folder, "we have a couple of choices to look at."

She was ready, almost relieved, to get to this stage.

"There are routine insulin shots and a possible worsening of your condition to include all sorts of other problems related to diabetes, which we'll need to discuss, or there's the possibility of moving to an insulin-free maintenance with proper lifestyle changes. Which route do you want to take?"

Mary Ellen smiled at her doctor, but her eyes were seeing the slim and dynamic figure of her mother.

Living with Reality

For many people, being diagnosed as diabetic becomes a life akin to that of an intravenous drug user. But for others, it is a great incentive to begin and stay with a program to implement a major change in their daily habits. But first, it is necessary to consider the deception of the "American Way." For the sake of something tasting good for the few seconds it is in our mouths, we totally overlook what it is doing to our bodies.

Actor Wil Brimley has appeared in movies including *Cocoon*, *Absence of Malice*, *The Natural* and currently has a successful television show, "Our House." Recently he developed diabetes. One segment of his show even featured his breakdown of health and consequent diagnosis.

Brimley's current health regimen includes a daily two-mile walk and a strict diet, but he states he took charge of his health only after he developed diabetes. "I had no semblance of self-discipline in my life, not a whisper of it," he says.[33]

By his own admission, the motivation for staying with his lifestyle change is a conviction that his former favorite foods aren't worth what they might cost him in health. "I've already had my pumpkin pie and my ice cream in life. It's a question of whether I want to enjoy the rest of my life or another bowl of ice cream. It's a pretty simple choice."

But Brimley's new choices have resulted in a big plus for him: he has continued to lose weight, and recently gotten the word that he no longer needs insulin. Today he takes no medication.[34]

The story behind Wil Brimley and millions of other diabetics is that the average American has little or no concept of what it means to really feel good.

But health is, after all, much, much more than the absence of illness.

ONE IN A HUNDRED AND YOUR IMMUNE SYSTEM

I stared at her as she locked the door of her sleek BMW, the ebony metallic surface flashing in the morning sun. Watching closely for a view of her face, I stood, transfixed, as slowly and painfully she labored across the parking lot, intent on reaching the safety of the curb. Her steps, halting and measured, were hardly the steps of a twenty-five year old. I must be mistaken.

But there was no mistaking that splendid piece of metal in the parking lot. It was the big one, the one the rest of us could never afford. The one she always kept waxed and polished, stunning in its unabashed elegance. And the one her husband used to drive. Before . . .

There was no mistaking her hair, either. Its sable radiance reflecting the sheen in her car, the coarse tendrils blowing across her face in the spring breeze of a California morning.

But surely that couldn't be the face of Whitney Reed, half hidden by the looming shadows of the store, or the body of my well-favored friend from gymnastics class. I'd call her when I got home. A phone call was always better than making a fool of oneself in the parking lot.

I recalled her story, spliced into times of waiting for our children to finish their hour of gymnastics every week. From the first, it had been difficult to imagine her a widow. The age, the face, the precious child, the ultimate finality of a husband's death from a ruptured aneurysm at twenty-six. Life's exorbitant exchange rate extracted far too many penalties to be covered by life insurance. Even an extravagant policy.

There was yet another eclipse in her young life — a mysterious progression of ailments brought on by a backfiring of her

her immune system. Oppressive aching in her joints, low grade fevers, blotchy patches seeping over her face, neck and arms, and near kidney failure at times. It was ironic that a child so loved and needed as little Lynly Ann was the catalyst that triggered the onset of these trials.

The fashionable Whitney I knew had always seemed to contradict her portrayal of pain. "Remission," she called it. How long it would last, she never knew. But whenever it departed, the days and the hours were blackened into a nightmare of agony.

The phone was ringing. Would she answer?

"Hello?" Her voice was faint in the receiver.

"Whitney. It's me. Are you okay?"

"Oh, hi. I'm doing pretty well." An outright lie, I thought to myself.

"Listen, I'm going to run a few errands and want to stop by. Will you be there?"

"I'll leave the door open. Please come on in. I'll be in the family room." She sounded tired.

But she wasn't there when I arrived, and the door wasn't unlocked. A note was taped to the mail drop. "Gone to mother's. Call me there." And the phone number.

So I called, wondering where this saga would end. From my morning's memories, I should have known. Yet for a moment, I thought I had walked into the wrong hospital room.

But there she was, waiting for me, looking for someone to share her smiles and eternal optimism, however thinly they masked her pain. Casualness is not an easy role to assume in the presence of bottles and tubes and needles — in the presence of sterile whiteness always moving quietly in the background — in the presence of someone whose eyes and hair and voice are the only remnants of a quickly fading memory.

"I'll be all right. In no time I'll be out of here." Was she trying to assure us both? "My dumb kidneys acting up again. I should have stayed with that medication. Not cut it down. But I hate taking it. I just despise taking it when I don't feel bad." Her bloated face was frightening to behold.

Lupus, they called it.

Autoimmunity: On the Rise

Whitney's disease, medically classified as Systemic Lupus Erythematosus, is a disease resulting from a malfunction of the immune system. It affects, among other things, the skin, the joints, and the muscle surrounding the heart, causing its victims the untold agonies of lesions, arthritis, and pericarditis. Women contract the disease nine times more often than men. Pregnancy can aggravate the onset of Lupus as a result of hormonal changes in the body. Renal, or kidney, failure is the most life-threatening of all Lupus complications. The prognosis for individuals suffering from this disease is not good.[1]

The prognosis is not good for those diagnosed as having Crohn's Disease, rheumatoid arthritis, or Multiple Sclerosis, all of which are classified as autoimmune diseases.[2]

AIDS, the blockbuster of all illnesses, has the worst prognosis of any affliction ever in the history of mankind. Although it is not an autoimmune disease in the same category as the others, the AIDS virus is, in effect, far deadlier, for it engineers a total devastation of the body's entire immune system.[3]

Cancer, too, is a part of this immune system picture. It currently strikes nearly one million individuals every year.[4]

What's happening to America's immunity? Why are these diseases on the increase? And why is our medical community so stymied in its efforts to promise us a cure?

Perhaps a look at the physiology of our immune system will help explain its complexity. This intricate system functions best when our bodies are finely tuned. An investigation into the immune system might consequently show us why poor health is a major contributor to the countless autoimmune disorders and immune system breakdowns that are becoming so prevalent in our society today.

The Battle of the Body

The immune system of the body is a study in organizational efficiency. Of our total one hundred trillion cells, only one trillion make up the immune system.[5] The odds against a problem developing may be one in a hundred under normal circumstances, but when this involves the health of our bodies, those odds are considerable, especially under certain circumstances.

In order for a virus to do its work of replicating itself in the body, it must get inside a host cell and take over. Cancer, for example, can be caused by a virus. By dividing our white blood cells into their various defensive roles against these viruses we begin to see the puzzle of the immune system fitting together.

Imagine the immune system as an army separated into numerous platoons, each having a specialized role to play in battle. When a virus gets into the body, this specialized army has a fascinating way of dealing with the intruder.[6]

The first warriors of the immune system are the macrophages. These cells are the general housekeepers of the body. They are constantly picking up waste products and will even sacrifice their lives to dispose of debris such as asbestos fibers. When they encounter a foreign organism, for example, a virus, the macrophages consume a few, but more importantly, they grab the antigens of that particular virus. We might think of these antigens as the ID cards of the virus.[7]

Once the macrophages get the ID card of the invading virus, they present it to the Helper T cells, so called because they originate from the thymus, the small mass of lymphoid tissue which lies in the upper chest at the base of the neck. These Helper T cells are like a band of roving scouts circulating through the bloodstream, ever on the lookout for an enemy. When presented with the ID card of the enemy virus, these Helper T cells sound the alarm at the spleen and the lymph nodes.[8]

This alarm rouses the Killer T cells into action. These infantrymen head out with orders to take no prisoners. In other words, they will kill outright not only the invading virus, but also any body cells that the virus may be hiding in to do its work of replication.[9]

Besides arousing the Killer T cells to battle, the Helper T cells also activate the B cells. These cells produce the biological warfare most of us are familiar with, called antibodies. When the Killer T cells destroy the invaded cells, the contents of the cells, including the foreign invaders, spill out. The exposed viruses are then pounced upon by the B cells, or antibodies, which attach themselves to the invader and paralyze them. Then these antibodies fire their deadly chemicals, destroying the virus.[10]

Because of their ferocious defense of the body, these antibody cells are like pit bulls. They don't know when to stop fighting. Rather than taking orders from the Helper T cells who initiated the action, they instead receive their direction from a completely different officer of the immune system, the Suppressor T cells.[11]

It is at this point that the diseases of the autoimmune system, such as Lupus, Rheumatoid Arthritis, MS, and Crohn's Disease, come into play. The theory behind these illnesses is that the Suppressor T cells fail to do their work and actually stop the action of the B cells, or antibodies. Simply put, the body's immune system begins to develop autoantibodies which, instead of attacking the bad guys, attack the good guys. The result may be arthritis-like symptoms, as in lupus, or actual arthritis, as in Rheumatoid Arthritis, the most common of the autoimmune disorders. The onset of MS and Crohn's Disease follows a similar etiology, or cause.[12]

Once the battle is over, defensive cells known as Memory cells are left to roam the bloodstream or lymph system for years. Their specific duty is to keep a lookout for the same type of virus, enabling the immune system to subdue the invader in an accelerated and particularly intense way if it should make another attempt at replicating itself inside the body.[13]

In contrast, AIDS, or Acquired Immunodeficiency Syndrome, is a relatively new virus. What is so unique about this invader is that it is the only virus known to completely commandeer the Helper T cells. If they are incapacitated, then there is no sending out of the troops. Thus, the AIDS virus has free rein throughout the body.[14]

In light of this last statement, nuclear warfare seems hardly so grim.

Future Shock

The Centers for Disease Control in Atlanta have stated that before 1979, there were only eight documentable deaths due to AIDS in the United States.[15] However, according to conservative projections, within ten years there could be as many as eight to ten million Americans infected with the virus, with hundreds of thousands dead or dying.[16]

The prediction of the *Medical Journal of Australia* is even more urgent. As much as twenty-five percent of Africa's population will be dead from AIDS in little more than a decade.[17] This mortality figure could represent sixty to seventy million people in the coming ten years.

Dr. William Grace, Chief of Oncology at St. Vincent's Hospital in New York City, suggested that by 1991, all of New York's hospital beds could be occupied as a result of the AIDS crisis. He states emphatically: "I think AIDS is going to devastate the American medical system. Last year (1986), coronary-bypass surgery cost $1 billion in this country . . . In 1985, the 12,000 patients with AIDS cost this country $6 billion. Do you realize that in five years (1992) there are going to be over a quarter of a million cases? The virus is already incubating in one million people, and what we're seeing now is that the incubation period can be eight or nine years. We're also seeing that a steadily growing number of those with the virus are actually getting AIDS. We're seeing other viruses like the AIDS virus — viruses that aren't even talked about in the press. There will be many more."[18]

Abortion, the greatest killer of the century, has taken untold millions. But even if abortion is not checked, these figures will pale in comparison to AIDS, which will slay tens of millions, or even more.

The Versatile Killer

It has been widely reported that the AIDS virus is a fragile one when outside of body fluids. Yet scientists at the Pasteur Institute, where this unimaginable virus was originally isolated, have suggested that the virus might be more rugged than had been previously thought. Their studies on the durability of the virus indicated that it can live for up to ten days at room temperature, even when dried out in a petri dish.[19]

How many of us are aware that the ". . . live AIDS virus has been isolated from blood, semen, serum, saliva, urine and now tears. If the virus exists in these fluids, the better part of wisdom dictates that we assume the possibility that it can also be transmitted by these routes. It seems reasonable, therefore, that AIDS victims should not donate blood or blood products, should not contribute to semen banks, should not donate tissues or organs to organ banks, should not work as dental or medical technicians, and should probably not be employed as food handlers."[20]

William F. Buckley, writing in the *National Review* concerning the death of actor Rock Hudson, commented: "Well, then, how come they acted as they did in Paris? There you may have read (in the small print) when Rock Hudson was discharged, all the nurses who attended him—and this was in a modern hospital, not a witch doctor's hut—were made to burn their dresses. The patient was fed on paper and plastic plates, with plastic forks and spoons—which were then destroyed."[21]

While most of us know that contracting the AIDS virus will most assuredly be akin to receiving a death sentence, we are generally ignorant of the fact that this lethal virus, in addition to wiping out the effectiveness of the immune system, also directly attacks the brain. The condition is called "AIDS induced dementia," and is probably the most grotesque of all the attacks wreaked on the body by this deadly virus. AIDS, with its commonly known infections, causes grievous pain and slow death. But AIDS induced dementia transforms the brain into an eventual black hole of imbecility. Few conditions can be as dehumanizing.[22]

Gene Antonio, author of *The AIDS Cover-up?*, has stated that the AIDS virus is probably the human equivalent of a "lentivirus." The Latin prefix "lenti" means "slow." This suggests that the virus usually has a relatively long incubation period. It was because of the many cases of AIDS dementia being uncovered that researchers were led to suspect a lentivirus, which in sheep causes progressive brain degeneration. Lentiviral infections in animals are so lethal, and effective vaccinations have been such a failure, that the only successful means of control has been the wholesale slaughter of the animals.[23]

One of the early signs of lentivirus in sheep is lung infection, with resultant mucus, and coughing. Lentiviruses are known to be rather easily transmitted through coughing, for example.[24]

According to Dr. James Slaff, Medical Investigator at the National Institutes of Health, "fully 30 to 45 percent of those presently infected with the AIDS virus will develop the symptoms of the disease within five years. The long range prospects beyond five years are probably much worse. If the lentivirus follows the same lethal course in man that it follows in sheep, then it is possible that infection with AIDS will leave few, if any, survivors.[25] In sheep the death rate reaches one hundred percent within about two-thirds of the normal lifespan of the infected animal."

In effect, the AIDS virus has an immense capacity not only to replicate itself, but to hide in the body for years while the carrier unknowingly spreads the disease.[26]

The Torture of AIDS

Infection by the deadly AIDS virus resembles a three-act tragedy. Like the movies of the early twentieth century, the first act is silent. The carrier experiences no symptoms. This stage is referred to as the asymptomatic carrier state. For years the individual harboring this silent, secret virus may enjoy good health. All the while the virus gradually but firmly establishes itself within the cells of the body. The eyes, lungs, liver, spleen, and kidneys, as well as the brain and other organs, are targeted.[27]

It can no longer be denied that the virus is toxic to body organs other than the immune system and the brain. The Associated Press ran a story which told of two people who received AIDS infected organs — one a kidney, the other a liver. The tragic irony of the situation was that the donor had originally been tested and declared safe. Yet sadly, both recipients tested positive for the virus following their transplants.[28]

At an International Conference on AIDS in 1985, former Secretary of Health and Human Services Margaret Heckler concluded: "Acquired Immunodeficiency Syndrome kills. The danger of the syndrome's deadly thrust is compounded because, like the iceberg's mammoth underwater size, usually seven times larger than what we see, the long gestation period of AIDS gives no initial warning of the omnipresent danger."[29]

Dr. William Haseltine of Harvard emphatically asserts: "Once infected, a person remains infected for the rest of his life. Once infected, a person is infectious. It is not safe to assume otherwise."[30]

By the time the second act of this human tragedy gets under way, the player begins to realize his is a solo performance and the curtains to backstage are closed. The action is intense, and the once silent stage becomes engulfed with the cries of an immune system under siege. Night sweats, swelling of lymph nodes, chronic fatigue, unrelenting diarrhea, weight loss — over fifty identified symptoms may creep defiantly on-stage. In the darkness of the mind, the symptoms of dementia begin to take root. Seizures, loss of coherent speaking ability, memory loss, deteriorating muscle control, and psychiatric problems — all may be manifested in their most horrifying states. This second act, a plethora of terrors, is called ARC, or AIDS related complex. Sometimes it is referred to as pre-AIDS syndrome. Either way, the tension on-stage mounts as the actor anticipates the final act yet to come.[31]

With the onset of this final tragedy, which is played out in the shadows of death and dying, countless diseases, called opportunistic infections, march threateningly down the aisles. This is full blown AIDS, referred to as stage III.[32] It is always the final act, for the immune system is too dysfunctional to call the infections to account. The audience watches with trembling revulsion the final scenes of what have become a real-life spectacle:

Kaposi's sarcoma: characterized by purplish spots and deadly taints because of its penchant for involving the internal organs. Extremely malignant, it can develop in the lymph nodes, liver, stomach, intestines, lungs, and other organs.

Pneumocystis carinii pneumonia: likened unto emphysema. Its progression leads to a growing sense of suffocation characteristic of the obliteration of lung function.

While these two diseases are the most common occurrences of AIDS opportunistic infections, there are others that may couple together:

Candidiasis: a fungal infection of the mouth, and the most common sign of AIDS;

Herpes zoster: painful skin eruptions involving the mouth, nose, and rectum;

Cytomegalovirus: a relatively common, but devastating, viral infection that is ordinarily dismissed by a healthy immune system. The lungs, as well as the retina, are attacked. Damage to the eye may result in blindness;

Herpes simplex: causes painful ulcers of the mouth and the perineal area. Severe inflammation of the colon, known as colitis, may occur.

Oral "hairy" leukoplakia: causes lesions on the borders of the tongue. This is another virus of the herpes group.

Malignant lymphoma: a virulent form of cancer associated with a mean survival rate of less than one year.

Tuberculosis: long thought extinct like polio and smallpox, is now making a marked comeback, thanks to AIDS. But tuberculosis, or TB, is not considered an opportunistic infection, because tuberculosis is more virulent than the other diseases and can be transmitted independent of an infection by the AIDS virus.[33]

In reality, we don't truly know the enormity of AIDS. As of August, 1987, the CDC's in Atlanta were classifying as AIDS patients only those manifesting full-blown symptoms of the disease—those in stage III. AIDS patients in stage I, the asymptomatic carrier stage, and stage II, the ARC stage, are not included in the national figures of those reported to be suffering from AIDS. Individuals dying of AIDS-induced dementia also are not included in the AIDS statistics.

There can be little doubt that AIDS is the ultimate disease of this century, or of any other century for that matter. Those sounding the alarm about AIDS call for a prudent lifestyle, which includes avoiding the "high risk" behavior so commonly associated with homosexuals and AIDS patients.[34] But can we afford to disassociate the connection between individuals indulging in a homosexual lifestyle and the rest of us indulging in the all-American lifestyle of too much fat and sugar and too little exercise? Either way, our habits are destroying our bodies' ability to fight off disease if and when it comes knocking.

And most assuredly it will come, if not knocking, then tugging at our heartstrings.

Where Are the Answers?

The phone rang.

Jane Powell sighed as she folded her newspaper. Dinner was in the oven and the kitchen was lustrous from a thorough cleaning.

"Hello?" Her voice sounded rather dubious.

"Hi Jane. It's Giny." Jane's friend, Giny Dunn, didn't wait for the usual courtesies. "Can you meet me for lunch? Something awful has happened at school. We've got to talk."

Running a brush through her hair, Jane tried to imagine what might have gotten Giny so excited. She hadn't even said which school, or which kid, for that matter.

"What on earth's the matter, Giny?" Jane could hardly wait for the waitress to leave before asking.

"Oh Jane, this has got to be the worst thing imaginable. I hardly know where to begin." It was obvious that Giny's distress was not exaggerated. "Last night I got a call from Sally, Brent and Sydney's health teacher. Peter and I had just had dinner with her and Jack the night before, so I was surprised." Giny paused as their waitress brought a basket of chips for the hot sauce.

"Yes?" Jane unfolded her napkin and took a chip.

"She told me to sit down, that she had some classified information." Giny looked at Jane.

"So is this going to be one of those 'don't tell anyone who told you' stories?" Jane smiled at her friend.

Giny ignored the question. "Jane, this will probably be on the front page of tomorrow's paper." She leaned forward to whisper. "Scott Harper has AIDS."

The chip in Jane's mouth suddenly went dry, almost choking her as she struggled to swallow. Somewhere in the distance she heard Giny's question about what to do now, but her thoughts were miles ahead of an answer. Where did he get it? Could he expose his classmates? How close did Sydney sit to him? Would he be allowed to continue school? What were his chances? What was AIDS, really? And finally, what would she say to June Harper, Scott's mother?

"Oh, Giny," was all she could manage to say.

If the remainder of the lunch had been served from a brown paper bag, neither woman would have noticed.

"Where did he get it, Giny?" Jane asked the obvious question. "Do they know?"

"That's the terrifying part. No one knows. Scott's never had a blood transfusion in his life. Obviously he's not homosexual or an intravenous drug user." Giny was at loss for reasons.

"So how was it discovered?" Jane wondered aloud.

"According to Sally, Scott had been losing weight. He'd also been having a lot of diarrhea and was always tired. Returning from three days' absence, he acted so confused that Sally called his mother. On the way home, in the car, he had a seizure. Of course June drove straight to the emergency room. Apparently it was in the hospital that the doctors discovered a condition similar to thrush in his mouth. That led them to run tests." Giny's tone was one of disbelief.

Jane shook her head. Diarrhea, weight loss, confusion? And a seizure? What did that have to do with AIDS? Weren't AIDS patients afflicted with Kaposi's something or other?

Giny read her thoughts. "Don't ask me. All I know is that the social reverberations of this issue are going to be felt far outside this town. If Scott didn't get it from the usual sources, then who's to say that any of his family[35] or friends won't get it from him in the same mysterious way he contracted it?"[36] Her voice was intense.

"But Giny, everything we've read in the media leads us to believe that the only way to contract AIDS is through promiscuous behavior, transfusions, or dirty needles."[37] Jane was insistent.

"Then you don't care if Sydney sits next to him in the cafeteria and drinks after him at the water fountain?" Giny gave Jean a hard look.

Nobody said anything for a moment.

"Do you remember all the court hearings for that poor little boy up north who contracted AIDS from a transfusion? First he had to leave school, then he was allowed to return, then he had to leave. I don't know how it all ended," Giny attempted to recall.

"Maybe school was over." Jane tried to be helpful.

"Or maybe he died." Giny's tone was fatalistic. "Anyway, Sydney is a girl. She probably washes her hands every hour and her hair every day. She can stay a long ways from dirt and from Scott. But Brent . . ." Her voice faded away momentarily. "Boys are so dirty in comparison. They get into everything." She took a long breath. "Jane, I don't want my boy using the same bathroom as Scott Harper. Or lunchroom, or classroom. I mean it. I'll go to court to see that it doesn't happen."

But he's just a little boy, Jane was thinking. Why did he have to be in the middle of such antagonism? Just when he would be needing more love and understanding than ever before in his twelve years, he would be abandoned, and left to face the inevitable alone.

Then, suddenly, a thought ripped through her like a dagger searching for her heart. On Sydney's dresser, off to the left corner, was a small brass, bell-shaped object. It was a mouthpiece for her French horn that she had borrowed from Scott Harper until a replacement arrived.[38]

What Are Your Odds?

Apart from all the known ways of contracting AIDS, six percent of the cases involve no known factor to transmit it.[39] Millions of us have already been and will continue to be exposed to this insidious destroyer of the immune system. Diseases of the autoimmune system are on the increase. Cancer, which is very often caused by a virus, continues to be the number two killer, right behind heart disease. What can we do to decrease our chances of harboring these life-threatening viruses? Obviously, when we look at what we can do to strengthen our immune systems, we have to look at some things that are destructive to it. Chemicals such as radiation and chemotherapy may destroy cancer viruses, but like the Killer T cells, they also destroy body cells and devastate the immune system.[40]

Smoking depresses the immune system,[41] as does extended bereavement, such as in the death of a spouse.[42] Guilt is a major factor, also.[43]

Dr. Anthony S. Fauci, director of the National Institute of Allergy and Infectious Diseases, has made some recommendations for carriers of AIDS that could apply to the rest of us. He has emphasized getting enough rest, eating nutritious foods, refraining from smoking, using alcohol prudently or abstaining altogether, getting plenty of exercise and fresh air, and learning to manage stress.

Dr. G. Fernandes of Austin, Texas, states that "moderate dietary restrictions and dietary manipulations can enhance immune function as well as prolong life and lower the incidence or delay the onset of autoimmune-type diseases."[44]

Granted, there is much confusion as to what constitutes a nutritious diet. After a couple of decades of overdosing on saturated fats in meats, we have been told to replace more of those fats with unsaturated or polyunsaturated fats. However, the evidence is mounting that the only safe course is to reduce total fats in the diet altogether. Dr. Fernandes points out that while dietary consumption of animal fat is down some seven percent since the turn of the century, vegetable fat is up by some three hundred percent. Cancer statistics are up, too.[45]

In fact, evidence is mounting that by exchanging saturated fat for more refined polyunsaturated and unsaturated oils, we may be merely exchanging a reduced risk of heart disease for an increased risk of cancer. Studies are beginning to suggest that the concentrated vegetable oils are responsible for creating more unstable free radicals than saturated animal fat. And the presence of free radicals suppress the immune system, are co-carcinogenic and increase the risk for cancer.[46]

To enable the body to rid itself of the free radicals produced by such large intakes of these concentrated vegetable oils, we need to be getting adequate but not excessive (as in supplementation) amounts of antioxidants, found in vitamins C, A, E, and selenium.[47] And the best sources for those vitamins are fruits, grains, and vegetables.[48]

Don't forget that daily brisk exercise has the effect of "pasteurizing" the blood for several hours. Therefore, exercise is a very definite enhancer of the immune system function.[49]

One final recommendation for promoting a healthy immune system is to maintain a positive mental attitude. Especially since we're up against the awesome odds of one in a hundred.

MYTHING OUT ON LIFE, OR "DO YOU HAVE ANOTHER DIET PLAN FOR ME TO TRY?"

The all-American spirit is indomitable. It refuses to be beaten, to give in, to succumb. Or to quit.

At least that's the way it is for the sixty-five million Americans who are constantly on a diet.[1] In spite of the odds against success, they keep trying the latest plan, promotion, or preparation. American adults are burdened by some 2.3 billion pounds of excess body fat.[2] Imagine a double line of bumper to bumper eighteen-wheelers, each loaded with twenty tons of fat. They would stretch from New York City to Los Angeles! Moreover, this figure does not take into account the alarming increase in childhood obesity.

For those who indulge in the all-American sport of consuming whatever appeals to the senses whenever it does, a gain of one quarter pound a week can amount to a fortune of weight in ten years; perhaps 120 pounds. This does not take into account what may happen after twenty or thirty years of indulging the appetite. So diet plans abound, and eager entrepreneurs, ever ready to reap the benefits of this indomitable spirit, laugh all the way to the bank. Consider the Jeneric family, who are traditional all-Americans in their approach to eating and, consequently, to dieting.

Fat for Life

After another day locked behind his office door, Joe Jeneric sighed as he headed down the hall to the elevator. He knew he should take the stairs, but was too tired to care. In front of him a couple of freckle-faced junior high boys with matching punk hairdos giggled as they shared a comic book between them. Probably paper boys. Joe thoughts were elsewhere as he crowded against them, squeezing his body away from the closing doors.

The mass of compressed humanity remained speechless, heads tilting so each pair of eyes could watch the lighted panel over the double doors. Even the matched freckle-faces behind him were quiet. Joe smiled to himself, wondering why people always behaved the same on elevators. He silently watched to see which floor was coming up.

The car bounced to a stop, knocking the woman in front of him backwards, and pushing Joe into the teenagers behind him. One of them had his foot widened as Joe stepped back, trying to keep from falling. As the mass of humanity emerged, Joe caught juvenile references to "fat old man" and "crippled forever" floating by.

Even the suffocating July heat that enveloped him as he headed for the parking lot was not enough to derail his train of thought. He had a right to get steamed up, he thought, pushing headlong into a higher zone of heat in his car. Grumpy and indignant, he stretched the seat belt over the bulge in his middle.

"I'm going to do something about this extra baggage," he resolved, down-shifting the Mustang to make a run off the ramp for the freeway. "Maybe Jean will get serious with me; she's always trying some new diet plan or other."

Dinner for the Jeneric family was especially rowdy that evening. Jeffrey, a high school senior, and Jennifer, a sixth grader, could hardly eat as Joe detailed the drama in the elevator. Even Joe's wife, Jean, had to cover her mouth with a napkin to hide her laughter.

"Come on," Joe insisted. "This isn't supposed to be funny. Can't you imagine how insulted I felt when those two little punks called me fat?"

"Punkers, Dad," corrected Jeffrey.

"Well, whatever." Joe was beyond caring. "And old! I'm only thirty-eight and a few pounds to the heavy side." He stabbed at his meat in indignation.

"Oh, Dad," Jennifer held her sides and leaned away from the table. "It's just the way you described them. The hair and the freckles and the comic book."

"Yeah, they probably never even saw your face." Jeffrey's face was still smiling from laughter.

"Right, just my circumference," Joe interrupted.

"But honey, it is a very humorous story." Jean wiped her eyes with her napkin.

"Well, I'm not trying to provide entertainment for anyone, just trying to get a little sympathy from my own family." Joe was enjoying the attention.

Jennifer clapped her hands. "I know, Daddy! You and Mom can go on a diet together. Mom's always trying out new ones. The two of you can help each other."

"Yes, and we could be the support system." Jeffrey's generous offer held overtones of irony.

"I've already thought of that." Joe buttered his bread as he spoke. "We'll let your mother see what she can come up with. And perhaps the two of us will allow your opinions to be expressed at the dinner table." He took a bite of bread and smiled at the kids.

That night before turning out the light, Joe and Jean had a short discussion about Joe's new resolve.

"Joe, this is great," Jean exulted. "There's something about turning the corner on forty that makes you want to be skinny again, isn't there?"

"No," Joe reflected on the day. "Actually, there's something about being called 'a fat old man' that makes you want to be skinny again." He punched some buttons on his clock radio and, sighing, climbed into bed.

"Well honey, we've gotten into this together; we'll just get out of it together." She smiled at Joe before turning out the light.

The Ultra-Nutra System

"Mom, tell Dad about this new diet plan you've discovered!" Jennifer's excitement set the mood for dinner several nights later. Joe was busy making inroads into Jean's lasagna, ignoring, for the most part, the salad accompaniment.

"Well, Jean, let's hear about it." Joe reached for more French bread. Jeffrey was silent, savoring his mother's cooking. "Oh honey, I think you'll be interested in this. There is a new franchise that has opened in the Meadowlake Center which has a money-back guarantee for those who sign up." Jean helped herself to more salad.

"Money-back guarantee?" Jeffrey chortled. "Sounds like you can't lose. Ha, ha."

"Now wait a minute," Joe broke in. "That's great marketing strategy. I bet the average person who doesn't lose weight on the plan is not going to ask to see the manager to admit he's still a fatso."

The table erupted in laughter.

"What's the name of the plan?" Joe asked with interest.

"It's called Ultra-Nutra," Jean responded.

"Ultra-Nutra?" Joe was incredulous. "That sounds like cow feed to me!"

More laughter. Jennifer cut in. "At least it sounds more serious than the 'Cookie Diet' or that 'Grapefruit Diet' you tried last month, Mom."

"Yeah," Jeffrey added, "and hopefully it has better endorsement than *The National Enquirer*."

"Just a minute everyone." Jean tried to get control of the conversation. "The focus of this plan is to try to help the individual understand why he or she has a tendency to obesity."

"Who needs counseling for that? People get fat because they love to eat." Joe helped himself to more lasagna. "Maybe I could get a job there nights."

Jennifer and Jeffrey laughed. Jean shook her head.

"Listen Joe," she tried again. "They have professional counselors who help you to modify your eating habits. But the real difference, it appears, is that you buy their prepackaged food so you can't go off their diet."

"That's it!" Joe was getting excited. "This franchise got a deal on K-Rations from the Army. With some spiffy repackaging and a little advertising, they're making a killing."

Jean and Jeffrey laughed. Jennifer wanted to know what "K-Rations" were.

"I'll explain it later, honey," Joe grinned at his daughter.

"But Joe, we really should take a look at this," Jean was insistent. "The facts are that this is a rapidly growing franchise with a money-back guarantee."

"So what does it cost for both of you?" Jeffrey questioned.

Jean answered, "The two of us can go for a little over $80 a month each for six months of counseling. Our prepackaged meals average about $2 per person per meal."

"You can't even eat at McDonald's for that, Dad," Jennifer contributed.

"Just think, everyone," Joe added. "No more home-cooked meals. Just like on bivouac! All you need is a canteen of water and K-Rations—those so-called 'nutritionally' balanced meals that taste like they have been prepared by Georgia-Pacific Paper Products." He looked over at Jennifer.

Jeffrey had an idea. "Say Dad, why not save yourself some money and re-enlist?"

"That's a thought," Joe responded, momentarily recalling his former trim self in full dress Army uniform. "What I'd like to know," he continued, "is what happens when the K-Rations are gone? When do you quit buying their products? All their counseling is superfluous if I can't do it on my own, in my own kitchen. And what about eating out?"

"That's simple," said Jeffrey, trying to be helpful. "You just look for another 'Ultra-Nutra' store."

"Besides," Joe added, looking at Jean. "I have no intention of your selling that set of waterless cookware neither of us could live without after seeing the demonstration."

"But Dad," Jennifer was serious. "Mom would still have to cook for us. Jeff and I don't need to eat that kennel ration stuff."

Everyone laughed but Jennifer. Joe looked at his daughter. "K-Rations, my dear. Kennel Ration is dog food." More laughter.

"I hadn't thought of that," mused Jean. "It would be hard to cook for the kids and then open one of their little tins of tuna for myself."

Jennifer giggled. "It sounds like baby food, Mom."

Joe consoled her. "Maybe they have a little picnic area where we could make reservations, to keep us away from the kitchen and subsequent temptations. By the way," he continued, "have you sat down to figure out the cost of this plan?"

Jeffrey was quick to help. "Eighty dollars a month each for six months—that's $480 apiece."

"Don't forget the K-Rations," Joe reminded him. "At two dollars a meal times six meals a day, we're spending an additional $350 a month, just for the two of us. Not to mention what it costs to keep Jenn and Jeff here in potato chips and cokes. Say, Jean" Joe had an idea. "Why don't you look into the cost of one of those franchises? It sounds like someone could make a great living off of fat people." Joe was in the mood for humor.

"Okay, Joe" Jean gave in. "We'll drop this one. We've got to be mutually agreed on a diet plan, and it's obvious that you only want to laugh at this one." She laughed herself. "I just thought this idea of the 'prepackaged' concept for control was pretty good."

"I'd rather spend the grand on five-star restaurants," Joe retorted. He looked at Jennifer. "Would you pass the cookies, please? I'd like some with my grapefruit."

The "I Love the Big Apple Diet"

The back door opened and slammed just as Jean was pulling the evening's meal of oven fried potatoes and broiled flounder from the oven. "Home gang," called Joe, flinging his briefcase on the couch. "What's for supper?"

"Looks like it's the 'I Love the Big Apple Diet'." Jeffrey picked up Jean's latest diet book from the counter. "Another diet plan to discuss?" Jennifer was excited at the prospect. "What's this?" She glanced at the cover. "You eat apples to lose weight?"

"Now hear this." Joe waved his arm in a semi-circle. "Your mother and I will ask for your opinions on the diet of our choice when we want them. Until then . . ."

He was interrupted by Jean, calling the family to the table.

Jeffrey announced from the dining room as the family assembled "Calling to order the official meeting of D.I.E.T—'Diet Information Exposed Tonight.'" He took his place at the table.

Following Joe's blessing, the family launched into a lively discussion of Jean's latest find in the field of diets. As usual, the exchange made a good accompaniment for her meal.

"Now everyone," Jean begged. "Before you get critical, let me tell you that this plan is endorsed by doctors and other health professionals." She passed the asparagus tips in cream sauce. Joe passed them right on to Jennifer.

Jennifer looked at her father. "Dad, aren't you having any?" She handed the bowl back to him.

Joe looked at Jean and then at his daughter. "Oh. Yes. Of course." He carefully placed one delicate strand on his plate, then smothered it with sauce.

"Who are these health professionals?" he asked. "I hope not the American Dietetics Association."

"And what's wrong with them?" Jeffrey wanted to know.

"Don't you know," his father answered, "that most of their members work in hospitals, and that hospital food is specifically designed to lengthen your stay?" He smiled, waiting for the inevitable reaction.

"Based on my last stay, I have no quarrel with that statement," Jean responded. "The food is so over-cooked it's almost pre-digested." She looked around the table, hoping no one was offended.

"So what's the scoop on this 'Big Apple Diet'?" Joe wanted to know. "Why did you choose it?"

"I found this quote in the book by some doctor who had tested the diet on a group of families." Jean paused, leafing through the book. "Oh, here it is. 'This dietary regime was readily acceptable by the family and required no change in the family diet habits.' Plus it was a bestseller in New York and the recipes looked pretty interesting." She cut a bite of flounder, savoring it.

Jeffrey took a swallow of water. "So I'd like to know how you guys think this plan will work if it requires no change in the family diet habits? Who are they trying to kid?"

"'Whom,' Jeffrey," Jean corrected.

"No, Mom. Get with it. 'Whom' is now considered archaic." Jeffrey smiled at her.

"What's wrong with that?" Joe was interested. "That's just what I'm looking for. Get this Crisco off my waist without having to change my basic diet." He reached for the book.

Jennifer was thoughtful, "But Dad, if what you've been eating has caused you and Mom to get fat . . ." "'Gain weight' is a better term, Jennifer," Jean corrected.

"Okay, 'gain weight.' Then how can you lose with a diet that's the same?"

"Now let's not jump to conclusions, Jenn," Joe was adamant. "Let's hear Mom out." He looked at Jean. "Why don't you tell us the features, honey?"

"Okay." Jean took the book back from Joe. "Basically, there's a one week crash program where some claim to lose as much as ten pounds. You eat up to seven times a day, get about four eggs, plenty of tea, coffee, and all the diet soft drinks you want plus about thirteen servings of various meats during the week. And supposedly this is a low calorie, low fat diet."

"If it is, then the servings must be small, to say the least," interjected Joe.

"What's this about eating up to seven times a day?" Jeffrey was curious. "Back sometime around the fourth grade when we studied the basic food groups, we were told that it wasn't good to eat in between meals."

"Funny you should remember that now," Jennifer interjected, "when you could hardly finish your homework last night without the Doritos."

"Well, I'm not on a diet," Jeffrey defended himself.

"Maybe the principle behind all this snacking is because your calories are so restricted at mealtime, the snacking during the day helps you to forget you didn't get very much at lunch or dinner." Joe's voice sounded hopeful. "You know it's easier for dieters to fall off the wagon if they're restricted to only two or three meals a day," Joe continued, trying to make some sense out of the plan.

"But what are all those calorie-free stimulants doing to your body?" Jean questioned. "Maybe you do lose weight by keeping your digestive system in constant motion without giving it anything, really, to work on. But at what price to the nervous system?" She shook her head.

"Well, this conversation has gone over my head," Jennifer commented. "Would someone please pass the potatoes?"

"Jean," Joe questioned, "do you like this plan or not? It doesn't sound too bad to me." He looked around for the dessert.

"It's carob brownies." Jeffrey read his thoughts. "I'll get them." He headed for the kitchen.

"What kind of brownies?" Joe asked in wonderment.

"Oh, just a new mix I found at the health food store this morning," Jean was casual.

She continued. "Back to this diet. Reading the cover and introduction, I was really excited to try it. Plus, the recipes looked great. But when I started reading through the book, I'll admit I had to question the 'healthfulness' of what I was reading—that is, from a basic nutritional standpoint."

"Both of you have to agree to go on one together," Jennifer reminded her parents.

"Just listen to this," Jean added, flipping through the book. "After you complete the first week, you get to reward yourself with a binge."

"A binge!" Jeffrey could hardly believe what he was hearing. "Is that related to the bingeing and purging we've been discussing in health science?"

"It's probably what started it, Jeff," Joe grinned at his son.

"Well, they call it a 'controlled' binge," Jean stated matter of factly. She continued reading. "You get to enjoy 'potatoes, pasta, blue cheese dressing, bread and rolls, rice, beef stew, chopped liver, peanut butter, commercial breakfast cereals, margarine, your favorite cheeses, cole slaw, condiments, and cakes and desserts.' Yet the program promises 'you won't gain an ounce, and you could lose several pounds.'"

"You know what I think?" Jeffrey finished off a brownie, "This diet would offer more success if it just stuck to apples."

"Well, I'll tell you what I think." Jennifer stacked the dishes. "I'm going to keep my weight where it should be so I won't ever have to go through this when I get old." She stopped suddenly, looking at her parents.

Jean ignored her daughter's comment. "I think I've learned something from our discussion tonight. We're going to have to find a plan that does more than just tell us how to rein in a bad lifestyle. The average American diet will soon be the death of all of us. I don't care how good your intentions are to stay skinny." She looked at Jennifer.

"So this one's out?" Joe wanted to know.

"As far as I'm concerned," Jean answered.

"Well, see if you can't find one that steers clear of K-rations and apples for our next get together," her son admonished.

The Snacklee Plan

Several days had passed since the last Jeneric discussion on diets. Jean had been making a conscious effort to restrict foods that were commonly known to be fattening, such as the usual morning doughnuts, and had even replaced the evening serving of red meat with chicken or fish. Still, both Joe and Jean wanted outside help from a diet they could trust, and yet one that would have some results.

"What's for dinner tonight?" Jeffrey charged in from the back yard, where he had been playing catch with a next-door neighbor.

"It's a surprise." Jean glanced at him, then at Joe, reading the evening paper.

"I know," Jeffrey grinned, "it's another D.I.E.T. convention."

"Well, we certainly put the quietus on the last two plans." Joe looked up. "Got another one to critique, dear?" he grinned.

"Do I ever," Jean responded good naturedly. "And it's tied in with dinner tonight."

"Does that mean we have to like the plan to get any food?" Jennifer walked into the kitchen.

Jean took a plate from the microwave and put another one in its place. "No. You kids are having leftover spaghetti. Your dad and I are having something a little different this evening." She set the hot plate at Jeffrey's place on the dining room table.

"This program has what I would call 'fringe' endorsement." Jean reached for the glasses.

"The kind that rhymes with 'binge?'" Jeffrey wanted to know.

"What I want to know," commented Joe, ignoring Jeffrey and getting concerned, "is what I'm going to be eating tonight." He moved towards the table suspiciously.

Jean set a crystal parfait glass at Joe's place and her own, then took out a blender full of something pink from the refrigerator.

"What you're having, dear, is fourteen vitamins, six minerals, eleven grams of protein, seven grams of fat, and a few grams of natural fiber." She poured the blend into their glasses.

Jeffrey looked at Jennifer. He spoke out of the corner of his mouth in her direction. "This is going to be a good one."

"Wait a minute, Jean." Joe was getting panicky. "Is this all I get for dinner? We're just discussing diet plans. We haven't decided on any yet, have we?" He looked over at Jeffrey's steaming plate of spaghetti. "Don't I get any leftovers?"

"Here, Dad," Jeffrey was helpful. "Allow me to get you a straw."

Jean brought Jennifer's plate from the microwave. "Shall we say grace?"

As the family began to eat, Joe cautiously tried a sip of his drink. "Jean! What is this? It tastes like soaked tree bark!" He pushed the glass away.

Jean, tasting her drink, looked at Joe. "The directions said to use water or milk; maybe I'd better try the milk." She gathered the glasses and headed for the kitchen. After a few whizzing sounds coming from the direction of the kitchen, she returned with what resembled a chocolate milk shake. Joe was doubtful.

"Come on, Mom. Don't keep us in suspense any more." Jeffrey was enjoying his spaghetti and meatballs. "What's this new plan you're springing on Dad?"

Joe could smell the leftover spaghetti. He wondered if there was any more in the refrigerator. "I love leftover spaghetti," he thought to himself.

"The reason I said this plan had 'fringe' endorsement," Jean paused to take a sip of her drink, "is that it is based on supplementation of the normal diet."

Jennifer wanted to know what supplementation was.

"Vitamins, honey," Joe responded. "And you're not going to find too many health professionals excited about pushing those kinds of pills."

He took a swig of his drink. "Not had, Jean, since you added the milk. But I want to know when I get the hamburger and fries to go with it."

"Joe," Jean sighed, "we're trying to go on a diet."

"Listen, dear." Joe looked at Jean. "Here's my interpretation of supplementation: It's like foreign aid. You only need it if you're unable to manage the resources you already have."

Jennifer spoke. "What's it called, Mom?"

"The Snacklee Plan, honey." Jean looked out the window, avoiding Joe's eyes.

"But Mom," Jennifer continued. "I thought we agreed last time that snacks were out."

"As you can readily see, Jenn, it doesn't have to be a snack. This is the sum total of my dinner." Joe was morose.

Jeffrey offered his opinion. "It sounds like a hype to me. Do you ever get to eat real food?"

"According to the plan, once you've reached your ideal weight, then you use this 'protein' drink along with your meals, or at least once a day," Jean explained.

"So this is a 'protein' drink?" Joe looked at his glass. "I'm reminded of the Scarsdale diet of a few years ago."

"Well, we did lose quite a few pounds with it, Joe," Jean recalled.

"Yes, but according to Dr. Bateson, we were in danger of losing our kidneys along with the weight."

"How do you lose your kidneys with your weight?" Jennifer wanted to know.

"From what I can remember," Joe responded, "it had something to do with all the protein overload on the kidneys. You don't lose them, honey, just damage them."

"But Joe, if we're careful to curtail our other intake of high protein food, then the protein in this drink can't hurt us." Jean was getting discouraged. "Don't you want to lose weight?"

Jeffrey offered a suggestion. "You both could just carry around a little protein chart in your pockets."

"Joe, let's give it a try. I've purchased a month's supply of the weight control formula, in addition to the daily supplements." Jean looked for Joe's response.

"A month's supply! You mean I've got to eat this stuff— excuse me—drink this stuff for a month? You've got to be kidding! If I'm going to go on a diet, it's got to be more normal than if I had my jaws wired shut." Joe's thoughts were still on the spaghetti.

Jennifer and Jeffrey laughed at this exchange.

Jean continued. "The company does offer a program to make a little extra money selling the Snacklee products."

"You mean it's multi-level, Mom?" Jeffrey asked.

Joe answered matter of factly, "Your mother plans to pay off the mortgage in a few months." He looked at Jean.

"Now Joe, in all fairness, the Snacklee plan expects you to eat healthfully in addition to the suggested supplements and protein drink. They just suggest that the soil has been depleted of nutrients from all those pesticides and poor crop rotation, so their vitamins help take up the slack," Jean explained.

"Wait a minute," Jeffrey wanted the floor. "We just studied about that in biology. The quality of a plant's nutrients is more dependent upon the variety of that plant than on the condition of the soil.³ Plants will draw from the soil what they need to grow. Anyway, we learned that eating a variety of fruits and vegetables should take care of any lack of nutrients." He was proud of his contribution.

"Okay, you guys. I can see you've ditched another diet plan." Jean began cleaning the table. "I'm going to stick with this and see how it works . . ."

"With a month's supply in the pantry, I guess that would be a good idea," Joe contributed, pushing his chair back.

"Why don't you find a diet plan for the family round table to critique?" Jean noticed Joe looking in the refrigerator.

"Okay, Jean," he responded, "just so long as you don't plan on putting the silverware out at the next garage sale."

The Diet Sinner Plan

"Jean, this one may be the one!" Joe was near breathlessness after his hundred foot run from car to newspaper to house.

"That's great, honey. I'm just in the process of drinking my last meal, so I'm ready for — what is it — diet plan number four?" Jean sounded uncertain.

Joe was quizzical. "How could your month's supply already be gone?"

"Remember, she's paying off the mortgage this month." Jeffrey walked in on the conversation from the family room where he had been studying. "She's been selling inventory."

"Well, actually, I've given out some of my supply as samples," Jean admitted. "But I have lost about three pounds this past week, even if I haven't made any money."

"Good for you," Joe complimented her. "I've gained at least two since we started looking for this perfect plan. I think I eat more when I get anxious. And the thing I'm most anxious about is running into those two freckled newspaper boys in my present condition." He smiled, remembering the event.

"Hi, Dad." Jennifer waltzed downstairs from her room. She looked at her parents expectantly. "Are we going to discuss another diet plan?"

"Yes, Jennifer," Joe responded. "It's time for our weekly 'Diet Convention.'" He looked at his waist and sighed. "We've got to find something soon."

"But," he continued "I've done my homework, Jean, and I think you'll like some of the features of this one. What's for dinner?"

"Pizza," Jean answered. "And we're going to eat here at the deck rather than set the dining room table." She reached for the cold drinks in the refrigerator.

"Where is it?" Joe looked in the oven as he spoke.

The doorbell rang.

"At the front door," Jeffrey called over his shoulder as he ran to get it.

"So let's hear about your program, Dad." Jeffrey set the box down and reached for a slice. "Okay, everyone. Listen," Joe searched his pizza for something. He looked in the box, then at Jean. "Where's the pepperoni?"

Jean smiled at her husband. "Honey, this is the 'Vegetarian Sampler.' There is no meat."

"But there's enough cheese to make up for it." Jennifer strung her mozzarella out, trying to bite through it.

"Oh." Joe's look was predictable.

"Well, go on with your diet plan, Dad," Jeffrey urged.

"Yes. As I was starting to say, this program is just what I need. It has a negative motivational factor incorporated into it." Joe helped himself to another glass of Dr. Pepper.

"Honey, you're generally such a positive person. Why do you need negative reinforcement?" Jean was curious.

"Let me tell you what it is, first. It's called 'The Diet Sinner Plan.' That's S-i-n-n-e-r. A plan for those of us who abuse our bodies. This program constantly reminds us of how bad it is to eat 'normally.'" Joe smiled at his family, anticipating a lively discussion.

"Do these people think it is sinful to go on a diet, Dad?" Jennifer wanted to know.

"No honey, just sinful to be as overweight as I am," Joe smiled at his daughter.

"Dad, those kinds of gimmicks are for the backs of cereal boxes," Jeffrey laughed. "We've got to hear about this one."

"Well, Jean, this one is a bit like your 'Ultra-Nutra' plan of a few weeks back," Joe continued, "in that you receive professional counseling. You just don't have to buy the K-Rations. They just require weekly meetings to keep you pumped up like a bunch of Dale Carnegie Course rejects." He reached for a third slice of pizza. "These veggies aren't bad," he remarked, "when you're as hungry as I am." "Now, Jean, before you start finding fault with my diet program, let me add that there is more than adequate positive reinforcement for the weak and lame. But as for us strong-willed people, they like to keep our ears boxed." Joe motioned for more drink.

"But Dad," Jeffrey broke in, "if you're so strong-willed, why do you need any diet program at all? Just do it yourself."

Undaunted, Joe replied, "Because, this strong will needs direction, son, not impetus. That's all."

"Would you please explain to me why negative reinforcement is so important in the issue of losing weight?" Jean wanted to know.

"Okay," Joe eyed the remaining pieces, then reached for one. "Historically, fat folks have used food for positive reinforcement. And while it is true that the meal table should be a place of happy enjoyment, both in fellowship and eating, such as we're doing right now, most of us have begun to use food as a reward for good behavior. . . ."

Jennifer interrupted, "Like the times Mom has promised us cookies or some other goodies if we say please and thank you and brush our teeth after each meal?" Joe smiled at his younger child. "That's right, honey. But in addition, most of us heavies use food as an antidote for the bad times that occasionally beset us all. So, what The Diet Sinner Plan seeks to do is to sell its clients on the idea of eating only out of necessity — not for any other reason."

"Do you mean you can't even enjoy your food?" Jean looked questioningly at her piece of pizza, then at Joe.

"Oh no. It's okay to enjoy your food. You're just not supposed to use it as a reward for either the good times or the bad," Joe explained.

"Do they care what you eat?" Jean questioned, cutting the last piece in half.

"Oh sure," Joe got up and looked in the refrigerator. "But not excessively. The idea is somewhat like your 'Big Apple' plan where you eat mostly what we normally eat. You just learn to eat less. He turned to Jean. "Is there any of that meatloaf left from last night?"

Jeffrey and Jennifer looked at each other and grinned.

"What's the matter?" Joe wanted to know.

"Well, here you are talking about eating less while you're grazing in the refrigerator," Jeffrey laughed.

"I'll have you know I'm not committed to any diet, yet," Joe assured his family.

"Let me see if I get this straight." Jean looked at Joe. "This 'Diet Sinner Plan' is not particularly interested in a reeducation of my tastes and habits, but rather only in control of my present ones. True or false?"

"Basically, that answer is true," Joe conceded. "Look at the odds. Over ninety percent of all people who lose are going to gain their weight back. Those diet inventors have little faith in the ability of Joe Jeneric to change a lifetime of health-threatening habits short of a heart attack as a motivator."

"Dad, don't talk like that." Jennifer's concern was obvious.

Joe patted her arm. "I'm sorry, honey. I was just trying to make a point."

"You could look at it this way," Jeffrey had a suggestion. "The people who put these programs together like to sneak a few Snickers, too. They're not about to suggest something that is more far out than what they are willing to do themselves."

"Jeffrey," Jean responded, "that is an excellent point. I see it as trying to superimpose a few good habits over a lot of bad ones. Doesn't it make sense that the bad has got to be rooted out before the good can flourish?"

"I see that we're back to the old issue of what will happen when the diet program takes its 'arm of influence' from around our shoulders," Joe sighed. "We'll be right back where we started, maybe even worse."

"It seems to me you're right back where you started in the discussion anyway," Jennifer commented. "Dieting, or trying to figure out how, seems like a real drag."

Joe and Jean looked at each other. Then Jean spoke. "Okay, you two have listened to four plans. You have a basic idea of what we're looking for . . ."

". . . and what we're not looking for," Joe interjected.

"Yes," Jean continued. "The next one is up to you." She motioned to Jennifer and Jeffrey. "See what you can find. It can't be any worse than the four we've already covered."

Jeffrey jumped off his bar stool. "All right. You've got a deal! We'll take you up on it." He grabbed his sister and swung her around.

The Revolving Diet

A few nights later, Jennifer and Jeffrey met their father at the back door as he came in from work. "Hey Dad! We found it! We've got the plan for you and Mom to try!" Both competed for his attention at once.

"Okay, okay." Joe tried to get in the door and get rid of his briefcase and newspaper. He looked around for Jean. "Dinner ready, hon?" he called.

"Hi Joe," Jean called. "Give me ten minutes. Jennifer, would you please set the table. I'm ready to start the stir-fry." So saying she poured a summer's worth of fresh vegetables into the smoking wok.

Joe's eye caught the myriads of greens, purples, oranges, yellows, whites, and reds, drawing him to the counter where Jean was quickly stirring the mixture. He leaned over the wok, taking in the aroma of the fresh blend, and gave Jean a kiss as he straightened up.

"What a good cook I married." He smiled at her. "Say, how are you cooking those things?" he asked, noticing there was no oil.

"Oh, just basically steaming them," Jean replied. "It's what Julia Child refers to as the 'new way to sauté' in her latest book — you just rub the skillet with oil, then add a little water to continue the cooking by steaming."

"And you can skip all the oil, Dad." Jennifer bounded into the kitchen for the napkins.

"Where are you finding out all these things?" Joe was curious.

"Well Joe, until we find a diet we can both live with, I've just been reading what I can about healthful cooking and trying to make a few improvements here and there."

"And wait until you see what the improvement is on the pork." Jeffrey was headed for the table with pamphlets and paper.

"Pork?" Joe became suspicious. "Aren't we having sweet and sour pork with these vegetables, Jean?"

"Now honey, you know we're trying to curtail our use of red meat . . ."

Joe interrupted, "Oh, then you must be substituting chicken."

"Wrong, Dad," Jennifer answered, coming back from the dining room. "It's a surprise," she continued as Jean gave her a look.

Following the blessing, Joe inspected the food as it was passed. "Brown rice first. Well, Jean, you've finally gotten that one past me," he conceded, taking a large helping.

"Here Dad." Jeffrey handed him the glazed vegetables.

"Mmm, I love this sweet and sour sauce you've fixed for the vegetables, Jean." Joe was hungry. "What's this?" he queried as Jeffrey handed him another dish with small whitish-brown cubes.

"That's the surprise, Dad." Jennifer was smiling.

"I figured that out," Joe responded, "but what is it? It doesn't look like it was ever alive," he commented, taking a small amount. "Where do they go?"

"On top of the vegetables. Here's the soy sauce." Jean handed him the bottle. "Just give it a try, Joe. Then we'll tell you what it is." She smiled at the kids.

Joe took a bite, hesitantly chewed, swallowed, then reached his fork into the mound of food for more. "I don't know what you've cooked up here, Jean, but it's delicious. This mystery stuff is really light, but very crispy and tasty. Game's up. What is it?" He looked at his family. They were all watching him.

"It's tofu, Dad," both kids virtually shouted at him, grinning. "You've just eaten 'sweet and sour tofu.'"

Joe smiled good naturedly. "I hate to take all the fun out of this game, but I'm sorry, I don't have any idea what 'tofu' is. Is it some kind of fish?"

Jeffrey and Jennifer both looked to Jean for an explanation. "I'll get into it later, Joe," she said. "Why don't we look at Jeff and Jenn's diet plan?"

"Oh, I almost forgot," Jennifer smiled at her father.

"I didn't. I've got the info right here." Jeffrey patted the stack of materials beside his plate.

"Let's hear it for number five, son." Joe was eating with gusto.

"Please, let me tell about it," Jennifer begged.

"Go ahead, Jenn. You tell how we discovered it," Jeffrey conceded.

"Well," Jennifer tried hard to explain, "we were in Rover's Grocery Store and they had this contest going where you could sign up to lose weight. . . ."

"All right! Where do I go to sign up?" Joe kidded Jennifer.

"Dad!" Jennifer objected. "Anyway, with this plan there were 100,000 people in Los Angeles that lost two million pounds."

Joe couldn't resist. "Wow, with all that weight reduction maybe California won't fall into the ocean after all."

"What's it called, honey?" Jean tried to be serious for Jennifer's sake.

" 'The Revolving Diet,' Mom."

"Well, if that doesn't just fit my past dieting history," Joe joked. "The merry-go-round of gaining and losing and mostly gaining. Just one big circle of fat." Joe had come to enjoy these family discussions. He silently wondered, though, if he would ever get serious about losing weight.

"You see, Mom and Dad," Jeffrey sorted through his pamphlets, "the reason for the name is that you go through three weeks of dieting, the first and the third weeks are the same; the second week is a bit of a break. That's where the name 'Revolving' comes in."

"Okay kids, tell us about the regimen." Joe tried to get interested.

Jeffrey began. "The first week you eat a fairly balanced diet of 600-900 calories a day. Assuming you get through that week, then you get a reward of 1200 calories the second week."

Joe cut in, "Survive that and you get to reward yourself with another first week, right?"

"Have you seen this plan, Dad?" Jennifer wanted to know.

"Not this one, honey, but about a hundred just like it. But we'll take a good look at it," he assured her.

"Jeff, I'd like to take a look at the types of food you can eat." Jean reached for a pamphlet and leafed through it. "Oh look, Joe. This was developed by a professor at UCLA."

"So what can we eat?" Joe wanted to know.

"Dad, it seems to me that if you're going on a diet, you'd want to know what you can't eat." Jennifer looked at her father.

"Well, what you can or can't eat. It's all the same. It's usually just the amounts." Joe began to wish he'd never broached the subject of dieting with his family.

"Joe, it says here thirty percent of the calories can come from fat. That seems a bit high to me, for a diet." Jean perused the information some more.

"Don't you see, Jean, from a university standpoint, no one is going to offend the meat and dairy industries. Might get those big research grants cut off." Joe covered his mouth as he yawned. He looked around. "It's been a long day," he apologized.

"Well, Dad, Jenn and I thought you and Mom would be intrigued with this 'revolving' bit. It gives you a bit of a change." Jeffrey was still leafing through the material.

"Yes, dear, I'd like to know what you think about that feature." Jean started stacking plates.

"My biology classes are basically covered with cobwebs, but as best as I can recall, it takes the body a while to adjust to fewer calories. That's why you'd probably lose weight quickly that first week." Joe was pensive.

"It's probably the reason most diet plans work well for a short time," Jean agreed.

"No doubt. But then after a time the body readjusts its metabolic rate and weight loss is so slow it's downright discouraging."[4] Joe spoke from experience. "So most people just give it up. No doubt this 'Revolving Diet' keeps the body in such a state of confusion with all those changes that weight loss is achieved and then some sort of maintenance plan can be implemented."

"What's this!" Jean had come across some information. "There are recipes in here using pork. I can't believe it." "Mom, what's wrong with pork?" Jennifer wanted to know. "We used to eat it."

"From the reading I've done, the trend in healthy eating is definitely towards a vegetarian lifestyle." Jean prepared for an uproar. "Now let me finish, please. I said 'towards.' That doesn't mean you go the whole route, of course. Just move in that direction. Anyway, for a diet plan to recommend one of the meats highest in cholesterol . . . I don't know. I just don't think I could get excited about it." She shook her head.

"We are getting picky," Jeffrey commented. "Let's see what else we can find to finish this one off." He leafed through the material. Here! It says there's unlimited snacking. We've already decided that's off limits. Now what else is there?" He continued looking.

Joe looked at Jean, then at Jeffrey and Jennifer. He really was pretty picky, he decided, when it came to food and diets.

"Joe." Jean shook her head. "What am I going to do with you? Look how you start the day — with a snack, basically. Some sort of sweet something to send you off to the office for coffee and another snack before lunch. And the rest of your day continues in the same pattern. I'd like to know what would happen if I could get you to eat just three square meals a day." She sighed.

"The only diet plan we'd be looking for would be for you." Joe shrugged his shoulders.

"Do you really believe you would lose weight if you quit eating between meals, Dad?" Jennifer wanted to know.

"Well, maybe if I did that in addition to making some changes in what I eat," her father conceded. "I was going to share this with you, Jean. I found it in a diet and nutrition letter the other day.[5] When it comes to counting calories for dieting, the average person is never sure just how much corn, for example, constitutes 100 calories — it's easy to hit or miss on a one half cup serving. So, let's say I miss to the amount of only 150 calories each day — maybe just one ounce of salad dressing. By the end of one year, guess how much extra baggage I'll have picked up?"

Everyone is quiet.

"Fifteen pounds," Joe answered his own question.

"So, getting out of this dilemma is easy," Jeffrey offered. "Just design your own plan. And be sure not to call it a diet!"

"I wouldn't be so adverse to that," Jean responded. "I wasn't going to say anything to hurt you kids' feelings about your diet plan, but since we've become so introspective about this issue, I'll share this with you. Please don't take it personally." She looked at Jeffrey and then Jennifer. Jean pulled a clipping from her pocket. "When I saw you kids bring in your information about the 'Revolving Diet,' I checked my file. I thought I had clipped an article about it."

"So what does it say, Mom?" Jeffrey wanted to know.

"Basically, it tells of Rover's Grocery Stores sponsoring your diet, the 'Revolving Diet,' for the second time, calling it the 'Revolving Plus Diet.' It is mostly for people of normal weight and slightly heavier people who need only minor adjustments."

"You mean this has been at Rover's before?" Jennifer wanted to know.

"Apparently, over a year ago, and a lot of people signed up," Jean said.

"It must have been a popular diet, then," Jeffrey contributed.

"Maybe. But the second go-round — no pun intended — was a total flop. And can you all figure out why?" Jean looked at her family.

"Because no one kept off the weight they lost the first time around," Joe read her mind aloud.

The Jeneric family members looked at each other. Jeffrey shrugged. Jennifer leaned her head on her hand.

Joe took the lead. "I vote for one more attempt at finding the diet plan of the century. If this last effort fails, then the Jeneric family will design its own." He stood up.

"Hurray for Dad," Jennifer clapped her hands.

"And poor Mom," Jeffrey put his arm around Jean. "She's the one that gets to find it."

From the refrigerator, Joe called, "Where is this stuff called tofu?"

Fit Forever

"Say Jean, these burritos aren't bad." Joe reached for another. "What's in them?"

"Jennifer helped make them. Tell your father what you put

in them, honey," Jean responded, glancing at a book lying next to her place mat.

"Let's see," Jennifer thought aloud, "beans, avocados, lettuce, tomatoes, hot sauce. That's all I can remember. Oh yes, and the flour tortilla. It's whole wheat, Dad."

"You didn't have to tell him that." Jeffrey was always ready to bring out his father's lighter side at the dinner table. "I'm not as concerned over the color of the tortilla as I am over the missing ingredient in the burrito: what happened to the cheese?" Joe wanted to know. He spied Jean's book. "Ah ha! I see we're going to have another meeting of the minds over the latest diet plan. What's this one called?"

"Most appropriately, 'Fit Forever,'" Jean responded. "Isn't this to be our last round table discussion on diets?"

"I'll be glad when we're through with this," Jennifer commented. "There is always something wrong with every one of these plans. I don't think we're ever going to find the perfect one."

"Well," Joe swallowed another bite of his burrito, "let's give this one a fair chance. It certainly has a positive name."

"This has got to be quick. I've got a big test in biology tomorrow," Jeffrey added, "but I wouldn't miss this for anything." He grinned. "Since we have a basic routine for these discussions, I'll get right to the negatives." Jean took another burrito and passed the rice to Jennifer.

Everyone smiled.

She continued, "It does have some snacking; some of the food combinations are a little weird, and it drives the medical community absolutely wild."

"Well, now that we have that behind us," Joe reached for the book, "let's get on with the good points. If there are any." Everyone smiled again. Actually, Jean, I'd like to know why you chose this plan," Joe was curious.

"Because Joe," Jean answered, "this is the first diet plan that I've looked at that is truly different from all the rest. The direction is away from high fat foods."

"It's that 'creeping vegetarianism' again," Jeffrey contributed.

Joe ignored his statement. "What is it that has the medical community so astir?"

"Oh, the authors' contention that fruit is the only food that should be eaten before noon." Jean looked around at her family as she spoke.

"Mom," Jennifer was surprised, "this sounds like a real punk diet. Nothing but fruit until lunch?"

"Supposedly the body goes through its elimination cycle more intensely during the morning hours. And according to the information, it's easier to digest light foods such as fruit during this cycle." Jean was not sure she understood what she was saying.

"And it's this 'cycle' business that's driving the medical community nuts, right?" Jeffrey wanted to know.

"I see the red snack flag," Joe waved his napkin in the air. "If I can only eat fruit until lunch, guess who's going to be snacking all morning long? However," he pondered the information, "I could use a few more elimination cycles."

The Jeneric children snickered, then looked at their mother.

"Really, Joe, the table isn't the place . . ." Jean looked at her husband.

"So when do you get into the real food?" Joe wanted to know.

"You pick up your calories at the noon and evening meal. This plan is great for fitting in with the all-American habit of eating the biggest meal in the evening." She looked at her family, "But . . ."

Joe interrupted, "But who wants to recount the whole day in your sleep while your stomach keeps you awake digesting your food? I must admit I've been sleeping much better since you started serving us lighter dinners, suppers, or whatever you want to call them, Jean." He looked appreciatively at his wife.

"What about the low fat business?" Jeffrey glanced at his watch, thinking of his biology exam.

"There's a pretty heavy emphasis on fruits, vegetables, grains, and nuts," Jean answered. "Animal products like meat and dairy and poultry are considered unnecessary."

"Unnecessary!" Joe exclaimed. "I think this diet is unnecessary."

"But Dad," Jeffrey explained, "consider where most of your calories, cholesterol, and fat come from: meat, dairy products, and eggs."

"That explains what happened to the cheese in the burritos," Joe sighed. "First it's brown rice, then tufu . . ."

"Tofu, Dad," Jennifer interrupted.

"Well, whatever." Joe was past caring.

"While we're on the subject of unusual dietary concepts, there's one on enzymes you might be interested in. Would you hand me the book, please, Joe?" Jean requested. She leafed through it. "Here it is: 'To properly cleanse the body of toxins one should primarily consume food that is made up of seventy percent or more water.' "

"Can't we just drink water?" Jennifer wanted to know.

"Not according to this," Jean answered. "Water doesn't contain the necessary enzymes that fruits and vegetables do to properly cleanse those toxins."

"Can't we just make up our own plan?" Jennifer was getting lost.

"Wait a minute!" Jeffrey recalled something from biology. "Enzymes are merely catalysts of metabolic activity in the body. They don't have anything to do with moving out wastes." He was proud of his contribution.

"One more complicated part, then I'm finished." Jean continued to leaf through the book. "The authors stress that improper combinations of food, like potatoes and beans, will slow down digestion because they're both considered to be concentrated food. Consequently, all the extra energy needed to get these foods through the body will create more toxins through fermentation in the stomach. In a sentence, here's the whole idea behind the plan: these excess toxins are the linchpins of weight gain."

"Wow," Joe yawned. "I don't think I'm smart enough to take on this diet." He glanced at the book. "Look, the cover says this is the 'program to shatter all the myths.' I think I'd be safe in saying it's going to create a few new myths itself."

Jeffrey headed for his room. "Six up; six down."

Joe headed for the family room. As he passed the refrigerator, he looked in, then shut the door. "I vote for the 'Jeneric Plan' myself.

PART TWO

LIVING THE EIGHT PRINCIPLES IN FIVE WEEKS

INTRODUCTION
TO PART II

The Jeneric family, in its pursuit of a diet for all reasons, merely represents a microcosm of the universal problem afflicting one in four Americans at any given time. Because of the prevailing failure rate of the average American currently on a diet, large numbers of these disgruntled dieters, as we saw with the Jeneric family, have been implementing dietary changes on their own.

Many of these changes are nothing more than just plain common sense, such as steaming, rather than frying, vegetables, and drastically reducing, or even eliminating, the use of foods high in cholesterol. Other ideas for change come from reading and hearing about ways to improve health and longevity through diet and exercise.

The difficulty in deciding what changes to make is, as always, in determining the credibility of the influences that lie behind these suggestions. Obviously, advertisements promoting the benefits of eating beef or of consuming large quantities of dairy products, which have been appearing in major magazines and even in physicians' journals, should be taken for what they are: biased propaganda sponsored by those who stand to gain from our food dollar. It is better to listen to the voice of the American Heart Association, the American Cancer Society, and independent studies before deciding whether or not to continue eating and drinking these items. Dietary changes that promise immediate results should also be shunned. Time is a key factor in the complex restoration of a previously abused body.

There are many of us who have yet to reap the grim harvest of a life of indulgences; we continue to tempt fate with impunity.

Yet despite all who may manifest no overt symptoms from unhealthy choices, the great majority of us still have no concept of
what it means to really experience the vibrant life. Making the
decision to change to healthy choices can and will yield abundant returns, not only for the present, but also for the future by
preparing us for a rich enjoyment of all the seasons of life. From
the first flush of youthful springtime to the slowdown of life's last
wintry era, all seasons may be enhanced by the choices we make
right now.

Reduce Your Risks for the Great American Diseases

In the first portion of this book, we presented a rationale for
better choices. It is a rare family indeed that cannot identify with
at least one of these insidious, but preventable, lifestyle diseases,
whether directly or hereditarily. It is a rare person indeed who
wants to become the victim of heart disease, cancer, diabetes, or
one of the immune-related illnesses. Similarly, it is a rare person
past the age of thirty-five who doesn't want to lose weight.

Consequently, the objective of this second section is to introduce a plan for making responsible, informed lifestyle choices
that will help us — as far as is scientifically understood — to reduce our risk of participation in these Great American Diseases.
When we choose to follow these suggestions, we will also gain a
fresh and purposeful new grasp of the meaning of dynamic
health. And for the majority of Americans who choose to make
this plan a committed part of their lifestyle, there will be an
added bonus: weight loss.

Keys to Success

What are the keys for insuring the success of our new
choices?

First, this plan is simple. We don't need to be highly educated professionals to understand and implement the principles
of a healthy lifestyle. While it is true that the body is an exceed-
ingly complex system, its care and operation can be understood
and appreciated by any average fourth grader. In fact, caring for
our health is as natural as giving birth. Ninety-five percent of all
women delivering babies have no need for the high tech procedures so readily available in hospitals; similarly, ninety-five

percent of all Americans wouldn't need specialized medical care if they took care of themselves.

The point is that the authors respect the readers' ability to make responsible decisions based on reliable data without the interference of those professionals who are trained with the attitude that too much care is better than too little. Of course, individuals under care for a specific medical condition should discuss these suggestions with their physicians before continuing the plan.

Second, this plan is reasonable. Removing ourselves from the mainstream of everyday habits into some isolated corner may engender some temporary changes in our lives, mainly weight loss. But the inevitable return to "real" life may overcome the loss of everything gained during our withdrawal, or, to state this problem in more American terms, the gaining back of everything lost. Long term success is unlikely without redirecting the everyday habits that make up our total lifestyle picture.

This plan does not make us feel "removed" from mainstream living, but rather seeks to incorporate the rationale for making permanent changes within our everyday living. Evidence shows conclusively that the lifestyle of the future is the one we are suggesting. By following the plan now, we'll not only keep up with the Jones, but probably move ahead of them.

Third, this plan is effective. Although the first week of the plan may appear deceptively simple, those who implement these simple suggestions during the first week will find their investment in this plan more than repaid by tangible improvements in physical, as well as mental and emotional, health.

Fourth, this plan has staying power. It will last. Our daily choices are executed along one of two possible pathways. One is the pathway of preferences; the other, the pathway of convictions. Obviously, both choices play a role in our lives, but it is our convictions that give real substance and direction to our lives. Participants in this plan will be led to the conviction that lifestyle choices matter, not only for the present, but also for the future. They are not only for our good, but also for the good of our children, and yes, for the good of society.

Finally, the best plans are progressive. In addition to allowing for individual differences, this plan encourages the partici-

pant to continually seek out unbiased information that supports
a state of health far beyond the status quo. The best of health can
be the legacy of all of us who follow the plan of *Living Well*.

Time to Begin

The plan we are about to launch is set up within a five-week
time frame. After a specific presentation and rationale for each
of the five weeks, we will give an assignment to follow through
for that ensuing week. For the most effective results, it is best to
adopt the plan week by week, instead of trying to absorb all the
principles at one or two settings.

Many will find it interesting that the issue of what we eat is
not taken up until the third week. The reason for this delay is
simple. By addressing factors other than the food issue first, we
will gain a reinforced confidence in the ability of the plan to help
us overcome what is, for most Americans, the most difficult section—the one dealing with food choices and changes.

Just as children grow at different rates, every individual
body responds differently to change. So we should be careful not
to place too great a credence in our efforts to measure, exactly,
the success of a plan. Instead, our ultimate goal should be a
more finely tuned body, both internally as well as externally.

COOL, CLEAR, AND RESTFUL

Week 1: Water and Rest

During the first week of the plan, we will discover why our bodies' fluid levels must be maintained for optimum performance and weight control, and why thirst is a such poor indicator of our fluid needs. We will also discover the rationale for proper rest in strengthening the immune system and in improving the overall functioning of the body. Throughout this first week, we should concentrate on acquiring two key health attitudes—a proper appreciation of the role of water in our health, and a recognition of our bodies' need for regular rest.

Nature's Medium

Inertia seemed to loosen my seat belt as the American Airlines 727 surged down the runway of the Sacramento Airport. The heavily laden silver bird lifted effortlessly toward San Francisco, then gracefully banked 180 degrees toward Denver.

California was hot and dry. My view northward was blocked by the heavy haze of burning rice fields. Down below, nestled in the parched Sierra foothills, I could see the immediate area of our home. We were living in a cinder box, I thought to myself, as I surveyed the singed yellow landscape.

Off to the south, stretched tautly as though over a frame, lay patchquilt fields, varying in their shades of verdure. Water, I thought. The gift of the Sierras from last winter's snowfall. To skiers, reveling in the powder form, it's recreation. To farmers, irrigating with the liquid form, it's germination. Yet how many times do we anticipate the extravagant good times of skiing while complaining about the weekly grocery bill.

Our pilot aimed us toward Tahoe. In less than fifteen minutes we were crossing one of the most spectacular lakes in the world. This body of water just four to five miles wide and some twenty miles long contains enough water to completely cover my native state of Texas. In fact, below me was enough water to give every square inch of Texas an eight inch rain shower.

Leveling off above the floor of the Nevada desert, the 727 engines settled into the drone of cruising speed. Even at thirty-five thousand feet it was obvious that without water there was relatively little life below. So it is with our bodies. If we begin to reduce optimum fluid levels in the body, the effect is immediately apparent.[1]

Water, Water Everywhere

A quick glance at the globe reveals that the world's surface and our muscles have something in common. Each is about seventy-five percent water. Our body parts range in fluid content from the kidney, which is eighty-three percent water and through which our entire blood supply is filtered thirty times a day,[2] to the bones, which are roughly thirty percent water. Overall, the water content of the body averages sixty to sixty-five percent water, depending on the amount of body fat. Someone who weighs one hundred-fifty pounds carries about ten gallons of the liquid.[3]

Why do our bodies require so much water? One reason is lubrication. Occasionally, some of us take naps wearing our gas permeable contacts. If we sleep more than an hour, the eyelid slowly drags over the contact. Obviously, the contact lens has prevented the normal continuous lubrication of the cornea. The effect is similar to swallowing a corn chip without chewing. We need the lubrication of saliva to move food from our mouths to our stomachs.

Water plays a major role in the digestion and absorption of our food. When lubricated food slides into the stomach, fluid enzymes taken from the blood begin to digest the food. As the nutrients are absorbed from the food and flood into the bloodstream, which is eighty percent water, this medium delivers the food-fuel to each cell.

Water also plays a key role in elimination. Every living organism must expel its waste. These wastes are released out the pores through a fluid medium. The kidneys suspend their toxins, such as urea and ammonia, in a water-based solution and flush them out of the body in much the same way that an engine throws its wastes into the engine oil to be removed by the filter. If the oil in our cars is not periodically cleansed, then engine wear and damage are the inevitable result. Similarly, if the urine in our bodies is chronically over-concentrated, then we run the risk of a kidney infection or kidney stones. At the least, we risk chronic fatigue.

Without a fluid medium in the joints of our bodies, we would all move in slow motion, if at all. Our bodies' "thermostat" is also dependent upon fluid to create perspiration for maintaining stable body temperatures. Millions of chemical reactions take place simultaneously in the body, yet not one can occur without a water-based medium.[4]

Yet many people think that the primary purpose for fluids is to quench thirst.

Your Body, the Water Recycler

For over an hour we crossed the Nevada and Utah deserts with only an occasional ribbon of a road interrupting the sameness of the topography below. Less than ten inches of rain falls here annually, I thought, as I marveled that there was any life at all. Miraculously, the living things below, whether desert rat, sidewinder rattlesnake, or cactus, were specially created to be master recyclers of water. Various industrial firms consider it a great achievement if they recycle fifty percent of the resources they use. Unbelievably, plants and animals of the desert recycle ninety-nine percent of the water they consume, whether in the form of water again or as food.

Considering the complexity of the human organism, our bodies may be the greatest water recyclers known. If they were not master recyclers, we would quickly become dehydrated unless we were able to quaff two and a half gallons of water a minute — an unbelievable 2500 gallons per day![5] Fortunately, the average person needs only six to eight glasses per day, depending on his size, the work load, temperature, and humidity. I have drunk as many as twenty glasses of water during a day of cutting wood in northern California with July temperatures soaring near one hundred degrees. A number of years ago, some three thousand people attended a "Healthyourself" seminar (an eight-week course on improving lifestyle) on the campus of Southern Methodist University in Dallas. With so many people in attendance, it was expected that someone would get the instructions mixed up. One zealous soul was so intent on helping his body's water needs that he thought he'd better drink his eight glasses before he went to bed that night. The next morning he phoned the friend who had invited him to the seminar and sheepishly asked, "Do you have any idea where I spent the entire night?"[6]

While we don't need to replace more water than the body needs, it is an unfortunate fact that the average American is no doubt chronically dehydrated and doesn't even know it.

If our bodies suffer from lack of water, our entire mechanism can be likened to an overworked burro, trudging sluggishly up the switchbacks of the Grand Canyon. Fatigue, and more surprisingly, hunger, are often merely symptoms of a greater problem—water shortage. Because thirst is a delayed response, it is not a trustworthy indication of our bodies' true needs.[7]

Count Your Losses

We all know that water is lost through perspiration and the elimination of other body wastes, but few of us realize that every time we exhale, we are releasing highly humidified air. In fact, we lose about two glasses a day through exhaling and another two glasses through our pores. In addition, the kidneys and intestines expel some six glasses of water per day. And that adds up to at least ten glasses of water that we must replace daily for our bodies to function at the optimum level.[8]

Usually, just a bit over three of the ten glasses of this lost water are replaced by the food we eat. Consequently, we can supplement a portion of the water we need simply by eating.[9] One popular health plan advocates eating a diet that is at least seventy percent water, which means eating predominantly fruits and vegetables. And there is nothing wrong with eating large quantities of fruits and vegetables. However, logic should tell us that eating a peach does not produce the same catharsis that drinking a glass of pure water does. Besides, eating, or even drinking fruit juice, initiates digestion, which requires even more water, while drinking pure water soothes and cleanses without stimulating digestion.

Water Time Instead of Snack Time

If we withhold necessary fluids from our bodies, they cry out for moisture, causing the brain to tell us we need to take care of our bodies' needs. For the average American accustomed to continuous snacking, this message gets translated into a call for food. Few parents realize that all too often their begging children are not really hungry at all. Their bodies are merely crying out for moisture.[10] Assuming that our eight year-old daughter has had an adequate meal, we have found that encouraging her to drink a glass of water will most often cause the hunger pangs to subside. Indeed, she will almost always admit that she feels better just minutes after drinking the water. We usually hear no more pleas for food until the next meal.

The Energy Drink

For many years medical scientists have known that water, when freely used, will greatly reduce fatigue. When Sir Edmund Hillary completed the first successful ascent of Mt. Everest, water played a key role in his success. Previously, Swiss climbers were the first to attempt this arduously temperamental mountain. They seemed to have the best chance of conquering it, since they boasted some of the most renowned climbers in the world. But they were to fail.

The British decided that their team, headed by Edmund Hillary, would be next. The team physician, Dr. George Hunt, carefully reviewed the records of the failed Swiss attempt. In the high dry region of Mt. Everest, the Swiss climbers had drunk less than two glasses of water per day per man. Dr. Hunt ordered extra snow-melting equipment and strongly suggested that the British climbers drink a minimum of twelve glasses each day they were ascending. Unquestionably, the free use of water reduced fatigue levels of the British climbers who made it to the top.[11]

Since few of us have any desire to scale a mountain the size of Mt. Everest, let's take a look at an even more practical experiment involving water and fatigue. Over forty years ago, Dr. G. C. Pitts of Harvard tested a group of athletes with the purpose of establishing a relationship between water and fatigue.

Walking on a treadmill set at 3.5 miles per hour in a hot environment, the athletes were allowed to rest regularly while their body temperatures were recorded. In the first test they were allowed no water. After 3.5 hours the athletes had a body temperature in excess of 102 degrees and were exhausted. Because the body is both air-cooled and water-cooled, these athletes resembled cars in rush hour traffic that were low on water. Overheating was inevitable.

Conditions were identical in the second test with one exception: the athletes were allowed to drink unlimited water whenever they were thirsty. They lasted six hours until their body temperatures gradually ascended to the exhaustion level of 102 degrees.

In the final test, the athletes were prescribed an intake of water commensurate with the rate of water lost while exercising. After seven hours the experiment was ended as the athletes indicated they could continue indefinitely. Exhaustion was delayed with the increase of water intake, causing the body temperature to remain at a steady 99 degrees, well below the exhaustion level of approximately 102 degrees.[12]

Gauging Your Water Needs

A comparison of the second and third tests of the Harvard treadmill experiment tells us that thirst is not a reliable guide to how much water the body needs. More often our bodies need water long before the brain tells us the need exists. Actually, when the body enters a negative water balance of only a fraction of a percent, the brain releases the hormone ADH (anti-diuretic hormone) which is dispatched to the kidneys. This hormone then signals the cells of the kidney (called renal tubules) to siphon up the surplus water and dump it back into the blood.[13] This explains episodes of intensely colored urinations. If the brain enters a water-deprived state, the brain cells shrink slightly, causing the mental disturbances which account for the delirious behavior of severely water-deprived individuals.[14]

But if the brain is tardy with the thirst message, how is an individual to know how much water is enough? A good rule of thumb for determining the quantity of water each of us needs is to divide our weight by two to get the total number of ounces we need to drink daily. These ounces may then be divided by eight so we'll know how many glasses of water to drink. For example, a 150 pound person will need seventy-five ounces of water, or approximately nine glasses a day. Because of the tremendous amount of fluid necessary for the body to produce milk, nursing mothers should probably double their water intake. An even more precise method for measuring the adequacy of our water intake is to check the color of the urine. Unless we're taking B vitamins or have had asparagus for lunch, the color of the urine should approximate the color of water from the tap.[15]

The Water Habit

The fact that more soft drinks are swigged daily in the United States than good pure water is indicative that few of us choose the water habit. Notice we said the water habit. Rather than telling ourselves to reduce our intake of carbonated drinks, tea, or coffee, we need to develop the water habit instead. We may then allow this habit to crowd out the less desirable sources of fluids.

To reach each day's quota, we only have to remember to drink the first one or two glasses as soon as we get up in the morning. We may remember the rest through a natural memory peg system. Basically the water habit is this: what goes in must come out. When the water comes out, then that's our memory peg to put more in. Rather than trying to guzzle water at two or three intervals, we need to replace our lost fluids at frequent periods during the day.[16] When nature calls us to eliminate, we should compensate by drinking a glass of water.

For those who don't like a glass of water first thing in the morning, it might help to try it with a squeeze of lemon. Brushing the teeth or gargling is another suggestion to help make drinking water a bit more appealing. But this all-important first glass can go far to help eliminate the urgent need for a jolt of caffeine so common with many Americans.

There's yet another reason for that first glass of water. For
some six to eight hours prior to waking, our body has continued
to function. Even though the body's need for water has dimin-
ished somewhat, water has been lost in at least three ways:
through the kidneys, the pores of the skin, and exhaled air.[17]
After some eight hours of such activity, a low level of dehydration has set in. Consequently, many people become accustomed
to the water habit by beginning the day with two glasses and
then follow with another one after exercising. Incidentally,
habituating this water treatment also helps to keep us regular
morning after morning. During this first week many of us might
think the decor in our bathrooms needs changing as we increase
the frequency of our visits. Instead, we should be thankful that
we've assisted in maintaining a positive water balance within our
bodies. As the water habit becomes established, we will also discover that our water hunger will become more pronounced by
replacing our thirst for beverages that might satisfy, but only
temporarily.

A good way to remind ourselves to take in adequate amounts
of water when away from the home or office is to stop at every
water fountain we pass. Usually eleven to thirteen gulps will
about equal one eight ounce glass of water. At home or work,
many of us get busy at our tasks and find we forget to take a
break for several hours. By drinking water regularly, nature
automatically beckons when a break is in order. Interestingly,
this habit also increases our alertness, which consequently improves our work efficiency.

Don't Dilute the Food

Many people contend that they get additional liquids by
drinking with their meals. But let's consider why we feel we have
to have some sort of liquid when eating. If it's not to offset the
hot sauce, then we're probably dehydrated. When we fail to
serve our bodies water between meals, our mouths become low
on saliva. Consequently, we must assist our depleted saliva supply by drinking when we sit down to eat. Yet no beverage has the
necessary enzymes needed to initiate digestion. Liquids taken
with meals (with the exception of milk which becomes a partial
solid in the stomach) only dilute the proper concentration of

enzymes needed for digestion.[18] Not only is our digestion impaired, but there is a tendency for us to chew less and swallow faster because liquids are used to wash the food down.[19] Bolting food is a major factor in overeating. And no one needs a Ph.D. to conclude that overeating is a contributing factor in the all-American problem of obesity.

Furthermore, drinking with our meals can even set the stage for indigestion because the stomach enzymes work best in a concentrated, undiluted mixture.[20] Even cold or extremely hot beverages, when taken with meals, have a tendency to arrest the digestive process until the stomach can raise or lower the temperature of the mixture to body temperature.[21]

To assist our body's miraculous digestive process, we should try to drink our water at least thirty minutes before eating, and wait until at least thirty minutes, preferably an hour, after eating. Our stomachs will thank us.

Water Cures

Giving our bodies adequate amounts of water can result in many positive returns, from helping us to monitor our salt intake to assisting in fighting off infections.

Many people deny that they use too much salt because they don't add any. Yet hidden sources abound: processed meats, canned vegetables, soups especially, cheese, carbonated beverages, salty snack foods. Just about anything that is processed and packaged is high in salt (See Appendix C: Some Facts About Salt). Key words to watch in label reading are "sodium" and "soda." A tip for new mothers: cow's milk has triple the amount of sodium as mother's milk, so it is easy to guess why babies started on formula develop an early taste for sodium.[22] Once inside our bodies, salt crystals become very possessive little rascals, each requiring a drop of water to hold it in solution. By significantly increasing our intake of water, we can over-dilute the sodium concentration in our bodies to allow the excess water trapped by the sodium to be filtered out by the kidneys. So instead of gaining weight with our new water habit, it is actually possible to lose a little weight this first week by simply increasing our water intake to the point where some of the excess sodium is flushed out.[23] Obviously, decreasing our use of salt is going to help, too. All other things being equal, a gain in weight this first week with our increased water intake is an indication that we need to hide the salt shaker and have our blood pressure taken.

Increasing our intake of water has another bonus when it comes to watching our weight. Water can depress the appetite by helping to regulate glucose levels in the blood. When we sit down to eat we don't feel so hungry. It is therefore easier to allow reason to control the appetite instead of impulse.[24]

Downing a glass of cool, sparkling water instead of the usual caffeinated drinks also helps our bodies to stave off dehydration. Few people realize that water is a diuretic. This simply means it is one of those agents which tends to increase the flow of urine. Couple water with the caffeine in coffee or a coke and you get an accelerated diuretic effect which goes beyond useful action. In other words, with caffeinated drinks, the kidneys are stimulated to over-produce urine, making dehydration inevitable.[25] Even alcohol promotes water loss by blocking the action of the kidneys to conserve water.[26]

Water is often overlooked as a great aid to the body in overcoming viral and bacterial infections. Some years ago an excellent study demonstrated that drinking hot water can function as a natural decongestant for upper respiratory infections. Hot water can increase the mucus flow by up to twenty-five percent over normal flow, whereas cold water decreases mucus flow by up to forty percent.[27] When battling a cold, we might drink a portion of our allowance for the day in the form of warm, or hot water.

Another helpful water remedy is one that we refer to as the "water treatment." When we find ourselves coming down with a cold, the flu bug, or even a headache, drinking one eight-ounce glass of water every ten minutes for one hour is often a great aid in fighting off the illness. A fully hydrated body is best able to assist the immune system to assist itself.

Poor Substitutes

By this time, most readers will have recognized that it would be a good idea to replace almost all of our liquids with water. At least we should prefer water in place of the more common substitutes.

Four hundred million cups of coffee are sipped and gulped every day in America. The latest research indicates that while moderate coffee drinking, (two hundred milligrams of caffeine or two six ounce cups of brewed coffee per day), probably won't hurt us,[28] it is still partially responsible for raising the cholesterol levels in our blood.[29] Anyway, who wants to take chances with "probably"? Heavy coffee drinking, i.e. more than six cups a day, is by all accounts considered inadvisable.[30]

We must remember that caffeine is addictive. Anything that is addictive—whether nicotine, cocaine, or caffeine—causes damage somewhere in the body.[31] Unfortunately, even moderate coffee drinkers may experience tenacious withdrawal pangs when they try to let go. Yet coffee is still considered an acceptable beverage, if we listen to the media.

Anytime the nervous system receives a jolt of one hundred milligrams worth of caffeine in a cup of coffee, or sixty milligrams worth of caffeine in a glass of tea, there is going to be a corresponding reaction in the form of a slight depression which calls for another cup at break-time. Most people are aware, however, that the stimulation of the second cup is not quite so high as that provided by the first cup.[32]

Some people get their stimulation from cola drinks or other caffeinated beverages such as Dr. Pepper and Mountain Dew. Others enjoy the kissing cousin of caffeine, theobromine, which is present in chocolate and chocolate drinks, along with a nice dosage of caffeine.[33]

When we imbibe caffeinated drinks, we artificially stimulate the nerves, unnecessarily speed up our heart rate, and simultaneously provoke a corresponding rise in blood pressure. Caffeine also encourages clot formation, a dangerous stress factor which our fat-ingesting society doesn't need.[34] Yet we live in a world where untold billions are spent annually to reduce stress in our lives.

Even the caffeine-free coffees aren't panaceas. Following the decaffeination process, coffee oils called caffeols remain which irritate the lining of the stomach.[35] Since the first cup is usually downed on an empty stomach, the drinker is guilty of stomach abuse.

For the unborn child, whose enzymes for metabolizing caffeine are undeveloped, caffeine is a dangerous intruder, freely crossing the placenta. Chromosome damage is possible, and birth defects likely.[36]

Even teas, except the good herbal teas, are active carriers of addictive caffeine. An additional irritant is also present in the form of tannic acid. We need to watch the labels of the cold remedies in our medicine cabinet since many of them contain close to thirty milligrams of caffeine.[37]

While caffeine overly stimulates the kidneys, causing excess excretion of water, the good news is that water in copious amounts helps flush caffeine residues from the system and greatly reduces the period of withdrawal for those who wish to break the habit.[38]

By keeping the body tissues bathed in pure water, we are actually assisting our bodies in fighting disease.[39] This again raises the issue of the immune system. Every rational person is aware of the necessity of keeping the immune system strong. Helping to keep the body detoxified by drinking plenty of pure water strengthens the immune system. It makes sense to replace coffee, tea, and other questionable drinks with pure water for less stress and healthier living.

Tap Into Clean Water

As we contemplate increasing our water intake, we're bound to recall all the contamination and disease stories spread about the sordid conditions of our municipal water supply.[40]

A recent TV special "For Your Family's Sake" clearly raises awareness of the growing problem. There can be little question that our groundwater is especially becoming increasingly contaminated to the extent that some are calling the state of our drinking water the number one hidden health problem in this country. Of all the available drinking water some ninety-six percent comes from below the ground. Unfortunately eighty percent of all toxic wastes are also buried underground.

Pesticides, herbicides, lead, trichlorethylene, and other chemicals are to one extent or another fouling the drinking water of at least forty million Americans. In the same TV special, an EPA official suggested that the American public should not depend upon the government to keep their water safe. The most prevalent government procedure is the adding of chlorine for bacterial control. Yet in some cities the amount of chlorine present in the tap water nearly equals that of the local swimming pools.

Because of the heavy municipal addition of chlorine and the possible presence of other toxins, we would recommend your water be purified when possible. To strongly urge you to increase your water intake without minimizing your exposure to potentially damaging chemicals is irresponsible at best.

When it comes to water purifiers there is much hokum to wade through. According to the November, 1985, *University of California Berkley, Wellness Letter*, seventy-five percent of bottled water sold in the United States is simply processed tap water from local taps. Plus, it can cost more per gallon than gasoline.

Our recommendation would be to do it yourself for just a few cents a gallon. Distillation is a popular method for purifying water, but the process leaves behind many suspect organic chemicals; also, distilled water tastes flat because minerals are removed.

All things considered, reverse osmosis (RO) is probably the water treatment of choice. In fact, the April, 1987, *University of California Berkley, Wellness Letter*, states that the EPA recommends only reverse osmosis for removing lead from water. Excessive lead levels affect some fifty million Americans. RO treatment is particularly effective when a prefilter and a postfilter sandwich the reverse osmosis membrane.

Finally, removing chlorine from the water will greatly enhance its drinkability, making it a much more pleasant task to develop the water habit. A simple filter using activated granular carbon will work nicely and is quite convenient. Be sure, however, that the filter is treated to prevent the growth of bacteria. Remember, one of the functions of water is to help remove toxins from the body, not to add to the problem.

Stressed Rest

It was a cool March evening in Waco, Texas. Stretched out and unconscious, my next recollection was Kathy screaming, "He's coming in! He's coming in!" For a micro-second I remember thinking, "Who's coming in?," before an explosion of brick and sheet-rock spewing across the room shattered my serenity.

A drunken interloper in a gutsy Mustang had lost control on the corner banked around our house, careened sideways across the yard, collided with the outside bedroom wall of our peaceful home, and come to rest momentarily between Kathy, who stood in stark horror, and me, who dozed in peaceful oblivion on the bed. Through the settling dust of confusion, I could see the front of the car tremble as the deranged driver ground the gears, agonizing in his search for reverse and freedom.

As I tried to pull myself up between the chasm of dream and reality, our then four-year old daughter, Brooklynn, came running into the room with a look beyond terror stretched over her face. Suddenly, gazing at the empty gaping hole in our wall, the full force of the crime hit me. So this was "hit and run." Metabolic inertia grabbed me so strongly that it was some five hours later before sleep returned.

Relax and Restore

Although such manic disturbances of sleep are unusual, it is unfortunate that many millions of Americans are the victims of poor sleep habits and other sleep-related disorders.[41] While it is not within the scope of this book to address unusual sleep problems, there are some principles of good rest habits that we can share.

What is sweeter than a good night's rest? Who suffers more than one who cannot partake of its healing balm? Lady Macbeth, in the famous Shakespearian play, would have sold her soul for peaceful repose: "The death of each day's life, sore labour's bath/Balm of hurt minds, great nature's second course/Chief nourisher in life's feast."[42] Rest is restorative, whether for an insomniac guilty of such misdeeds as Shakespeare's heroine, or for any of the rest of us frenetic Americans on our eternal quests.

One of the primary reasons we have chosen to couple adequate rest to the water habit is self-control. Developing the water habit, along with the other lifestyle habits we will introduce in the succeeding weeks, requires rational thinking. A fatigued brain has the tendency to follow the line of least resistance. This translates into resuming old habits. We need to be alert for good sound thinking, and this means getting adequate sleep. Some of us may be like Albert Einstein, who is said to have slept up to twelve hours per night, but a few others' sleep habits may be closer to those of Thomas Edison, who seemed to get along quite well on about four hours per night. For most of us, however, seven to eight hours seems to fit our needs.

Mysterious sleep! While it was once thought that the body shuts down during sleep, it is now well-known that brain wave activity increases during sleep. Some twenty percent of the body's blood supply is used by an organ accounting for only about two percent of the average adult's total body weight. Only the liver rivals the brain in intensity of metabolic activity during this resting phase. This is no doubt the reason the brain is renewed most by rest. But rest also stimulates hypertrophy (thickening of muscle fibers) as a result of exercise.[43]

The principal secretion of growth hormones occur during sleep. Since this release takes place best early in the night, it is easy to see why a prompt and regular bed time is especially helpful to the growing child. The hormones of sleep also enhance the protein synthesis which is so critical for proper body maintenance.[44] Finally, it is during sleep that injuries, whether internal or external, heal fastest.[45]

Each of us has been created with internal biological "clocks" that govern the function of every living tissue. These "clocks" are apparently reset regularly when rising time is consistent. The operation of these "clocks" is referred to as Circadian rhythms. In a later chapter the value of regularity in not only our sleep habits but even our eating habits will be discussed in greater detail. However, it is important to note that the chief Circadian rhythm is that of sleep and wakefulness.[46]

Why do our sleep needs vary so widely, even within the same family? The answer to that question is unclear. It is interesting to note that in the animal kingdom, the most preyed upon animals sleep the least, while an animal such as a gorilla, which fears only man, sleeps a lot.[47]

Dr. Philip M. Tiller, Jr., conducted a survey of women who were divided into two groups. The first group slept seven hours a night or less, while the second group slept at least eight hours a night. The first group had five times as much tension, seven times as much fatigue, and twelve times as much nervous apprehension as the second.[48]

The threshold for fatigue obviously varies from person to person. But whatever that threshold is for each of us, research indicates that only a limited amount of sleep loss can be sustained before emotional and intellectual functions deteriorate. We need to watch out for those emergency room residents and interns who are called on to work eighty to one hundred plus hours or more per week![49]

Mark Twain, the Insomniac

At least part of Mark Twain's well-known crankiness can probably be traced to his chronic insomnia. The story is told of Twain's inability to sleep one night at a friend's home. He had convinced himself that the problem this particular night was one of poor ventilation. After fitful attempts at sleep, he impulsively snatched his shoe and flung it through the darkness in the supposed direction of the window. Sounds of shattering glass echoed throughout the room. Twain took a deep breath and gratefully fell asleep. In the morning, his rested eyes beheld a smashed, glass-enclosed bookcase. The room was still inadequately ventilated.

Obviously, poor ventilation was not the reason for Mark Twain's inability to sleep. However, a well ventilated room will help to increase everyone's quality of sleep. Just as our bodies need pure water to function best, our lungs likewise require fresh air to do their work properly. And fresh air enhances rest.

Artificial Sedatives

The sleep inhibiting effects of caffeine are well known. What is not so well known is the fact that alcohol in moderate amounts reduces the quality of sleep and becomes an outright risk for those persons with pulmonary and cardiovascular diseases.[50]

Traditional sedatives promise "safe and restful" sleep, but high altitude tests with well-conditioned athletes show that these sedatives reduce oxygenation during sleep.[51] Logically, this means that the organ calling the loudest for blood during sleep—the brain—is being deprived of oxygen. In these same high altitude tests, the so-called drug of choice was deemed to be Acetazolamide. Use of that drug was found to impair the buffering of lactic acid, a waste product of muscle metabolism. The presence of lactic acid is associated with muscle soreness and its prompt buffering is obviously desirable.[52] Dr. Jan Oswald of the Royal Edinburgh Hospital has these words of warning for the frequent sedative user: "The enormous quantities of hypnotic and antianxiety drugs consumed today cannot be defended on therapeutic grounds."[53]

As we move through these next five weeks of lifestyle changes, we will discover that each new habit will enhance the effect of the previous habit learned. All of our health habits are interdependent. Because good health habits are based on natural law, to abrogate one is to jeopardize the integrity of the whole.

Assignment for Week One

- Divide your weight by two and then again by eight to find out how many glasses of water your body needs daily.

- Beginning with one or two glasses of water before breakfast, make a daily, conscious effort to drink your required number of glasses before retiring at night.

- Try to cut down or even cut out caffeinated and highly sugared drinks.

- When you are tempted to snack, try drinking a glass of water and waiting fifteen minutes before eating.

- Make a mental note of your increased energy level as the week progresses.

- Determine the amount of sleep you need to function properly and make every effort to get your needed rest each night.

- Make sure your sleeping quarters have proper ventilation.

- Read through this chapter at least one other time this week.

OUTWARD BOUND

Week 2: Fresh Air, Sunshine, and Exercise

As we begin the second week of the plan, we will move out-doors in our search for those choices which will enhance our health and fine tune our bodies. We need to continue the first week's emphasis on water and rest so as to build our base for developing consecutive, life-long habits of preventive living. The benefits of drinking enough pure, fresh water to sustain and refresh our bodies daily and of getting adequate rest in a well-ventilated room should be greatly apparent to us after one week of habituating these choices.

This second week we will learn of the importance of good quality fresh air, how sunshine can truly be our friend, and why the combination of these two contributes greatly to the total picture of exercise.

Air: Our Life Force

The weight was deadening—crushing and flattening my chest, pressing it, pushing it, squeezing it down until my lungs seemed to collapse from the enormity of the burden. I fought back the covers, kicking and pushing against the intruder that threatened to suffocate the very life that flickered within me. In the blackness of the night my hands beat the air frantically, pushing helplessly, futilely, at infinity. The palpable roaring in my ears was unbearable, the rising and falling intonation of gasping breath stifling my silent screams for help.

Dale's voice, calling to me, reached over the abyss of panic, grabbing me, lifting me, holding me. But not calming me. For there is no respite for one awakening in the clutches of an asthma attack.

Lifeblood of the Lungs

Air. Oxygen. Life. To be deprived of this element most needed by all of us for our very survival can impart a healthy dose of appreciation for its benefits. For of all the elements available for sustaining us, air is probably the one most taken for granted. Yet seventeen thousand involuntary breaths daily can hardly be counted as insignificant. By breathing, we not only sustain our very lives, we also help lift blood from the lower body to the heart, provide massage for the liver and the stomach to aid in digestion, draw in large amounts of oxygen (a gallon or more with each deep breath) to vitalize our tissues, and receive the necessary oxygen to change our food into energy.

While we all need a certain quantity of air for life, many of us overlook the quality of the air that we are continuously taking into our bodies. For example, during the 1984 Summer Olympics in Los Angeles, it was predicted that for each day the athletes competed in the outdoors, they would be showered with about two thousand tons of organic gases, thirteen hundred tons of nitrogen oxides, four hundred tons of sulfur oxide, and fifteen hundred tons of pollutants.[1]

This pollution fallout amounts to more than ten million pounds of grit every day in Los Angeles alone. Painful breathing is an indicator that high levels of toxic airborne pollutants exist. On the average in the Los Angeles area, one day in every five is labeled a "stage two ozone alert." This means that for every one hundred million parts of air, there are at least thirty-five ozone particles. This stage two can also cause coughing and decreased lung performance.[2]

In spite of countless daily assaults on our lungs, most of us underestimate the ability of our bodies to adapt to these less than ideal conditions. Studies have shown that exposure to fifty ozone particles per one hundred million parts of air can cause as much as a fifty percent drop in lung performance. However, within five days most well-trained athletes adapt to the poorer quality of air.[3] For the rest of us, adjustment may take longer, but eventually it will occur, just as the body, while initially rebelling against those first few days of cigarette smoking, will finally compromise to the point of actually enjoying and then even craving the deadly smoke being pulled into the lungs.

Airborne Pollution

Indeed, air pollution is a major problem in many of our urban areas. Even nonsmokers who live in high air pollution areas have respiratory problems that are more often associated with smokers.[4] Some urban areas have such poor air quality that the oxygen-carrying capacity of the blood in normal, healthy individuals is reduced to that of a pack a day smoker.[5]

An article entitled "Health Effects of Areas of Urban Air Pollution," gives a comprehensive report on the quality of America's urban air and its overall effects on the general populace. The article points out that the regular pollution reports issued within urban areas fail to measure accurately what is happening to a particular person at a given time and place. For example, a city receives its data from a pollution monitoring station which may issue a report of moderate pollution for the day, even though pollution can soar into the dangerous zones for people stuck in a traffic jam.[6] This article also points out that pollution most severely affects premature infants, the newborn, the elderly, the disabled, those with chronic heart and lung diseases, certain asthma sufferers, and those who regularly inhale tobacco smoke.[7]

The polluted air that some of us continually breathe decreases oxygen in the blood and facilitates atherosclerosis. Carbon monoxide, a prevalent ingredient in polluted air, binds with the oxygen in the blood, rendering it ineffective.[8] Lack of oxygen can cause the inner layers of the blood vessel to separate.[9] The logical conclusion to this scenario is that impure air may be a contributing factor in cardiovascular disease.

Paying the Price

Even though our bodies can and do adjust to such harsh conditions, living with inferior air quality often brings with it severe penalties for abusing our bodies. Smokers reckon with a number of deadly penances for continued abuse of their lungs and body in the form of lung cancer, emphysema, heart disease, and multiple other needless complications. Smoking accounts for nearly eighty-five percent of all lung cancers, but research now shows that the remaining fifteen percent succumbing to this insidious and painful disease can to a great extent be laid at the feet of the smoking public.[10]

More and more nonsmokers are recognizing the deadly effects of their subjection to the smoke of others. In recognition of this, perhaps a new and timely response to the age-old question of "mind if I smoke?" might be: "Wrong question! The question should be, 'Mind if *we* smoke?' Sorry, but I'm a nonsmoker."

Another factor unrelated to the quality of the air we breathe, but one that can slow down the absorption of oxygen by our tissues is the typical Western diet high in fat. When we consume fatty foods, the fat causes our red blood cells to become sticky and clump together. This clumping makes it very difficult for the oxygen carriers to gain access to the body tissue because they are supplied by extremely fine blood vessels.[11] Lack of exercise is another major factor in decreasing the flow of quality oxygen to the cells of the body. Finally, research has shown that the insidious cancer virus prefers an environment of decreased oxygen in which to do its work.[12]

Negative Ions for Positive Attitudes

While most of us cannot change the quality of air which surrounds us, short of moving to a better location, we can do our best to improve our bodies' ability to utilize whatever fresh air is available. One way to help is through inhaling the benefits of negative ions.

The air we breathe is twenty-one percent oxygen, seventy-eight percent nitrogen, and one percent miscellaneous other gasses, including carbon dioxide. When an atom loses an electron, it becomes either positively or negatively charged. So far as air is concerned, the positive charges are carbon dioxide molecules, while the negative charges are oxygen molecules. It is the negatively charged oxygen molecules that benefit our bodies. Up to a point, the more negative ions there are in the air, the better. This ionization of the air occurs in a number of ways, including sunshine, a discharge of lightning, and the breakup of water droplets. It's no wonder that we feel a natural high from being in the presence of a waterfall or the beating of the surf.

Negative ions can hide in many places; they adhere to walls, air conditioning ducts, and fabrics. They benefit us by lowering our respiration rates and decreasing the effects of headaches, dizziness, nausea, and fatigue.[13] Exercise increases our intake of these negative ions. In fact, research shows additional benefits from these invisible little guys: a study reported over thirty years ago in the *Journal of Cancer Research* indicated that when tumor laden animals were placed in a negative ionized environment, the tumor growth was reduced by up to fifty percent when compared to animals allowed to breathe only common indoor air. As already mentioned, studies show that without sufficient oxygen, viruses can and do flourish.[14] With sufficient oxygen our immune systems can do a better of job of controlling these foreign invaders.

Give Our Lungs the Benefit

It is no secret that clean, fresh air is able to purify by rendering bacteria, viruses, and other harmful substances inactive, whether in the laboratory or on the clothes line. Besides assisting our immune system in its proper function, fresh air can also help prevent disease by helping to eliminate damaging toxins from our bodies.

Because pollution is also responsible for reducing the available negative ions, the most frequently used rooms in our homes should be aired out daily. We spend an average of fifty to fifty-five hours a week in our bedrooms, so we should see to it that pure, fresh air is allowed to purify and freshen this environment during the day, in addition to being available during sleep.

Deep breathing and good posture also aid in our bodies' intake of life-giving oxygen, allowing our lungs to function naturally and to their fullest capacity.

Air is vital. Its quality is important for sustaining our bodies in the best of health. Let's also see how sunshine plays a role in good health.

Sunshine: Maligned by the Media

Recent publicity has stressed the harmful effects of the sun in promoting a rash of skin cancer in this country. In addition, sun worshipers are known to age long before their time. Indeed, the incidence of skin cancer is alarming. Four hundred and fifty thousand people are diagnosed as having some form of skin cancer every year and some fifty-five hundred die annually of the type known as malignant melanoma.[15] If we look only at these statistics, exposure to the sun's rays could hardly be classified as beneficial. However, as with the use of any statistical information, the whole picture must be examined before we should our conclusions.

Most of us know that all life on this earth is dependent on the sun, and that the sun is the catalyst in the process of photosynthesis whereby energy is stored as carbohydrates, proteins, and fats for later consumption by man or animals. Up until the last generation, the history of man has been one of life under the sun. During the Great Depression of the 1930's, America was about seventy percent rural and thirty percent urbanized. Presently, the United States is roughly the reverse of those statistics. As we have become more urbanized, our exposure to the sun has lessened, yet our problems continue to increase.

From the ancient Greeks to the beginning of the twentieth century, medical literature indicates time and time again that the sun is a positive factor in the health of man. In 1877, two scientists by the names of Downes and Blount demonstrated the ability of sunlight to destroy bacteria; consequently, sunlight became a widely prescribed treatment for bacterial infections. The scourge of the early twentieth century was tuberculosis. In 1903, Niels Finsen won the Nobel Prize for using ultraviolet light to successfully treat skin tuberculosis. But with the discovery of the antibiotic sulfanilamide in the late 1930's, modern pharmacology began to rapidly develop as the choice treatment. Consequently, continued studies on the beneficial effects of sunlight were abandoned.[16] While it is true that many people suffer from an overindulgence of the sun's bounties, the great majority of these people are fair-skinned individuals[17] who have failed to condition their skin to the sun's rays before allowing their bodies to be exposed.[18] A still greater majority thrive on the all-American diet of foods high in fat,[19] which creates a basis for the formation of free radicals.[20] Indeed, there is a growing concern that all fats, especially the polyunsaturated ones, contribute to the aging process in which the cells of the body begin to lose their vigor.[21]

Refined fats, such as shortenings and the various vegetable oils, can promote the formation of these free radical — molecules that are very unstable and can damage every system in the body. Exposure to excessive sunlight intensifies the activity of these rabble rousers to the point that a deranged cell can have its genetic order scrambled and begin to act like someone gone mad.[22]

So while 450,000 people are diagnosed as having skin cancer every year, most of this cancer is in the form of a benign basal-cell or squamous-cell cancer,[23] precipitated by excessive sunburn, high fat diets, and low levels of vitamins C, A, E, and selenium, which are found primarily in foods of plant origin.[24] These three vitamins and mineral function as guardians of the cell, among other things, playing a major role in preventing the free radicals from doing any damage.[25]

Sunlight: Nature's Healing Balm

Most of us would be surprised to learn of the improbable number of beneficent uses of sunshine. These include preventing cancer,[26] improving energy and fitness,[27] lowering blood pressure,[28] decreasing resting heart rate,[29] lowering cholesterol,[30] increasing the storage of glycogen (sugar) in the liver which, in turn, lowers sugar levels in the blood,[31] to strengthening the immune system,[32] increasing the body's tolerance of stress,[33] enhancing the beauty of the skin,[34] directly killing germs,[35] and aiding in weight reduction.[36]

The sun is actually instrumental in reducing the incidence of colon cancer. Statistics show that the rate of colon cancer is significantly less in sunny states such as Arizona and New Mexico than in states farther north, such as New York, New Hampshire, and Vermont. An individual has almost triple the risk of developing colon cancer in New York as in New Mexico, even though the amount of available solar radiation is only forty percent less in New York than in New Mexico. These statistics have led scientists to conclude that it is the exposure to natural sunlight that may provide protection against colon cancer.[37]

In 1945, an experiment conducted at the University of Illinois demonstrated that ultraviolet light had a positive impact on the cardiovascular fitness and muscular endurance of college-aged young men. Both test groups exercised indoors for ten weeks during late fall and early winter when sunlight availability was at it lowest. These two groups both participated in a physical test before and after the test period. The only difference in treatment of the two groups was that the experimental group received full body ultraviolet exposure three times a week for one minute at each session for the first four weeks. The following four weeks the exposure in the test group was increased to one and a half minutes each session for three times a week. During the final two weeks, the full body exposure was increased to two minutes. After the ten week test period, the control group showed a 1.5 percent gain in cardiovascular fitness and a 11.8 percent gain in muscular endurance. But the experimental group demonstrated a 19.2 percent gain in cardiovascular fitness and a 15.4 percent gain in muscular endurance.[38] Exposure of the test group to ultraviolet light was minimal, at best.

The benefits in cardiovascular fitness to the test subjects help us to understand why exposure to ultraviolet light reduces blood pressure and decreases cholesterol levels in the blood. Lessening these two factors alone will increase the fitness of the cardiovascular system, making it easier for the exercise we take to positively affect our bodies.

For diabetics, the benefits of sunlight are also impressive. In as little as three minutes of exposure to ultraviolet light, the glycogen, or sugar, concentration in the blood is decreased as it is moved from the blood to the liver for storage.[39] Sunlight also plays a role in enhancing our natural immunity by strengthening the immune system in a number of ways.[40] No one can deny that a sparkling clear and sunny day lifts our spirits and promotes a positive attitude, increasing our resistance to disease. Sunlight also promotes the use of oxygen in the tissues.[41] The immune system thrives on rich supplies of oxygen. One of our most feared diseases, cancer, has many varieties that prefer to do their sinister work in a relatively oxygen-free environment.[42] America's most popular vacation spots often feature pristine beaches in leisurely, sunny settings. Sunshine is a known relaxer and mood improver.[43]

While light skinned people burn more easily, the good news is that sunshine, if used in moderation along with a diet that fights free radical formation, can actually enhance the beauty of the skin.[44] In addition, by decreasing the incidence of free radicals in the body through a low fat diet, the natural aging processes of our bodies may be delayed.[45]

Sunlight is the best known purifier of air. That's why we find operating rooms equipped with full-spectrum lighting for purification purposes.[46]

For the average American, the use of sunshine to aid in losing weight is a real bonus. By stimulating the thyroid gland to increase hormone production, sunshine in turn increases our rate of metabolism, thus burning more calories.[47] When we couple that benefit with a diet lower in fats and animal products and higher in plant foods, it is possible to see some real results in overall weight loss.

Vitamins, Naturally, for Protection

Because of the natural protective role that vitamins C, A, E, and the mineral selenium play in preventing free radical damage, many people are inclined to supplement these items in their diet. Logic dictates that those who choose to eat the standard high fat/high sugar diet should probably take supplements. However, research indicates that few of those who eat a good variety of food need any type of supplementation. The high level of nutrients in their tissues protect against free radical formation and the damage that can be done by the sun.

We must keep in mind that vitamin A does not occur naturally in nature. It is produced in the body from the dietary sources of carotenes as found in yellow vegetables and fruits. Keeping our intake of carotenes high raises the threshold at which the sun begins to burn the skin. There is also a greater tendency to tan if our intake of carotene is kept high.[48]

As for vitamin D, the vitamin that helps to convert calcium to bone, the sun is the best source. Studies have shown that the recommended daily intake of four hundred IU's of vitamin D should be the maximum for many people. The average dietary intake of vitamin D, primarily through dairy products and other animal foods, is well over 2400 IU's. This level may be toxic for some people. It has been associated with the lowering of magnesium in the body, which is needed to help protect us from heart disease.[49] But it has never been shown that an individual received a toxic dosage of vitamin D from sun exposure.[50]

Our Sun the Sustainer

The beams from our life-sustaining sun form a spectrum of visible and invisible light, reflecting hues of blues, yellows, and reds when bent into a rainbow. The really good rays, however, are the invisible ultraviolet ones that provide so many health-giving benefits when absorbed properly. Our warm friend is only an enemy to be shunned if we choose to abuse our bodies by overdoing our exposure or by consuming a typically high fat diet. In reality, this ever-present companion is a wonderful contributor to our health if we will use it in moderation and eat a diet which helps our bodies to effectively utilize the sun's goodness.

And nothing could be better than crisp, invigorating air and brilliant, transparent sunshine to beckon us to the refreshing world of exercise.

The Natural Stimulant

There are untold numbers of books and articles touting the benefits of exercise. In some areas it's becoming difficult to drive with all the joggers demanding a share of the roadways. Exercise and health clubs abound, advertisements portray the body beautiful in all manner of fashion, and everyone knows someone involved in body building. Even more recently, there has been an increased interest in the sport of power walking. By whatever method, exercise has definitely come into its own with our all-American focus on health and fitness.

When we choose to use the great out-of-doors as our gymnasium, exercise enhances the benefits of oxygen in our bodies and integrally involves us in the proper usage of the sun. Besides the overall feeling of well-being that exercise gives us, numerous other physical benefits accrue to our bodies when we intentionally exert them.

Exercise is a necessary ingredient for the overall health of the body. Obviously, the first thought most of us have about exercise is the increased metabolism and consequent burning of extra calories it effects. But in addition, exercise also helps to keep the appetite under control, neutralizes stress, lowers blood cholesterol, promotes digestion, and normalizes blood sugar.[51]

When muscles are at rest, they primarily use free fatty acids as an energy source. Stimulating activity however, increases muscle fuel consumption by as much as seven to forty times, causing our bodies to begin burning sugar. Hence the desired burning of those extra calories.

Diabetics, in particular, can benefit from the advantages of a good workout, especially one involving sunshine and fresh air. During serious exercise, blood sugar-glucose becomes the primary energy source. As a result, excess sugar is cleared from the blood, which is of benefit to the vast majority of diabetics who are not dependent on insulin.[52] In addition, exercise also increases the cell's sensitivity to the action of insulin, thereby decreasing its need.[53]

Studies have also shown that physical exertion enhances our self-concept well beyond what would normally be the case without it. Little cousins of morphine known as "endorphins" are released by the brain during sustained exercise, giving us an over-all sense of well-being, a "natural high," as many promoters of exercise refer to it.[54]

The effects of our sedentary lifestyles in general, and our jobs in particular, are far from beneficial. A study involving over one million men in Sweden directly correlated sedentary jobs with increased colon cancer risk.[55] The statistics indicated that even after-work exercise didn't seem to make that much difference in the subjects under study. But conclusions from this report should lead us to see the necessity of scattering more of our exercise throughout the day. Take the stairs instead of the elevator. Park farther away than necessary. Mild exercise stimulates colonic activity; consequently, it would seem logical for us to participate in some form of exercise more than once a day.

For those who have suffered a heart attack or who hope to prevent or increase the chances for surviving one, exercise is an invaluable ally.[56] Those of us with lower cardiovascular risk factors may be more interested in the value that exercise plays in keeping our immune system defensive and healthy.[57]

Another interesting fact that is surfacing regarding exercise is that some preventive-minded physicians are now prescribing rhythmic exercises as a "no side-effect" replacement for tranquil-izers.[58] These "replacements" include walking, jogging, cycling, and bench stepping. Evidence of success indicates that five to thirty minutes at only thirty to sixty percent of maximum exer-tion seems to be the most effective method.[59]

The Choice Is Ours

Whatever form of exercise we choose to add to our overall plan for health, we need to consider the importance of including sunshine and fresh air in conjunction with that choice. Our choices should include an activity that we can be comfortable maintaining, day after day, week after week, year after year. For most people that choice will be a combination of brisk walking and/or jogging for variety and consistency. But some people will prefer to add cycling, swimming, or some other aerobic sport to their list of possibilities. The most important consideration, however, is to relentlessly pursue this part of the plan, regardless of how many times we slip back into old habits.

We want also to continue our newly acquired habits from week one, adding them to the following goals for this second week, as we continue to build a responsible health plan for the well-being of our bodies, both internally as well as externally.

Assignment for Week Two:

- Take ten slow, deep breaths outside or in front of an open window each morning immediately following the first glass or two of water.

- Air out your sleeping quarters completely for a set time each day (such as while taking a shower) with windows wide open and sun shining in.

- Make a conscious, daily effort to sit and stand tall; ask others to help by reminding you.

- Begin a conscious reduction of all dietary fat.

- Spend more time and more of your food dollar in the pro-duce department choosing new varieties of fresh fruits and vegetables.

- Begin reading labels and noticing how others spend their food dollar (standing in the checkout line is a good place for this).

- Establish a set time for exercise in the sun and fresh air at least four times weekly.

- Find your level of exercise efficiency from the formula below and maintain a corresponding pace.

- Read through this second chapter of the plan at least one other time this week.

Formula for Maximizing Exercise Efficiency

Subtract your age from the number 220. The resulting number is the absolute maximum your heart should beat at any given time. For the best benefits from exercise, the pulse should stay between sixty and seventy percent of your maximum rate for a minimum of twenty minutes at least four times weekly. For example: If you're thirty-five years old, your maximum heart rate is 185 beats per minute. During effective exercise, your pulse should hover between 111 and 130 for at least twenty minutes four times each week. To take your pulse, count the beats for fifteen seconds immediately upon stopping and then multiply by four. If your pulse is below the sixty percent mark, increase your pace.

For those over age thirty-five or suffering from a health condition, it is best to check with your physician before beginning an exercise program.

NINE

EAT TO LIVE
Week 3: Nutrition and Self-Control

Having spent two weeks thus far in conditioning our bodies to the benefits of pure water, adequate rest, and invigorating exercise in the fresh air and sunshine of the outdoors, our focus this third week centers on health habits surrounding the table. Because most of us eat at least three meals every day, the unhealthy habits that have accumulated over years of reinforcement are tenacious, clinging with the insistence of a crying baby trying to avoid taking a nap.

As we move into this third week of the plan, we will begin to examine eating habits that are contributing to the breakdown of our health. During this time we need to keep in mind the increased energy and vitality that these first two weeks have contributed to our lives, as well as the possible weight loss many of us might have experienced, and consequently stay encouraged and positive about our decision to take control of our health. We also need to remember that our focus is on overall and lifetime health in contrast to the typical American approach to "health": a crash diet and membership at a fitness center. (For those who are wavering, it will help to reread those portions of Part I that apply to you.)

Hunger or Appetite?

The call to eat is familiar to all of us, but few of us realize the subtle difference between hunger and appetite. One is inherent; the other acquired. When our body signals us that it's time to eat, those signals are translated into hunger. But when we visualize specific and favorite food items, this psychological craving is defined as appetite. In other words, our body does not specifically instruct us as to what its needs are. It doesn't say "time for a Big Mac." Instead, our brain just says "feed me."

Appetite is an acquired phenomena. When hunger strikes, a west Texas rancher may crave a thick, juicy steak; a Louisiana roughneck, frog legs; a South Pacific Islander, fresh dog meat; a Mexican laborer, rice and beans. While hunger is as natural as breathing, an appetite is merely the sum of our favorite food habits we acquired growing up added to our choices as an adult. Fortunately, these habits can be changed in a relatively short time, depending, of course, upon our attitudes.

An analogy gleaned from an episode in Peter Jenkins' *Across China* might serve to further illustrate the power of the appetite. Peter accompanied an expedition to climb Mt. Everest, towering some twenty-nine thousand feet into the clouds. The climbers arrived at a Tibetan city situated at twelve thousand feet, and began the arduous task of acclimatizing. Gradually the group moved upward, slowly allowing their bodies to adjust to the reduction of available oxygen. For those not accustomed to this extreme altitude, adjustment might take weeks before the body could maximize its vital forces for an ascent to the top of the world.[1]

Adjusting to changes in altitude is a lot like adjusting to changes in appetite. Given proper time and a positive attitude, the body can conform to very significant changes. Unfortunately for most of us, adjusting to changes in the appetite may be more difficult than trying to adjust to life at fourteen thousand feet. At least it may seem that way if we look around us at the number of seemingly helpless overweight and unhealthy people who populate the richest country in the world.

For too many years we've allowed our bodily appetites in the form of cravings to control the brain. Consequently we allow our injudicious decisions about food rather than our brains to make healthy food choices for us. A good deal of what we crave is based on what we see and hear. Fast food operations teach every red-blooded American to salivate at the first few notes of their "You deserve a break today" ditty, conjuring up sizzling, crispy fries, tantalizing, juicy burgers with all the trimmings, and countless other overrated items to steal our money and our health. In reality, what we are allowing our appetite to crave is food items that are too salty, too sweet, and worst of all, too fattening.

In order to break these patterns of acquired appetite, we must "acclimatize" the brain to look beyond the initial craving for poor quality food. We need to understand that what fast food franchises don't tell us about their food is that it will be four seconds in the mouth, four hours in the stomach, and forty years on the hips, if we live that long. In other words, we need to reverse the pattern from "body telling brain" to "brain telling body." Eat to live, as the saying goes, rather than live to eat.

One of the best ways to get ourselves to see the whole picture before we indulge our appetites is to take responsibility for our health. No doubt the best way to accomplish this challenging task is to become educated on the subject of health. We must read, search, and learn. We should experiment with new and healthful recipes, be open to trying something different, desire the very best for ourselves and our families, including the "best" food for our bodies. But we must be forewarned that our attitudes swing an incredible amount of weight when it comes to food decisions and bathroom scales, not to mention unseen internal damage. And they can do it to us three times and more every day.

Obesity: A National Hazard

From a scientific standpoint, there are six types of obesity. Fortunately, only two of these types afflict the overwhelming majority of overweight Americans. But unfortunately, the majority of these people like to think that they fall into one of the more rare categories.[2]

The first category includes the person whose obesity is predominantly genetic. Classifying an individual in this group is a difficult assessment, however, because of various environmental factors.[3]

A second type of obesity is caused by the overproduction of certain hormones. It is extremely rare. Drug-induced obesity, which may be induced by the use of antihistamines, is a third category. It is also rare. A fourth classification is known as hypothalamic-induced obesity where there is too much insulin in the blood. This rare condition may cause hypoglycemia, which induces the individual to eat a considerable amount of calories throughout the day.[4]

The fifth category of obesity is not so rare. Physical inactivity is responsible for a good share of overweight individuals in this country. In fact, a survey of twenty-one states conducted by the Centers for Disease Control indicated that less than half of the American population is physically active at a level that is likely to be beneficial to their health. The percentage of men who indicated that they did not participate in physical exercise ranged from forty-four percent in Idaho to sixty-six percent in Tennessee. Among women, the percentages ranged from forty-one percent in Idaho to seventy-one percent in Tennessee.[5]

The last category is nutritional obesity. It contains the greatest number of obese individuals who consistently indulge in too many calories, especially of the wrong variety. Most all of us are aware that a high fat intake contributes greatly to obesity, but few of us realize that a high protein diet also promotes greater fat storage.[6]

In order to restructure our thoughts, our health, and our measurements, we need to modify some of our acquired habits to conform more closely to those "fourth grade health principles" we all learned, and all forgot.

Appestat: What's That?

Most of us—obese or not—fail to recognize that built into the digestive mechanism of the body is a minute device designed to tell us when we've eaten enough. Some scientists refer to this little device in the brain as the "satiety center," but the more technical term is the appestat. This control center tells us when the body needs nourishment, and, more importantly, when enough is enough.[7]

This tiny little appetite regulator is an ever present help in maintaining ideal body weight. Consider the number of people who weigh the same year after year and never concern themselves with counting calories. Most likely they are in tune with the functioning of their appestat, which in most people is very accurate. If our appestat were to have an error rate of even less than one percent, we would slowly gain weight throughout the years.[8]

In reality, the satisfaction gained by our eating is more a function of time than it is of the amount of food we consume.

Once we begin eating, it takes approximately twenty minutes before the appestat will signal the stomach that it's turning off the appetite. Consequently, if we eat rapidly, we will consume far more food during that twenty minute period than if we eat slowly. If we have only twenty minutes in which to eat, we will do our bodies a great service by eating slowly and thoroughly consuming only five hundred calories than by bolting one thousand calories down in the same amount of time. When food is not properly chewed it is poorly digested. When more food is consumed than is needed, we all know where the excess is stored: around the waist, on the hips, under the chin, and more insidiously, out of sight in the muscles and in the lining of the blood vessels themselves.[9]

Another fact overlooked by many of us is that the highly refined diet preferred by so many of us requires little effort to chew. Consequently, a much larger volume of this fiberless food can be consumed in the twenty minute period than could otherwise be eaten if high fiber, whole grain choices were included.[10]

While drinking water throughout the day helps keep us more alert, eating in tune with our appestat also helps reduce fatigue levels. Too much food in our stomachs is a major contributor factor to feelings of fatigue.[11]

Many readers may wonder if there is hope for those of us with appestats that have "malfunctioned" for years. Happily, our bodies are very forgiving. Despite lifelong habits, they adjust to healthy improvements. Eating slowly, chewing thoroughly, and exercising consistently gives us an excellent chance to restore the functioning of this tiny control center.[12]

Taste the Food

While most of us know that we get the nutrients we need through the carbohydrates, fats, and proteins we ingest, few of us are aware that the digestion of these nutrients actually begins in the mouth. Insofar as carbohydrates are concerned, this is a most critical issue, because there are no enzymes in the stomach to initiate digestion of these high fiber foods. It it is imperative that they be well chewed before they are swallowed.[13]

Good chewing habits are associated with a high intake of water between meals. In fact, in order to prepare the digestive

system, specifically the saliva glands, for a meal, it is a good idea
to drink a glass of water about thirty minutes before eating.
When we started our water drinking habit two weeks ago, we
were also paving the way for improved eating habits. A well-
hydrated body means the saliva glands will be fully charged and
ready to deliver the saliva needed for digestion. If we drink just
before or during our meals, the stomach juices needed for digestion are diluted.[14] If we crave liquids when we are eating, this is
a good indication that our bodies have not had enough water between meals.

Another consideration for chewing our foods thoroughly is
that the full flavor of the food is not released unless the food is in
a solution, particularly the saliva. People who chew their food
more completely actually enjoy it more. In addition, it is likely
they will eat less.[15]

Failure to chew our food thoroughly can inhibit the digestive
processes in much the same way that a compressed block of yeast
will take much longer to dissolve in a liquid medium than will
powder-like particles of yeast sprinkled over the same liquid.
The digestive juices and enzymes do their work more quickly
and efficiently if the food is chewed to a virtual cream before
arriving in the stomach.

People who are hooked on antacids to relieve suffering from
indigestion or "sour" stomachs may benefit from these simple
principles of chewing in much the same way that we all rely on
refrigeration to keep our foods from spoiling. If digestion is
retarded, either by overeating or poor chewing, then the excess
or undiluted foods will begin to sour in our stomachs for lack of
proper or timely digestion.[16]

One final thought on proper chewing concerns the intake of
calories. A positive side effect of eating more slowly is that we reduce the number of calories consumed. Laboratory tests have
shown that reduced caloric intakes reduce the risk for cardiovascular diseases, kidney problems and even cancer.[17]
Reduced risk for cancer is the result of a combination of factors,
but it is known that cutting back on calories enhances the
response of the immune system.[18]

Eating more slowly and chewing our foods thoroughly may
be among the most difficult habits to cultivate. Chewing is a de-

cision that we make hundreds of times throughout the meal. However, once we begin enjoying savoring our food for a change, and accept the benefits of eating more slowly and chewing our foods more completely, these new habits will become ingrained into our patterns of living.

Other Aids to Avoid Rolaids

There are a number of other overlooked principles that encourage good digestion. Not the least of these is the concept that we should "eat breakfast like a king, lunch like a prince, and supper like a pauper." Although we all use the term "breakfast" daily, few of us realize that the word suggests that the purpose of this first meal of the day is to "break a fast." Since our bodies have been without nourishment for almost twelve hours, they need much more food at this first meal of the day than at either of the other two remaining meals.

Because of our high-paced, frenetic days, dinner has become the largest meal of the day for most of us. Accordingly, we have developed eating patterns that are out of harmony with our natural bodily rhythms. It isn't sensible to ask our digestive systems to deal with the most taxing burden of the day when nighttime is upon us and rest for the entire body should be in order. It is during the evening hours that the energy demands of the body are on a downward curve in preparation for the night's sleep.

But what about those people who insist that they fall into the classification of "night people"? People who stay up until all hours, eat a good share of that time, sleep until the last possible moment, then dash off to work on an empty stomach that has worked most of the previous night to rid itself of the onslaught of food taken in the previous night? People whose morning intake of nourishment exists primarily in the form of hot and cold chemical stimulants, coupled with various other snack items that can be begged, borrowed, or bought? People who growl at anyone who dares to smile before the noon hour?

I used to be just such a person. The adjustments most newlyweds suffer pale in comparison to what happens when a "night" person hooks up with a "morning" person. I never even headed in the direction of the bedroom before eleven o'clock P.M. By the time all the rituals of bedtime had been performed, the midnight chimes were usually waiting in the wings. It was then time to relax, and relaxing to me meant reading. But Dale couldn't sleep with the light on. Relaxing to him meant sleeping. In fact, relaxing to him meant heading in the direction of bed around nine o'clock P.M., just as I was tying my running shoes and heading out the door for my daily exercise.

Mornings were even more exciting. Dale at first wondered why this wife he had married could never manage her mornings to be out of bed in time to fix him any breakfast, not to mention join him in exercise. At last, he would toss me a piece of toast as I flew by him in my eternal quest to not be the last person at my desk before the tardy bell rang. After all, I was the teacher.

The differences in our "morning" and "evening" personalities were immense. Dinner, if I was fixing it, was a three course meal, preceded by a salad, and followed by a wind down of various "snack" items as I graded papers and prepared for my classes. Supper, if Dale had the menu, was popcorn, toast with various spreads, and fresh fruit. He had a set time every evening for brushing his teeth and for turning off the light.

Our lives might have continued their patterns of opposition, and at the worst, have taken us our separate ways. At the least, it could have insured that we never had kids. But then my body rebelled.

It happened one morning during a coffee break in the lounge. I stood up to head out for my next class, only to discover that the ceiling had become the floor, and the floor the ceiling. Then they tried to change places again. Our school nurse made an appointment for me to have a glucose tolerance test, explaining that I couldn't eat breakfast the following morning. I assured her that wouldn't be a problem.

In a way, I was relieved to discover that I was one of the thousands of "hypoglycemics" lurking around the recesses of snackdom, because I was secretly envious of my husband's supreme control of his body, his discipline, and his consistency in striving to maintain his health and physique. I was on the losing end. Half the time, I didn't exercise at night. Either my stomach was too full, I had evening obligations, or I talked myself into doing something more "important." I never felt rested in the mornings. Of course, I always attributed this to my perpetual and breathless lateness. It was enough to exhaust anyone, but so is a stomach that has to work the entire night.

But if I can change, there's hope for everyone. After twenty-five years of being a self-proclaimed "night person," I can now humbly assert that I hold membership to the exclusive club of "morning people." It took reversing a lot of things, like my tendency to stay up late, eat heavy meals in the evenings, snack for hours, skip breakfasts, and compensate by snacking most of the remaining day.

Let no one be deceived. It takes a determined effort to change life-patterns. It's not easy to run early in the morning when your eyes are barely open. But it got easier as my body acclimated to all the unexpected benefits. We must remember that our bodies can and will adjust to most habits, whether they weaken our bodies' fine tuning and consequent total health, or whether they harmonize with what is most healthful and beneficial for our physical and mental needs.

By following this pattern of eating a large breakfast, a significant lunch, and a light supper, many people discover that perpetual snacking is no longer necessary, especially when they continue to drink enough water between all their meals. The idea that we need to eat snacks in between our three meals, whether fruits, vegetables, or candy bars, simply flies in the face of good physiology. By initiating digestion all day long, the stomach, liver, pancreas, and small intestine all become overworked. The digestive system needs a rest between meals; in fact, there are many people who do very well on two well-balanced meals a day.[19]

Several years ago a study was conducted to test the role of the stomach in the process of digestion. The subjects were individuals who, for various reasons, had tubes inserted directly into their stomachs. A few hours following their first meal, the contents of the subjects' stomachs were examined. Some of the subjects were given snacks between the major meals. A couple of hours after each subject ate, the contents of their stomachs were again examined.

Taken after the evening meal, tests showed that those who ate only three meals regularly spaced throughout the day had digested all but part of that meal. Tests of those who had eaten every two hours, or snacked between each major meal, showed that a part of what these subjects had eaten for breakfast remained in their stomachs in an undigested state, along with portions from every other meal eaten throughout the day.[20]

The explanation for this phenomena is that the digestive juices which aid in breaking down our food are initiated each time more food is eaten. Consequently, when new food enters the stomach several hours into the digestion of the first meal, the stomach promptly stops digestion of the first meal and begins anew on what has just appeared. If this pattern continues all day, it is late into the night before our exhausted stomachs can finally get some relief.[21]

Logic tells us that if our eating habits are weakening the digestive system, then that same weakening, even if it is not felt physically, could extend to the immune system.

Besides giving our stomachs a break, another aid in promoting good digestion is a leisurely walk following our meals, especially if we can take in some good deep breaths of fresh air at the same time. Another important tip for promoting good eating habits is to concentrate on maintaining a light, happy atmosphere at mealtimes, leaving the controversial or unpleasant subjects for later. A relatively stress-free mealtime is known to have an excellent influence on digestion.[22]

Finally, we should mention the "potluck" principle. Most people might think this principle concerns overeating, since that's what most of us do when we show up at a potluck. But this principle is actually concerned with variety. Variety may be the spice of life, but too great a variety of food taken at any one meal can delay digestion because of competition among the various enzymes available for digestion. Generally, three to four varieties of food at a meal is adequate.[23]

A study reported in the *American Journal of Clinical Nutrition* indicates that when a specific food is eaten, its taste and appearance decrease in appeal with time. However, the attractiveness of the other available food remains relatively unchanged. Consequently, too great a variety of food can make gluttons out of us all. The conclusions from this study were to avoid serving too great a variety of foods, and also to avoid serving the food in courses. If possible, we should place all the food to be eaten on the table. The greater the variety, the greater the temptation to overeat.[24]

Once these suggestions concerning healthy "table" etiquette become an integral part of our daily eating habits, we will find that we have a greater feeling of well-being about us. As we strive to make these habits permanent, we will aid our bodies in the strengthening of our overall immunity and will give ourselves the gift of increased vitality. Most of us will also see a continuing pattern of slow, but measurable, weight loss.

Assignment for Week Three:

- Spend fifteen minutes writing down your appetite cravings. Whenever you find yourself craving something not on your list during this week, add that new item to the list and make a note of what brought that craving to mind.

- Evaluate your list of cravings. From your reading, decide which food items are a responsible choice and which are not. Make every effort to replace the less healthy items with good choices.

- For just one meal this third week, choose the amount of food you think you should eat and set a timer for twenty minutes. Eat slowly, chewing your food well. Evaluate your level of hunger satisfaction at the conclusion of this period.

- If bolting large volumes of food is a problem, continue to portion your food out before you begin eating, putting the remainder of the food out of sight, and concentrating on savoring each bite of well-chewed food.

- Make an effort to concentrate on chewing each bite thoroughly. Make a family game of this new habit to help everyone remember.

- Begin fixing larger breakfasts. They should include several fruits, whole grain cereals and toast, waffles or pancakes with fruit toppings, and scrambled tofu with oven-fried potatoes. Check recipes in the back of this book for suggestions.

- Try to see that the family gets a hot lunch and a light supper instead of the reverse. Remember, new patterns take time. Don't get discouraged.

- Make every effort to cut out snacking, permanently. Remember the water habit to help you get through the withdrawal stage.

- Following at least one meal during the day, go for a leisurely walk, taking the family if you can.

- Refuse to discuss controversial matters at the table.

- Keep the variety of foods to a minimum at any given meal.

- Reread this chapter at least once during this third week.

TEN

INSIDE NUTRITIONAL MYTHS
Week 4: More On Food

When it comes to decisions about food, there are always two angles: what we should and what we shouldn't put into our shopping carts and our mouths. Either way, most of us have some preconceived ideas about nutrition or the lack of it. As we progress through this fourth week, we hope to be able to examine and resolve many of the controversies in today's world about diet.

Before beginning this fourth week, it would be a good idea for us to take a look at the three previous weeks' assignments and assess our strengths and weaknesses in adhering to the suggestions for better health. If we discover a failure or a lapse, we should take time to reread the information that clarifies the issue in question. Education and an open mind are two of our best friends when it comes to changing lifelong patterns, especially in the area of our willful appetites.

The Changing Times

Years ago, Joseph Lister noticed that his colleagues were examining patient after patient without washing their hands. He also noticed that a high number of these patients died after being admitted to the hospital. With a bit of politicking, he was able to institute a handwashing policy, thus greatly reducing the mortality rate at the hospital. The doctors at this hospital, however, thought his recommendations were too time consuming, so they threw him out and returned to their practice of not washing their hands between patients. All of us know the rest of the story. People started dying again.

Tradition dies hard, especially in such well-entrenched insti-
tutions as universities, mammoth corporations, and hospitals.
Over four hundred years ago, Montaigne stated: "Whenever a
new discovery is reported to the Scientific world, they say first,
'it is probably not true.' Thereafter, when the truth of the new
proposition has been demonstrated beyond question, they say,
'Yes, it may be true, but it is not important.' Finally, when sufficient time has elapsed to fully evidence its importance they say,
'Yes, surely it is important, but it is no longer new.' "

We find much the same situation surrounding what constitutes a healthy diet in this day and age. We believe the statistical
evidence stands by itself, once all the cream is skimmed away.
But there is also much "fat" to be poured off in the area of medical
research.[1] The issue of protein in the diet is a classic example.

Too Many Bricks

For years Americans have been on a quest for protein. There
are high protein diets, protein drinks, protein powders, protein
candy bars, protein discussions, protein disputes over the necessary RDA; the list is endless. When the subject of abandoning
our time-honored and favored sources of protein comes up,
especially if it is in reference to that nasty word, "vegetarian," we
always hear a lot of shrieking from the protein people, both
those who stand to gain (or lose) from our food dollar, and
those standing in line at the fast food outlet whose appetites
control their choices.

We find few diet centers or plans suggesting that a change in
our tastes is a prerequisite to changing our size. Instead, the
usual emphasis is on modifying our intake of food. But this
never lasts for long, judging from the statistics and the fat
around us. Such diets never do much on a permanent basis to
benefit the internal operations and consequent overall health of
our marvelously designed bodies.

Those who are familiar with "protein discussions" will recall
that there are twenty-three amino acids occurring in nature that
are absolutely essential for life. Of these twenty-three, eight cannot be manufactured by the body; consequently, they must be
obtained from our food choices. The interesting fact about the
protein issue is that animals, too, must find these eight amino

acids from outside sources. Since these essential amino acids are originally synthesized by plants, it would seem reasonable for man to get the amino acids from the original source as do animals. In other words, if cows can flourish on grain, common sense dictates that man can, too, rather than having to get his protein from a secondary source, namely animal products.[2]

Proteins might be called the building blocks or bricks that help create the structure of our cells, whether in the skin, hair, nails, or the like. What we see when we look at an individual is basically protein. Protein shapes the outer shell, or frame, of our bodies. Carbohydrates, by contrast, provide the best fuel sources. Unfortunately, most people think of protein as being a good energy source. Yet protein only yields roughly sixty percent of its weight in energy, whereas carbohydrates give up some ninety-five percent of their weight in energy.[3] This simply means that as soon as the body utilizes all the protein it needs for growth and repair, the excess is cast off in the form of toxic wastes, like ammonia. In fact, too much protein is a much greater problem than too little.[4] Few people realize that protein deficiency is almost impossible if sufficient calories are being consumed.

Over the years the government has gradually lowered the recommended daily allowance for protein, in part because of recognition of the problems caused by excess protein consumption.[5] In fact, one of the more current and effective treatments for chronic kidney disease is to lower the patient's intake of protein. Years ago it was thought that the average one hundred-fifty pound male needed approximately one hundred grams of protein every day. Later, the recommendation was lowered to seventy grams. In the 1970's, a suggestion was made to lower the RDA to forty grams of protein daily.[6]

As can be imagined, this last proposal caused an uproar in the protein producers' households; the dairy industry, the poultry industry, and the meat producers rose as one body to defend the health of America. After much haggling, the government nutritionists and the high protein producers agreed on a forty percent error factor to be built into the recommendation. Forty percent of the forty gram recommendation is, of course, sixteen grams, which, when added to the original number of forty, yields a recommendation of fifty-six grams daily, the current federal recommendation for the average male.

It is unfortunate that big business can so direct our thinking, and consequently, our eating. Any number of studies have shown that even physically active men can do well on thirty grams of protein a day, especially since there are people in other countries surviving on less than twenty. The average American consumption of protein is one hundred grams or more per day. Furthermore, research shows that too much protein is much more than expensive. It is detrimental to our health![7]

For the record, it is entirely possible to get more than adequate protein on a plant diet. Here's how. One gram of protein yields four calories of energy.[8] If we believe that we need at least fifty grams of protein a day, then we will need to consume at least two hundred calories of protein daily (fifty grams multiplied by four calories). For physically active people watching the scales, a total of two thousand calories per day might be a reasonable goal. So of those two thousand calories, two hundred, or ten percent, must come from protein sources.

Let's assume that we eat six hundred calories of fruits and vegetables a day. Fruit is quite low in protein, with the banana being about the highest of the commonly eaten fruits. Less than two percent protein would be an average. Vegetables such as broccoli and cauliflower, on the other hand, can range upwards of twenty percent protein. Staying on the conservative side, we will say that the six hundred calories of fruits and vegetables average only four percent protein. Four percent of our six hundred calories (600 multiplied by .04) gives us twenty-four calories that come from this source of protein. And if it takes four calories of protein to yield one gram of protein, then twenty-four calories divided by four grams equals six grams of protein.

Continuing this same calculation, assume that we eat eight hundred calories from whole grains such as brown rice, whole wheat bread, maybe millet cereal for breakfast, corn bread for lunch, etc. These grains range in protein content from about eight percent for rice all the way up to eighteen percent for wheat. Again, staying on the conservative side, we will assume that the eight hundred calories of grains yield only ten percent protein. Ten percent of eight hundred (800 multiplied by .10) means that eighty calories come from protein. And eighty divided by four amounts to a total of twenty grams of protein from our selection of whole grains. Added to our six grams from fruits and vegetables above, we now have a total of twenty-six grams of protein.

Finally, suppose we eat six hundred calories from legumes (peas, beans, peanuts) and nuts. All nuts are high in fat as well as calories, so we want to eat sparingly of them. The olive is technically a fruit, but because of its high fat content, it also falls into the category of foods that should be used sparingly. In percentage of protein, the legume/nut category is quite high, soybeans having as much as forty percent protein. Most of the beans and peas fall into the twenty to thirty percent range. Again, staying on the conservative side, we will use the twenty percent protein value for our six hundred calories. Twenty percent of six hundred calories (600 multiplied by .20) equals one hundred-twenty calories of protein. And one hundred-twenty divided by four yields thirty grams of protein. If we add that figure to our previous twenty-six grams of protein, we have a total of fifty-six grams of protein, all derived from a vegetarian diet without the help of the dairy, poultry, or meat industries.[9]

In spite of the fact that traditional dietitians who keep up with the literature now concede that it is possible for a total vegetarian to get more than adequate protein, some people still have concerns about what to eat to maximize their protein intake when they are trying to move away from animal products.[10] A good rule of thumb is to remember a growing favorite food combination — rice and beans — prepared in the kitchens of those spicy "South of the Border" restaurants. This memory peg may be expanded to include any combination of a grain (rice, corn, wheat, oats, barley, millet, rye, etc.) and a legume (peas or beans grown in a pod). Adding nuts to either category also gives us a very high quality protein. These combinations do not need to be eaten together at the same meals, just sometime during the same day.[11]

Clean Burning Energy

For years, the word "carbohydrates" has raised a red flag of warning for America's millions of perpetual dieters. But are these energy sources really that wicked? Or has the world of media and dieting managed to deceive us again? After all, what can be more basic than a slice of bread and a baked potato? Would the real truth please take a stand?[12]

Actually, carbohydrates are the cleanest burning energy sources we have available to us. It is because these plant products convert so easily and efficiently (about ninety-five percent) into energy that for years they were considered a major culprit in obesity. They became forbidden foods that diabetics and the rest of us would-be dieters should only eat in secret, and then accompanied by great feelings of guilt.[13]

Now, however, their role in the diet has gone full cycle to the point that carbohydrates might be considered king of the nutrients, but only in their unrefined form. The real value of these nutrient sources lies in our eating them in their complex form instead of their refined, simple state.[14]

In this country, the average adult consumes over fifty percent of his calories in the form of "empty" or "refined" foods.[15] These include sugars and syrups, free fats and oils, refined breads, cereals, and alcohol. Except for the free fats and oils, these food items are defined as "simple carbohydrates," while plant foods that are whole and unrefined are called "complex carbohydrates."

Whenever the food industry takes natural food and refines it, as in the case of white bread, we might as well expect poor health to follow. Few people know the story behind the milling industry where, in order to produce the soft, white, highly refined and prized flour so characteristic of most baked goods, all the nutrients and bran were literally stripped from the grain, leaving a product so devoid of anything that the government stepped in and ordered "enriching" to insure that we all didn't begin dropping like flies. For wheat supplies one-fifth of our total food energy.[16] Once we discover that the milling industries have taken over twelve vitamins and minerals from our wheat and replaced them with only three of the B vitamins and one mineral—and only at governmental insistence—few of us feel very "enriched."

Another problem besides the loss of nutrients in refined carbohydrates is the lack of fiber in these foods. Unrefined whole wheat bread has five to six times as much fiber as white bread.[17]

Potatoes lose nutrients and fiber when peeled, but this is nothing compared to what happens when butter and sour cream literally smother this defenseless favorite. These fat laden additives can turn an innocent one hundred calorie potato into a four hundred calorie fat generator.

The digestion of complex carbohydrates is characterized by a much slower absorption rate of the necessary blood sugar due to the fiber content of these nonprocessed foods. This is especially advantageous to the noninsulin dependent diabetics, as well as for the rest of us who are not diabetic.[18] A high blood sugar level (hyperglycemia) soon crashes (hypoglycemia), thus rushing us toward another between-the-meal treat which, as we have learned, disrupts the whole digestive process. The difference between getting our apple whole and getting it in a glass is evident in terms of blood sugar levels. The fiber in the apple slows down the absorption rate, keeping our blood sugar levels on a more even keel.[19] As a consequence, we should go easy on fruit juices since they are little more than sugar water with vitamin C. Granted that fructose, or fruit sugar, is absorbed more slowly than sucrose, or table sugar. But the best rule is still to eat foods in as natural a state as possible. For example, applesauce is better than apple juice, but the apple is better than applesauce.

While we are on the subject of blood sugar, it is important to point out that hyperglycemia, or high blood sugar situations, are known to greatly inhibit the ability of the immune system to ingest and kill invading organisms.[20] This should help us overcome the temptation of a candy bar over an apple the next time we feel the urge to indulge.

While the average American is eating approximately forty to fifty percent of his calories in carbohydrates, many of those food choices are in the form of simple, refined carbohydrates. The ideal diet would probably contain about seventy to eighty percent carbohydrates, mostly of the complex variety, ten to twenty percent fat, and ten percent protein.[21]

Fiber Facts
Once regarded only as a substance found in wood pulp for paper mills, fiber has more recently become the star attraction of the health-oriented community. As usual, those who stand to

gain by the ignorance of the majority have introduced all manner of potions to salve our "fiber consciences," from fiber pills and tablets to high fiber bran cereals and other prepackaged and processed fiber aids. All of this is at great cost to the consumer — and great success for these charlatans of "health."

Once again, Americans have been deceived. We're told that fiber is an elusive and mysterious aid to health that must be sought out in special shops labeled "health food stores," or diligently sought in specially packaged jars of "miller's bran" or other high-priced concoctions. In reality, the fresh fruit and vegetable bins of our local grocery are some of the best, and least expensive, places to locate the stuff. So is the aisle containing all the breads. We should simply take time to read the labels and be sure our money is spent on "one hundred percent" whole grains. The biggest problem with fiber in this country is not so much in what we fail to buy as it is in the thousands of packages of refined sugar, and preservative-loaded goodies that consume most of our food dollar and our health. These leave little space in our kitchens, money in our pockets, room in our stomachs, or desire in our hearts for nature's wholesome and "whole" foods.[22]

Actually, the idea of fiber in the diet is not new. Champions of the benefits of these complex carbohydrate foods range from Sylvester Graham, originator of the now adulterated "graham cracker" in the nineteenth century, to Dr. Dennis Burkitt, whose studies on the elimination habits of Africans have rendered him more infamous than he might ever have imagined. It was Graham who originally promoted the use of the whole kernel of wheat to prepare his crackers. How surprised he would be today if he were to read the ingredients on boxes labeled with his name. The very items he spent a lifetime promoting have been milled out, replaced with refined, white flour, sugar, and caramel color in a pitiful attempt to outwardly imitate the original product. Burkitt's research in the seventies helped generate a surge of interest in these beneficent plants which has taken root in our current diet conscious mentality. Indeed, it came just in time, for America was in the throes of concern over constipation.[23]

What, exactly, is fiber? Fiber is basically the non-digestible cell walls of plant material. For this reason it has been overlooked for years as having any nutritional benefits. But the facts are now indisputable: fiber is a multi-faceted necessary food-stuff that is present in the majority of those foods we should all be eating.[24]

For a quick review on the two types of fiber, Type I and Type II, most of us will remember that Type I is good for increasing the bulk of the stool by absorbing water and hurrying the body wastes to the outside like little "scrubbing sponges." In addition, these inflated particles help prevent all sorts of colon problems from constipation and hemorrhoids to diverticulitis. Current medical studies even show that fiber may be helpful in prevent-ing colon cancer, the number two cancer directly behind lung cancer. The best sources for Type I fiber are the whole grains.[25] Type II fiber performs the important role of lowering cholesterol and assisting in the management of blood sugar. Key sources for these fibers include oats, brown rice, barley, nuts, fruits, and vegetables. In other words, fiber is not going to be found hiding in the dairy or meat counters, which is a major reason animal products are less than ideal foods.[26]

Well-read opponents of a vegetarian, high fiber, high energy diet often cite an article from the *American Journal of Clinical Nutrition* which seems to indicate that a high fiber diet does not help control cholesterol, blood sugar, and insulin levels. But again, the complete picture must be taken into account.

One group under study was given a relatively low fiber diet of twenty-two grams while the second group ate a relatively high fiber diet of fifty-nine grams of fiber. Each group ate the experi-mental diet for four days and then for nine days ate their normal diet. Then the two groups switched experimental diets.

Conclusions showed that both groups tolerated their diets reasonably well, except for complaints of cramping and ex-cessive visits to the bathroom during the high fiber diet and of constipation during the low fiber diet. The side effects alone tell us that constipation is a serious indictment against the low fiber diet. As for the distress of those on the high fiber diet, we can see that the body was trying to adjust to what it needed: faster trips through the large intestines. For those choosing to make high fiber a regular part of their diets, the cramping dissipates in a few days, especially if fiber intake is gradually increased.

As for the claim that high fiber in the diet doesn't lower cholesterol, sugar, or insulin levels, the complete diet of the two
groups, aside from fiber intake, must be examined. Included in
the subjects' menus each day were one glass of whole milk, one
egg, one egg yolk, and two pats of butter, keeping cholesterol
levels well above the three hundred milligrams per day level that
the American Heart Association recommends. By taking in that
much cholesterol daily, the subjects under study did not show
any appreciably lower levels of cholesterol, regardless of how
much fiber they were consuming.[27]

As for a weight loss program, another study in the *American
Journal of Clinical Nutrition* presents a good case for a high fiber
diet. Both obese and non-obese subjects were involved in this
study. Two diets were used: one a high fiber diet, and the other a
low fiber diet. Interestingly, the low fiber diet was called a high
energy density diet and the high fiber diet was called a low
energy density diet. The sublets were tested over a five day
period. At each meal they were encouraged to eat to satisfaction.
For those subjects on the high fiber, low energy density diet,
satiety was reached at 1570 calories per day. By contrast, it took
three thousand calories for those on the low fiber high energy
density diet to reach satisfaction. Obviously, those on the high
fiber diet were giving the appestat time to block the stomach's
call for more food, while those subjects eating the low fiber diet
reported a greater tendency to eat to the point of discomfort. It's
harder to be a glutton when eating a diet high in fiber.[28] Our
previous chapter on the benefits of pure water comes into play as
we move into a diet filled with more high fiber food items, especially the kinds that fall into the category of Type I fiber. Because
these fibers absorb water for expansion, it is important to
remember to keep up our habit of drinking plenty of water for
our bodies' needs.

Fat Is Not the Enemy
A few myths about this maligned nutritional subject should
be dispelled. The first is that our bodies don't need fat. On the
contrary, fat is necessary for proper cell physiology and the production of hormones. These fat-soluble vitamins, A, D, E, and
K, are held in the body and transported by fat, as opposed to

water-soluble vitamins like C, which are easily passed out in the urine. Even cholesterol, which our bodies need in small amounts, is manufactured from fat. With a modest amount of fat in the diet, there is no need to introduce additional cholesterol to our bodies through the eating of animal products.[29]

The problem with fat is that most Americans eat about forty to forty-five percent of their daily calories in fat, yet studies show that survival is dependent upon a diet of only about seven percent of fat calories per day. Some Chinese even eat less than four percent of fat in their diets, and appear to be surviving without problems.[30] The low level of fat our bodies actually require to function, in contrast to the unbelievable amount we feed them, may be compared to a need for eight glasses of water a day for good health while drinking five gallons. Our lungs would most likely begin to fill with water to the point of drowning us.

Our bodies are dependent upon fat for proper functioning, but needing seven percent and getting forty to forty-five percent is another indication of the American diet dilemma. Because fats add flavor to food, we find the adjustment period needed to greatly reduce these foods from our diets extremely difficult. Everyone thinks that bland food is for hospital diets. This helps explain why the average American eats something fried[31] three times a day. Our high intake of fat is also a major reason why heart disease and cancer are at epidemic proportions in this country. For those diagnosed with one of these diseases, the sacrifice of lowering our fat consumption to around ten percent is a small price to pay to survive, regardless of our previously-conditioned taste buds.

Another misconception about fats relates to their effects on digestion time. Because the small intestine cannot handle the fats as quickly as other nutrients and requires special help for proper digestion, a meal high in fat can take up to four to five hours to exit the stomach. A meal high in complex carbohydrates, on the other hand, will pass through the stomach in three hours or less. Consequently, there are some who believe that fat extends the feeling of satisfaction. A more likely scenario is that too much fat slows the emptying time to the point that fermentation occurs. The resultant irritation to the stomach can cause premature hunger pangs. So all across America it's snack time again.[32]

To look at commercials and advertisements pushing polyun-saturated fats, one would think they are the health food answer to America's problems with cholesterol and consequent risk of heart attacks. In reality, the latest research points to the need for all of us to not only avoid animal fats whenever possible, but to take it very easy with these refined oils from vegetables and soy-beans. Such tremendously concentrated foods are extremely tax-ing on the digestive system, regardless of whether they come from animal or plant sources. According to tests run on foods we consume, oils are the greatest promoters of cancer in animals.[33] Few people realize that it takes fifteen ears of corn to get just one tablespoon of corn oil.[34] And few of us could pronounce the names of the innumerable additives and petroleum distillates used to refine these vegetable oils for household use.[35]

Fats are also a poor source of calories. While each gram of protein yields four calories, as does each gram of carbohydrate, every gram of fat more than doubles this yield with a whopping nine calories per gram.[36] Although we don't need to think of fats as our enemy, we should treat them like a friend that quickly wears out his welcome. Brief contact should be the key to the re-lationship. For more extended stays, invite the nut family for modest visits, along with olives and avocados. These are all high fat carriers, but the fat in them is more digestible when eaten along with the natural fibers of the plant.

Calcium Chasers and Other Minerals

The dairy industry has been doing us a public disservice by teaching our children that milk is essential for strong bones and teeth. Through the use of colorful charts that helpfully point out the four basic food groups, every one of us has been conditioned to believe in the absolute necessity of meat and dairy products for a sound diet.[37] Ask any group of elementary school children to name the most important mineral needed by the body. The majority of them would no doubt respond with the correct an-swer of calcium. But few of us, if any, realize that these charts are, in actuality, printed and distributed to the school systems by the National Dairy Council, and various food producers.[38]

It is true that calcium is one of the more essential minerals used by the body; indeed, it is found in more plentiful supplies than any other mineral. It assists in the blood clotting mechanism of the body, is used in enzymatic activity, and aids in proper functioning of the nerves and muscles.[39]

It is also true that milk is a good source of calcium, in addition to protein. But we need to back up twenty or thirty years to the time when the food industry first developed infant formulas. Working through doctors, particularly pediatricians, these giant corporations were able to convince mothers that by using these new formulas, supposedly superior to mother's milk, we would be raising the healthiest kids in the world. The truth of the matter is that obesity is running rampant among the young. Never have there been more children with such weakened immune systems as we have now. While cow's milk is not wholly to blame, few can deny its role in the development of these problems.[40] One thing is certainly true about the dairy producers' claims that milk is the perfect food — that is, if we're talking about baby calves. A calf grows at a much faster rate than does a human baby; consequently, it makes sense for cows' milk to have triple the protein (eight grams) as contrasted to human milk (2.5 grams). And when calcium is compared, we see that cows' milk also has more than triple the amount of calcium (288 milligrams per cup) as human milk (eighty milligrams). Yet even during the fastest growing period of a child' life, when his birth weight doubles in only six months, his need for protein and calcium can be satisfied totally with his mother's low protein, low calcium milk.[41]

So are we hearing false information concerning our national crisis of osteoporosis, the condition where calcium is taken from the bones to supply other needs to the point that the bones are severely weakened? The answer is no. While America has one of the highest rates of calcium consumption in the entire world, her people still suffer from the highest incidence of this disease. The problem is related not to our intake of calcium but rather to our absorption of calcium. On the average, Americans absorb only from twenty to thirty percent of their calcium intake, while others absorb as much as seventy to eighty percent. As a result, many authorities are calling on Americans, especially women, to increase their intake to the 1200-1500 milligram per day range. Currently most Americans are getting roughly half that amount.

However, the World Health Organization has stated that many cultures do fine on four hundred-fifty milligrams of this mineral per day with little or no incidence of osteoporosis.[42]

If our problem centers around absorption, then there must be ways we can stop our bodies from losing so much calcium. One of the first is to limit our protein intake. A high level of protein in the diet causes an acid urine which draws out calcium from the blood.[43] Another method for maintaining adequate absorption of this important mineral is to decrease fat intake, because high levels of fat in the diet can decrease bone density. Lowering sodium intake, which otherwise would increase urinary loss of calcium, is another way we can help our bodies to absorb calcium. So is eliminating caffeine from our diets. The individual who consumes one gram of caffeine (ten cups of coffee) per day can lose approximately one hundred milligrams of calcium. It is also of great benefit to stop smoking and drinking and to exchange carbonated drinks for healthier beverages. The high content of phosphorus found in meat and soft drinks binds with the available calcium, leaching it from the body. Eliminating or controlling stress and nervousness can greatly help to keep our levels of calcium up. Even the wisest man, King Solomon, warned thousands of years ago that "a crushed spirit dries up the bone." Finally, the biggest benefit of all in helping our bodies to absorb calcium is in daily exercise, especially when it involves the weight-bearing types such as walking and jogging.[44]

Those who choose not to eat animal products should pay close attention to these suggestions for maximum calcium absorption and, in addition, get plenty of sunshine for vitamin D. Good sources of calcium are dark, leafy greens, tofu, nuts, and seeds. But virtually all foods, when eaten as grown, have varying degrees of calcium.[45] Foods that are not necessarily on the best seller list but that nevertheless are good for us, such as fresh fruits and vegetables, wholesome grains and hearty legumes, and small portions of nuts, still concern many people who have been told for so many years that such a diet will not support all the vitamin and mineral needs of the body.

Women have been convinced they need extra iron, for example. The key function of this mineral is to provide the make-up of hemoglobin, the blood protein that carries the oxygen. But when we see that good sources for iron are readily available in green leafy vegetables, legumes, prunes, dried apricots, raisins, and whole grains, it is easy to see how a prudent diet can easily accommodate quality sources of this mineral.[46]

A mineral that a plant diet is often thought to be deficient in is selenium, which is a valuable antioxidant, protecting against the formation of free radicals, and consequently functioning as one of the guardians against cancer.[47] Yet for the vegetarian, sources of selenium are readily found in grains and onions.[48]

Zinc, a critical mineral affecting many bodily functions such as growth, healing, and appetite, is found in abundance in both whole grains and legumes.[49]

Finally, there has been a tangle of criticism over the last, and most elusive of the B vitamins, B12.

The Mystery Vitamin

Probably the only thing most of us have ever heard about vitamin B12 is that its deficiency causes some sort of anemia in those gaunt, strange looking health food store frequenters that most of us picture with dirty feet, baggy clothes, and hair pulled back into ponytails. The truth of the matter, however, was reported in a study by Dr. Victor Herbert, a world authority on the B12 issue. Dr. Herbert studied ninety people with megaloblastic, or pernicious, anemia. Of those ninety individuals, only five were vegetarians, which points to the fact that the B12 issue is not really that much of an issue for vegetarians who eat a wide variety of foods.[50]

This evasive vitamin, only recently discovered in 1948, is needed by every cell in the body, especially the blood cells and the gastrointestinal lining. Since it is used in protein metabolism, logic tells us that the higher an individual's intake of protein, the greater his need of this vitamin. A deficiency in this vitamin threatens the integrity of the nervous system, causing pernicious anemia, a deadly disease characterized by progressive destruction of the red blood cells.[51]

So why the controversy over B12? Because people who choose to incorporate only nature's healthiest plant foods into their diets are continually asked their source of B12. Indeed, the medical community has for years encouraged these individuals to supplement their diets with this vitamin, since it is supposedly available only through animal products. But we should examine exactly where this vitamin originates. Vitamin B12 is synthesized by bacteria. Animals eating plants with the dirt on them take in small amounts of this vitamin. The theory is that those who don't eat animal products, but who do wash their vegetables, will be unable to find adequate sources to support their health.[52]

However, supplementation is not necessarily the answer. Dr. Herbert is highly skeptical of the benefits of laboratory-produced B12. He states that supplements are often mere analogues when measured by standard methods, meaning that while researchers have been able to produce a chemical compound that appears to function like B12, in reality it is structurally different. This difference raises serious questions as to the benefits of B12 supplementation.[53]

An article in the *Journal of Seminars in Oncology* spoke of the role that vitamin A plays in inhibiting the growth of cancers. The author recommended daily consumption of foods containing this vitamin, but drew the line short of recommending supplementation, stating that supplementation needs more study. This may be true for all supplementation except in relatively rare cases, where for one reason or another, the individual is unable to absorb certain vitamins and minerals from his diet.[54]

Before we discuss where vegetarians can derive their B12 naturally, we need to know how much of this vitamin is necessary in the diet. Like other RDA's, the recommendation for B12 has gone down over the years. Some researchers believe that 0.1 micrograms (not milligrams) per day is adequate for those on the "standard American diet," sometimes called SAD. Most researchers, however, say 0.5 micrograms are needed.[55] In 1987 the RDA was lowered to 0.2 micrograms. Interestingly, cow's milk yields about 0.4 micrograms per cup, while mother's milk yields such a fraction of that as to be hardly measurable. We must remember that it is during this time in an infant's life that the most rapid growth period takes place and B12 demands would be the greatest.[56]

Because of their low protein intake, it is quite likely that vegetarians require only 0.05 micrograms per day of B12, one tenth of the highest recommendations for those eating the SAD way. In addition, we can reduce our B12 needs by not smoking. Those of us who take large doses of B12 by supplementation increase our need for the vitamin. Dr. Herbert reported that all ten multi-vitamin/mineral supplements that were tested contained products which break down vitamin B12, as do high doses of vitamin C and oral contraceptives.[57]

Even in reduced amounts, B12 is still a necessary vitamin. In spite of the controversy surrounding it sources, those who contemplate dietary changes will be glad to know that B12 has been found in green vegetables, turnips, yeast, olives, wheat, soybeans, unsprayed fruit, water, and even 0.25 micrograms are produced daily in the mouth.[58] It is also synthesized by the small intestine.[59]

Fleshing It Out

When it comes to the more sensitive issues in nutrition such as meat eating, many people want the facts up front before they will decide to implement any changes. As we begin examining the whole picture of animal protein, a different portrait than what the advertisements and media have presented begins to emerge.

It is no secret that animals are becoming more and more diseased. Over fifty years ago, an article in the *Journal of the American Veterinary Medical Association* reported that diseases from cattle were transmissible to man.[60] This was well before antibiotics, hormones, and other pharmaceuticals had made their way into the production of cattle and other food animals.

Orville Schell, a modern-day Upton Sinclair, has reported some alarming facts in his book *Modern Meat: Antibiotics, Hormones, and Pharmaceutical Farm*. According to his research, farmers are using plastic hay, cardboard, computer paper, and newsprint as roughage for their cattle.[61] Obviously, we have no idea how our health will be affected by the ingestion of all this ink, glue, and wax, as well as by the many petroleum by-products of plastic. Farmers use oral insecticides that pass through the cow and kill the fly eggs that are laid in the manure. At this writing, no one seems to know what effect these poisons will have on the health of those eating this meat. Because of the odd tastes left in the meat of animals fed these antibiotics, wormers, molds, and waste products, it has been necessary for the meat industry to turn to synthetic additives such as flavors and aromas to mask the overwhelming chemical flavors permeating the meat.[62]

Mr. Schell raises numerous concerns about the widespread use of growth hormones given livestock, since research has proven that some of these are known to cause cancer. Indeed, the concern over feeding livestock growth hormones is analogous to the questions raised about the sanity of allowing athletes to take steroids to increase their bulk.[63]

The U.S. Centers for Disease Control have recorded serious cases of drug-resistant salmonellosis in people who have eaten hamburger meat. This meat came from cattle that had regularly been fed low doses of antibiotics.[64]

Another factor to consider is that while the USDA has set standards regulating antibiotics and growth hormones, these chemicals are administered by the very individuals who stand to profit from bigger animals, regardless of the health of those animals. If a small amount produces larger animals, then we can see the rationale behind administering larger doses.

Some people who are concerned about the quality of their meat purchase it from friends or individuals who raise "clean" meat. Yet while science knows little about the effects of chemical manipulation on humans, it knows next to nothing about the effects on the offspring of these animals. Who is to say how many generations of livestock will be affected genetically by the use of these drugs?

One final observation on this issue concerns the way meat is handled by our bodies, especially as it relates to cardiovascular disease. A study designed to show a positive correlation between meat consumption and ischemic heart disease (the obstruction of the blood flow) revealed a thirty percent increase in the risk for ischemic heart disease in a group of men aged forty-five to sixty-four who ate meat daily when compared with those who did not. This association was not related to the eating of high cholesterol products such as eggs and dairy products. Obesity, marital status, and smoking were other factors that were neutralized out by the study, making meat eating the only causative factor.[65]

Another significant study was reported several years ago in the *Journal of the American Medical Association*. Its subjects were twenty-one vegetarians whose staple diet had been whole grains, vegetables, legumes, and fruit for an average of three years. On the average they consumed fish, dairy foods, and coffee only two to four times per month. They ate eggs once a month and meat and poultry less than once a month. During the study, these individuals ate nine ounces of beef per day for four weeks. At the end of the four week period their total cholesterol rose by nineteen percent. Even blood pressure increased significantly. And this was over a four week period, not four months, or even a year.[66]

While not a "flesh" food, cheese and its use has become a concern of those studying the effects of animal products on our bodies. This high fat, moderate sodium food item is the product of concentrated and fermented milk. The putrefaction process necessary for the aging of cheese results in a whole host of waste products that cause irritation to the nerves and the gastrointestinal tract. Rennet, taken from the stomach lining of baby calves, kids, or pigs so young their stomachs have never digested anything but milk, is used to curdle milk for making cheese. There are few manufacturers of this product that use vegetable sources of rennet.[67]

Milk, when pasteurized for approximately thirty minutes at one hundred-thirty degrees, can still have bacteria remaining, not to mention the ever-present viruses that are far more resistant to destruction by heat than are bacteria.

Many times the onset of chills, fever, diarrhea, and abdominal cramping are the result of salmonellosis food poisoning from a diet of eggs, poultry, or dairy products. The sufferer passes the symptoms off as a bout with the flu when in reality the consumption of contaminated animal products is the cause.[68]

Even fish are known to carry and transfer disease from over-polluted environments to man. A fish tapeworm identified in people living in and around the Michigan area causes a variety of symptoms, including numbness of extremities, along with fatigue, weakness and dizziness. Symptoms can continue for years before proper diagnosis is made.[69] In essence, animal products are eager hosts for a variety of diseases that are readily transmissible to man.

It has been quite a few years since Americans were first warned to stop smoking. The health benefits for those quitting this devastating habit have been phenomenal. With the latest Framingham study showing the need to greatly reduce the nation's cholesterol levels[70] and with increased research for animal-transmitted diseases continuing, we will begin to see more and more people moving in the direction of a diet based on the goodness of the earth.[71]

As we approach the game plan for this fourth week we need to keep in mind that most of us are, or have been, voluntary slaves to our appetites. Changing these appetites requires more than ordinary motivation. So as we begin the assignment for week four, we suggest that you continue on with the following chapter "Staying Power" to help make this plan one for a lifetime.

Assignment for Week Four:

- From the recipes in the back, plan at least two main meals without the use of animal products for this fourth week, trying to serve these meals at lunch, if possible.

- Plan to add one main meal each ensuing week that is free from animal products.

- Take a thoughtful trip to the grocery store this week, stocking up on an abundance of fresh fruits and vegetables, and limiting yourself to a maximum of one to two prepackaged food items.

- Buy and eat only 100% whole grain breads and breakfast cereals, avoiding those with preservatives.

- Drastically reduce the use of all fats, paying special attention to those hidden sources of polyunsaturates in prepackaged, refined food items.

- Instead of frying foods, begin steaming, baking, or sautéing in a skillet rubbed with olive oil (see recipe section for instructions).

- Try one of the alternate milk recipes at the back for use in cooking and on cereals. Mix with regular milk until tastes become adjusted.

- This fourth week keep suppers light, using suggestions in the recipe section.

- Make every effort to eat a hearty breakfast each morning.

- Make a note of the money you save by purchasing more fresh fruits and vegetables, in addition to cutting down, drastically, on your use of refined, prepackaged items and animal products.

- Have a physical and blood panel with HDL and LDL levels separated.

- Have another blood panel in sixty to ninety days to check progress.

- Reread this chapter at least once during this fourth week.

- Read through Chapter 11 "Staying Power: Assignment for Success."

E L E V E N

STAYING POWER
Week 5: Assignment for Success

As we move into this fifth, and last, week of our plan, we've no doubt had adequate opportunities to observe the matchless and bellicose power of our appetites, evidenced by the number of food fights we find ourselves losing. The counsel we receive when we desire to stop smoking and drinking—that is, to go "cold turkey,"—just doesn't work when it comes to eating. We must remember that we are not "quitting" but changing our habits. While the habits of smoking and drinking are harmful to our bodies, eating is a perfectly natural occurrence that takes place several times daily. It's just a matter of choosing those foods that will most benefit our bodies. Since we desire to make changes based on what we learn about what's healthy for our bodies, we should move gradually into this remodeling lest we fail, become discouraged, and then quit the plan altogether.

For programs involving the will power, there must be a plan for maintenance, a formula for continued success. We must be able to depend upon a Power that can compensate for the times when our will is weakest, for the times when we're ready to give it all up and toss the book over our shoulder, our progress out the window, and the good food in our refrigerator down the disposal. Those with strong wills can succeed. In fact, most of them don't even need a plan. But we soon realize that few such people actually exist when we start looking around us. In this prosperous country, health seems to be a nebulous and intangible attainment if we simply focus on the latest health fad. But for those of us desiring a lasting commitment to a plan that refines the total body, both inside and out, there is a Way.

New Start

I was single, twenty-five, and in graduate school, proud of the extra twenty-five pounds my weight-lifting, body-building sweat-outs had produced. I enjoyed the indulgence of a meat diet twice a day, ignored the notion that "sugar in the morning, sugar in the evening, sugar at supper time," might be less then ideal, and deliberately violated my upbringing with a beer now and then, even more on the weekends. Health, I was convinced, was a reflection staring at me from the mirror.

It was January 17, 1971. The day was a cool one. The crispness of winter in East Texas enhanced the sunlight shimmering through the pine needles. I loved Texas winters. Their mildness rarely asked for more than sweaters and cords instead of all the heavy trappings demanded of inclement weather farther north.

I should have been studying that bracing January day. Instead my thoughts had taken me away from my assignments, reflective thoughts that included my plans for the evening, my past, the death of my father less than two miles from the very place I was sitting, and my widowed mother, whose years of hard work and diligent perseverance had enabled me to get the education she so prized. And I thought of God. The God that I had loved as a child, but had walked away from as a man.

My friends would be expecting me in less than a half an hour. But my heart wasn't in it. The alcohol that I would consume was consuming me, filling me with a spirit of self-love and egoism, pushing out the needs of others as surely as it planted within me its insidious seeds of dependence. I glanced at the sun, melting its splendor over the western horizon. It was time to go.

Reason fought desire as I glanced at my watch. If there was any vestige of care within me, care for myself, my direction, my parents, then there had to be a caring God who shared this concern with me. And if He cared . . .

I stood up, but instead of stepping out into the coming darkness, I reached for my wallet. Pulling out the club card, I deliberately tore it in half, again and again, until the tiny fragments sifted gently into the swirling toilet, disappearing forever. I knelt down. Somewhere, there was a Presence, a Person, a Help. And I needed Him.

The First Step

Through the years following my choice to let God take over, Kathy and I have experienced many joyous advances toward better health. There have been some setbacks, but we have discovered an essential key to the best of health; a health that springs not only from the body, but one that includes the mind and the spirit as well.

The essence of turning our lives from a past imperfect tense to one of present perfect action requires choosing to trust, inherently, in the God who cares. Regardless of our personal belief system, believing that there is a God who desires only our best good is an absolute and essential motivation for making the best choices, choices that are not always easy.

It is this spirit, this knowledge that God desires only the best for His children, which should be present when we make culinary decisions, decisions that seem so insignificant at the time, but which, nevertheless, are actually determining a pattern in our lives. They are also decisions that are determining a pattern in the lives of those little people whose eyes never miss a choice that Mommy and Daddy make.

For example, if we have a choice between an apple or an irresistible chocolate dessert, most of us will be inclined to choose the dessert, thinking that one time won't hurt. Although it's true that an indulgence every once in a while won't kill us, it's the overall pattern of our choices that we must consider. We must also consider our strength to overcome these patterns, especially once we've progressed enough to realize how much better we feel, physically, when we're consistently considerate of what we put into our bodies.

Most of us do not have the strength within us, on a repeating basis, to make the better choice. However, if through our study we know that the apple is a better choice, and through our knowledge we know that God wants only the best for us, and through our faith we know that He will provide the power to make the right choice, then we can make the better decision even in the face of a clamoring appetite.

Health in the Past

Over the centuries the value of caring for the physical aspect of man has received varying degrees of emphasis. In Old Testament times, diseases were prevalent that were similar to those which afflict modern man today. But God told His people that if they would obey His health laws, "none of those diseases" would afflict them (Exodus 15:26, Deuteronomy 7:15).

By 400 or 300 B.C., the Greek philosophy of elevating the soul and the mind to the detriment of the body was beginning to dominate the thinking. Plato was the primary source of this teaching. The history and literature of this period reveal that, indeed, the body was relegated to a place of inferiority in the face of intellectualism. Choice and discipline gave way to inclination and permissiveness. Greek thought resulted in a glorification of the human body in sports. So the body was cared for, not for the sake of health, but rather in order to optimize the chances to wear the coveted garland. Obviously, this devotion to health involved only the few competitors entering the races.

During the height of Greek influence, we find the Apostle Paul instructing his readers to view their bodies as a temple of God (1 Corinthians 6:19-20). In fact, the Apostle admonished these Corinthians to glorify God in their bodies. Considering their physical conditions, this counsel from Paul must have astonished the Corinthians. Like many Americans, they were accustomed to pleasing their appetites, giving little consideration to their bodies. Yet Paul was trying to tell them that God cares about the total person. Without a healthy body it is not only more difficult to work or play at one's optimal level, but more difficult to worship as well.

While it is true that the diet in Biblical times was different than what we see as being important for healthy living in the 1980's, our choices must be made within the context of the culture in which we live. In fact, we could conclude that Paul might very possibly have recommended a diet similar to what we have examined these past few weeks had the world then been experiencing the increasing incidence of cancer, heart, and other lifestyle diseases that have been associated with our present diet and lifestyle.

Putting Failure Behind Us

Failure is a word that slumps the shoulders of everyone experiencing it. Fear of failure drives some toward excellence and others into the despair of apathy. Failure, like success, is often perpetuated by its own inertia, for while success breeds success if complacency can be avoided, likewise failure breeds failure if complacency is tolerated. The fact that sixty-five million Americans at any one time are on a diet indicates a great distaste for failure. Because most dieters fail and eventually regress to their former weight and often beyond, the experience of being on a diet becomes their attempt at success. Yet the benefits of dieting are all too often tenuous at best. So we find the vast majority of unhealthy people remaining in a vise-like grip with the body controlling mind rather than the way it should be.

As we begin to implement this plan in our lives, we need to be aware that discouragement is one of our greatest enemies. Too often we blame our failure to gain control over our lives on a litany of excuses from "I don't care" to "my problems are hereditary." We must make our commitment to health in the form of a conviction that offers no excuses and refuses to tolerate failure. True, most of us will experience what we might label failure, but we need to see this setback as merely a temporary plateau in our upward progress towards better health. In all fairness, this program is not designed to avoid these temporary setbacks; instead, it is designed for continual growth. So if we find ourselves stretched out on a plateau, we need to gather our forces, renew our resolves, pack them on our back, and start climbing again.

Another key to failure is to rely upon our own will power. There are many who teach, and millions who believe, that within the individual there is power to achieve almost anything. But if that is the case, then the race is only for the strong-willed person. What about the rest of us who are weaker? Must we suffer from our failure of will power? The good news is no. Philippians 2:5 confidently assures us that "I can do all things through Christ which strengthens me."

Keys to Success

There can be little doubt that the road to good health is cluttered with the weak and frail who have stumbled and fallen. But in Christ we have a Source of strength that is greater than any challenge that can come our way. Instead of trusting ourselves, or even the "Living Well Plan," we should trust in the One who can save us from our own willful selves. We should ask Him daily for His help.

The great evangelist, Dwight L. Moody, appealingly articulated the key to success, regardless of the area of our lives needing help:

"Trust in yourself, and you are doomed to disappointment; trust in your friends, and they will die and leave you; trust in money, and you may have it taken from you; trust in reputation and some slanderous tongue may blast it; but trust in God, and you are never to be confounded in time or eternity."

With the proper focus on trust in God, we are better suited not only to make the best choices for our health, but also to have the power available to achieve the desired results, and to maintain these desired results.

Another key to our success with this plan is realizing and dealing with the difference between physical and psychological cravings. With the habit of smoking, the psychological addiction is much more difficult to break than is the physiological addiction. Physical cravings are often overcome in a matter of days, but like Linus's security blanket, the psychological addiction can continue for weeks, months, or even years.

Such is also true of the appetite. The physical appreciation for new foods and an elimination for other foods can be rapidly accepted by most people; the problems arise when circumstances create temptations to return to old habits. Thankfully, these temptations can be weakened by mental preparation before they occur. We should practice feeling thankful for our new lifestyle, often praising God that He cares for every aspect of our lives, even the health of our bodies. This habituation of praise to God will strengthen us to endure the temptation to regress when it occurs. But most important, we can claim His power for victory, and that victory can be ours, for to trust in ourselves is to ensure defeat.

Practicing the program itself is another key to succeeding. As we acclimate our bodies to the principles of health we have studied, these very principles strengthen us to practice them again and again until we are comfortable with our new lifestyle. Conversely, we must remember that to violate these principles of health predisposes us to greater violations of other healthful principles.

Success for a Lifetime

One of the primary motivations for a better lifestyle is to improve our appearance. This is undoubtedly the major reason that keeps sixty-five million Americans on some type of a diet. But if we were to compare our bodies to a beautiful, sleek car that barely limps down the road due to lack of proper maintenance, few of us would desire this kind of attractiveness. Few, if any of us, could care less how attractive we appear when we're prostrate on some bed of affliction due to a body "breakdown."

Consequently, it is a good idea for us to seek a physical examination by a doctor and request a full blood panel as we continue with this program. The importance of having the cholesterol level divided into HDL (high-density lipoproteins) and LDL (low-density lipoproteins) can be seen in the chapter on heart disease. After several months on this new lifestyle, the positive results from a new blood panel will be a boost to all of us who are concerned with the inner workings of our body as well as its outward appearance. These internal, clinical encouragements are also a significant motivation to continue to grow in our new lifestyles.

Sharing this plan with others is a natural outgrowth of our exuberance over our new body styles, both internal and external. However, we need to be aware that our personal testimonies can be received as personal rebukes from those who lives exemplify the standard American lifestyle. Consequently, we need to understand that our enthusiasm will be better received if we focus on the benefits of the plan, rather than the methods.

From the beginning of time there has been one other principle of life that God has sought to teach man: the need to rest on His Sabbath Day. Spiritual needs aside, it is a precept of the way we are biologically programmed to rest, completely, one day a week. This principle of the Sabbath rest not only nourishes us spiritually, but recharges our bodies to be able to perform more efficiently the other six days of the week. Properly observed, the Sabbath gives us the time to renew our commitments to God, the family, and ourselves.

The Apostle John, (3 John:2) says, "Beloved I wish above all things that thou mayest prosper and be in health." Health, like prosperity, is most often the result of right choices coupled with dedicated efforts. As we experience the bountiful rewards of following and assimilating these health principles, let us regularly pause and praise the One who truly "healeth all of thy diseases." (Psalm 103:3)

Assignment for Week Five:

• Each morning, perhaps while exercising, ask God for help in maintaining the healthy habits of this program to give your body only the best. Ask especially for a release from unhealthy desires.

• Before eating, thank God for your immediate progress and ask Him to keep you temperate in your eating.

• Share the benefits of the "Living Well Plan" with others.

• Refuse to give up if you fail. Ask for Divine help and continue on.

• Reread portions of this book that will inspire you to continue when you feel your resolve weaken.

PART THREE

FOOD
FACTS
AND
RECIPES

TWELVE

BASIC FOOD FACTS

Menu Planner

Upon Arising: Two glasses of water (or your allotment).

Breakfast: For a hearty breakfast, try to at select least three from the following:

- Whole grain cereal with lowfat milk, alternate milk, or fruit topping
- Entrée (waffles, pancakes, scrambled tofu, etc.)
- Whole grain bread with cashew, almond, or peanut butter, tahini (sesame butter), or fruit spread
- Fresh fruit
- Additional fruit (frozen, canned, or dried)

Mid-Morning: Two glasses of water

Lunch: Mix and match 3-5 selections from the following:

- Entrée
- Whole grain or tuber (potatoes, sweet potatoes)
- Cooked vegetable
- Salad or raw vegetable with dressing or dip
- Whole grain bread and spread
- Simple dessert (occasionally)

Mid-Afternoon: Two glasses of water

Supper: Select from the following choices, keeping this meal light:

- Fruit entrée
- Fresh fruit
- Whole grain bread with spread or topping
- Air-popped corn

Evening: One glass of water

The Process of Change Is Gradual, So . . .

• Go about Changes Slowly
It may take months to win your appetite and your family's over to new tastes, and you may find all sorts of resistance to new recipes and foods, but don't give in or give up.

• Have Good Choices on Hand
For any changes to happen, the desirable foods must be near at hand. If potato chips are on the shelf, the family' will reach for them and it will be back to the old habits. Stock your kitchen with popcorn, unshelled peanuts, dates, sunflower seeds, granola, and fresh fruit. Have the better choices readily available.

• Serve New Dishes as a Side Dish First
Try to have a sure-fire favorite with something really unusual. An eggplant dish with that suspicious name "ratatouille" seems much safer with an old favorite, such as fresh pineapple, and with the old standby, cookies.

• Avoid Repeating New Foods Too Soon
It is easy to be exited about success, but give the memory of it time to flow. Bean cookery, for example, might be a whole new area of interest for you, but when the kids start seeing them in

the soup, the salad, and the burritos, the complaints might begin, especially for a family whose most recent memory of beans was on the camp-out last summer.

• Serve Enough for Everyone to Get His Fill

Remember, by serving lower-fat foods, you also reduce calories.[1]

Good Planning and Organizational Strategy Will Help You Stay With Your Goals

• Plan a Menu and Make a Grocery List at the Beginning of Each Week

The thirty minutes it takes will be well worth the time and food savings throughout the ensuing week. Keep a file of old menus and use them again.

• Set Aside a Three to Four Hour Slot at the Beginning of Each Week for Baking and Food Preparation

Again, the time spent in this preparation for the week will prove to be invaluable.

• Try to Work Within Each Family Member's Schedule

Spouses who can't come home for a hot lunch can take a prepared meal to work in a microwave dish. And teenagers, with their higher energy level, could brown-bag it at lunch and reheat the noon meal in the evening. Where there's a will to make changes, there's always a way.

The Four Food Groups

• Beans, Nuts, Seeds:

Eat three to five cups of beans per week (kidney, pinto, lentils, navy, refried, in chili, etc.). Use nuts and seeds to spice up grains, beans, and vegetables. Don't be afraid of the fat from nuts and seeds when you're committed to moving in the direction of a plant diet.

- **Vegetables:**

Eat 2 to 3 cups per day, unpeeled if possible.

- **Whole Grains and Potatoes**

Eat 2 to 5 servings at each meal. Choose light, supper items from this group (bread, rice cakes, cereals, oats, etc.).

- **Fruits:**

Eat 3 to 4 pieces per day. Fresh fruit is preferable to juice.[2]

Food Suggestions for the Pantry

- **Grains**

rolled oats	wheat flakes
quick oats	rye flakes
brown rice	corn meal (not degermed)
millet	whole wheat flour
bulgar wheat	barley

- **Beans**

lentils	garbanzos
black beans	lima beans
pinto beans	navy beans
black-eyed peas	split peas
great northerns	kidney beans

- **Nuts and Seeds**

almonds	cashews, raw (used the most)
walnuts	pecans
sesame seeds	peanuts (actually a legume)
sunflower seeds	poppy seeds
unblanched almonds	

- **Dried Fruit**

pitted prunes	dates
figs	unsweetened macaroon apricots
raisins	coconut
apricots	

- **Miscellaneous**

pimientos
carob powder
cornstarch
baking yeast
black olives
onion powder
vanilla
Vege-sal
butter fllavoring
Spike Seasoning
clear gel (precooked
    cornstarch—ask for it
    in the kitchen of a
    bakery or restaurant)

food yeast flakes (nutritional
    or Brewer's)
McKay's chicken style
    seasoning (vegetarian)
vital gluten (as an aid in
    breadmaking)
lemons (preferable to bottled
    lemon juice)
Soyagen (soy milk powder)
Emes (pronounced "Emas")
    gelatin
Savorex and Vegex—
    beef-like seasoning

Protein—It's Everywhere

Eat the following to get approximately: [3]

- **8 Grams of Protein:**

1 cup milk
1 cup buttermilk
½ cup dry beans, cooked

½ cup lentils
2 tbsp. peanut butter
1 large stalk broccoli

- **7 Grams of Protein:**

1 egg
⅓ cup mixed nuts
¼ cup soybeans

1 cup cottage cheese
½ cup nuteema
1 small piece "soy" chicken

- **5 Grams of Protein:**

2 slices whole wheat bread
½ cup green limas

1 cup cream of mushroom soup
1 cup brown rice

- **3 Grams of Protein:**

½ cup spinach
½ cup oatmeal

½ cup Farina
1 cup cornmeal

- **2 Grams of Protein:**

½ cup whole wheat cereal   1 biscuit of shredded wheat
  1 slice of bread   ½ cup vegetables

1 Gram of Protein:

  1 apple   ½ cup fruit juice
  1 orange   1 banana

QUICK 'N EASY, HEALTHFUL RECIPES

Breakfast

Tips

- Natural rice, toasted and steamed with peanut butter and fruit topping
- Oatmeal cooked with raisins and a bit of honey, lowfat or alternate milk
- Creamed lima beans, navy beans, or peas on toast with fruit, fresh or canned
- Fruit soup over toast with peanut butter (see "Soups" section)
- Granola with lowfat or alternate milk, fresh fruit, toast, and skillet fries
- Waffles with peanut butter, fruit topping, and cashew cream
- Whole wheat toast with peanut butter topped with hot applesauce or hot pureed apricots

Delicious Millet

Millet, used mostly as bird seed in this country, is actually the "king of grains." It contains all eight essential amino acids, and is alkaline, whereas other grains are acidic.

     1 cup millet
     3 cups water
     ½ tsp. salt
     ½ cup unsweetened coconut
     ½ cup toasted almonds
     ¾ cup chopped dates

Yield: 4 Servings

- Cook first 3 ingredients 1 hour
- Stir in remaining ingredients shortly before serving
- Millet can be slow cooked overnight in oven at 200° or on a slow burner

Scrambled Tofu
A great accompaniment to any "sweet" breakfast entrée, such as waffles, pancakes, Musseli, and the like.

```
      1 lb. tofu
      1 bunch green onions, chopped, or 1 tsp. onion powder
      2 tsp. soy sauce
      1 tsp. margarine or oil-rubbed teflon skillet
   1½ tsp. chicken-like seasoning
      ½ tsp. tumeric
      1 tsp. parsley flakes
```

Yield: 4-6 servings

- Drain tofu, mash, and simmer with other ingredients until liquid is absorbed
- Serve as you would scrambled eggs
- *Variations:* add ¼ tsp. sweet basil and ¼ tsp. dill weed or ¼ cup baco chips

Skillet Fries
Great with Scrambled Tofu

- Scrub, but don't peel potatoes; cut out eyes and hard spots
- Slice, shred, or cube
- Rinse in colander
- Pour into hot, dry teflon skillet
- Salt lightly
- Turn occasionally until done and crispy brown

*May be baked in glass, sprayed dish at 450° until done

Yield: about one serving per potato

Sunflower Seed-Oat Waffles

In blender:

>   ½ cup sunflower seeds, or any nuts
>   2 cups rolled oats
>   ¼ cup any type freshly ground flour
>   ½ tsp. salt
>   2½ cups water (use only enough to turn blender initially)

Yield: 4 large waffles

- Blend until light and foamy, about 30-60 seconds
- Let stand while waffle iron is heating; batter thickens on standing; blend each time before using; may add more water if batter is too thick
- Spray iron with Pam (first time only) just before pouring batter in
- Bake in hot waffle iron 8-10 minutes
- Do not peek before 8 minutes
- Serve topped with peanut butter, fruit spread, and plain yogurt or Cashew Cream

Hurry-Up Hearty Hash

The yeast flakes enhance protein value; this is also good with Scrambled Tofu

>   ½ cup chopped onion
>   ½ cup chopped celery
>   2 unpeeled potatoes
>   2 cups cooked brown rice
>   ½ cup chopped Brazil nuts, or walnuts
>   ½ tsp. salt
>   ⅛ tsp. garlic powder
>   2 tbsp. soy sauce
>   ¼ cup Brewer's yeast flakes (with B-12)

Yield: 4-6 servings

- Sauté onions and celery in small amount of water

- Meanwhile, wash, scrub and remove spots on potatoes; shred on medium
- Cook potatotes in hot Silverstone skillet, turning when browned
- Add remaining ingredients
- Stir enough to mix well
- Cover, let cook on medium heat until browned, about 10-15 more minutes

Musseli

This Swiss breakfast treat will probably become a family favorite. Try topping it with sliced bananas, granola, and Cashew Cream

    3 cups oats
    ½ tsp. salt (optional)
    1 cup milk, soy, nut, or regular
    1 20 oz. can unsweetened, crushed pineapple with juice
    1 grated apple with skin
    2 tsp. vanilla
    ⅓ cup raisins
    ¼ cup slivered almonds, toasted
    3 tbsp. unsweetened macaroon coconut, toasted
    ⅓ cup frozen blueberries (optional)

Yield: 6-8 servings

- Mix oats and salt; add milk and pineapple with juice; mix in remaining ingredients
- Serve immediately, or refrigerate until cold; very good second or third day

Cashew Cream

    ⅓ cup raw cashews, washed
    1 cup water
    2-3 dates
    ½ tsp. vanilla

- Blend until creamy. Refrigerate until cold. Extremely rich; a great substitute for dessert topping.

Layered Applesauce

A surprisingly easy breakfast dish, yet fancy enough for company

 2 cups rolled oats
 1 cup chopped nuts
 ¼ tsp. salt
 2-4 tbsp. date sugar or honey
 1 qt. unsweetened applesauce

Yield: 4-6 servings

- Toss oats and nuts in Silverstone skillet until lightly browned
- Stir in salt and sweetener
- Beginning with rolled oats, layer oats and applesauce in 5 x 9 casserole dish, ending with oat mixture
- Bake for 20 minutes at 350°
- Serve with milk and canned, unsweetened peaches, pears, or apricots
- Scrambled Tofu makes a nice accompaniment

Johnny Cakes

 2½ cups cornmeal
 1 tsp. salt
 2 tbsp. brown sugar or honey
 2 tbsp. margarine
 ½ cup milk
 2 cups boiling water

Yield: 3-4 servings

Mix all ingredients, adding boiling water last

- Pour into preheated dry Silverstone skillet, cooking until brown; flip
- Serve with peanut butter and/or fruit toppings
- Great with Skillet Fries and grapefruit

Lightning Granola

Mix this in the evening and let it toast overnight

> 6 cups rolled oats or use 1 cup rolled rye, and/or barley, etc. with
> the oats for variety
> 2 cup mixed flours (whole wheat, corn etc.)
> 1 cup raw, chopped nuts
> 1 cup unsweetened coconut (optional)
> 1 12 oz. can apple juice concentrate
> 1 tsp. salt
> 4 tsp. vanilla
> 2 cups raisins
> 1 cup date pieces (optional)

Yield: almost 1 gallon

- Mix first four ingredients in large bowl
- Mix apple juice concentrate, salt, and vanilla
- Pour liquid over dry ingredients and mix thoroughly
- Spread on cookie sheets, keeping middle thin and sides thick
- Bake at 150° overnight or at 250°, stirring every 30 minutes until done
- Stir in dried fruit
- Store in airtight container

Strawberry-Pineapple Sauce

> 3 cups pineapple juice
> 3 tbsp. arrowroot or cornstarch
> 2 cups strawberries
> 1 tbsp. honey

Yield: 4½-5 cups

- Blend all ingredients until smooth
- Cook over medium heat until clear, stirring constantly
- Serve hot over toast, waffles, or pancakes
- When cool, may be used as a spread for bread

Apricot-Date Jam

⅔ cup dried apricots
⅔ cup soft dates
1½ cup apple or pineapple juice

Yield: 2 cups

- Simmer fruit in juice
- Whiz all ingredients in blender
- Serve on toast or waffles
- Store in refrigerator

Grape Conserve

¾ cup unsweetened frozen pear-grape concentrate (undiluted) or
   frozen grape juice concentrate (undiluted)
¾ cup water
¾ cup raisins or currants
2 tbsp. quick-cooking tapioca or Clear Jel

Yield: 1½ cups

- Simmer concentrate, water, and raisins 10 minutes; turn off heat; let stand 30 minutes
- Whiz briefly in blender to break up currants
- Conserve should have texture of jam
- Add tapioca or "Clear Jel" (precooked cornstarch thickener) to thicken

Carob Sauce
Very good on waffles or pancakes

1 cup water
2 tsp. vanilla
2 tbsp. honey
⅛ tsp. salt
2-4 tbsp. cornstarch
2 tbsp. carob powder

Yield: 2 cups

- Blend all ingredients
- Cook until thick, stirring constantly

Apple Butter
Excellent on waffles, pancakes, or toast

> 1 quart unsweetened applesauce
> 1 12 oz. can frozen apple juice concentrate (undiluted)
> dash of cinnamon

Yield: about 1 pint

- Spread applesauce, apple juice concentrate, and cinnamon on cookie sheet; stir until mixed
- Bake at 250°, stirring every 30-40 minutes until thick, dark and cooked down (about 2-3 hours)
- May leave in oven overnight 150° if desired

Quick Fruit Spread

> 2-3 cups any dried fruit (peaches, apricots, pears)
> 1 12 oz. can frozen apple juice concentrate
> ½ cup water

Yield: 2-3 cups

- Simmer ingredients 15-20 minutes
- blend
- Set out to cool
- store in refrigerator

Cooking Guide for Grains and Legumes

1 Cup Dry	Cups Water	Cooking Time /Hours*	Yield in Cups
Barley (Whole)	3	1¼	3½
Buckwheat (kasha)	2	¼	2½
Bulgur Wheat	2	¼	2½
Coarse Cornmeal (plenta)	4	½	3
Millet	3	¾ to 1	3
Rice, brown	2	¾ to 1	3
Rice, wild	3	1	4
Wheat, cracked	2	½	2⅓
Wheat, whole berries	3	2	2⅔
Black Beans	4	1½	2
Black-eyed Peas	3	½	2
Garbanzos (Chick peas)	4	2	2
Great Northern Beans	3½	1½ to 2	2
Kidney Beans	3	2	2
Lentils and Split Peas	3	½ to ¾	2¼
Limas	2	1	2¼
Baby Limas	2	¾	1¾
Pinto Beans	3	1½ to 2	2
Red Beans	3	1½ to 2	2
Small White Beans (navy, etc.)	3	1½ to 2	2
Soybeans	4	2½	2 to 3½

*Cooking time is after the Legumes have been soaked. To soak: cover with water overnight, or bring to boil, cover, and let set one hour off heat.

Weight for weight, ordinary dry beans, peas, and lentils contain about the same percentage of protein as does fresh meat. Peanuts and peanut butter contain more, and soybeans much more. Nuts are fully comparable weight for weight with meat and eggs.[1]

One-Dish Meals

Make it easy on yourself and delicious for your family!

Holiday Red Beans

So attractive and colorful; serve with cornbread for a quick, nourishing, and balanced "one-dish" meal. Haystack cookies make a nice closing.

In electric skillet rubbed with olive oil:

> 1 large red onion, sliced
> 1 large green bell pepper, sliced
> 1 large red bell pepper, sliced (or 1 4 oz. jar pimentos)
> 5 cups pinto or kidney beans, cooked with 2 cup of the liquid
> 1 tsp. cumin
> 1 large bunch fresh spinach, rinsed and torn into bite-sized pieces
> Spike and Vegesal seasoning to taste

Yield: 3-4 servings

- Steam vegetables 5 minutes, stirring occasionally
- Add beans and cumin; stir
- Place spinach on top, cover and let steam 5-7 minutes

Kathy's Curry and Rice

Another "one-dish" favorite. A salad dresses it up.

> 4-5 stalks celery
> 2 large onions
> 3-4 cans mushroom soup; OR
> 3-4 cups Cashew Gravy plus ½ cup sliced fresh mushrooms, simmered in water (use microwave)
> 1 tbsp. curry powder or to taste
> Cooked brown rice
> 2-3 avocados, diced
> 2-3 tomatoes, diced (optional)

Yield: 4-6 servings

Cashew Gravy

In blender:

> 1 cup raw cashews, washed
> 4 tsp. arrowroot powder or cornstarch
> 4 tsp. onion salt
> 2 tbsp. brewer's yeast flake
> 4 tsp. soy sauce
> 2 cups hot water (to wash out blender)
> Total 4 cups water*

*To blend cashews thoroughly, use a small amount of liquid

Yield: 4 cups

- Steam onion and celery in small amount water until tender
- Add vegetables to cashew sauce or mushroom soup; stir in curry
- Cook over low heat until thick
- Serve over brown rice and diced avocados and tomatoes (optional) for a terrific blending of textures (chewy rice and smooth avocado) and flavors (curry with mushrooms)

Haystacks

Ask your friends to each bring several ingredients; assemble meal in separate bowls on backyard table; layer in given order and enjoy. Rice and beans round out complementary proteins.

> Brown Rice
> Pinto Beans
> Chili Sauce (see below)
> Lettuce, shredded
> Tomatoes, chopped
> Green Onions, chopped
> Diced Avocados
> Sliced Olives
> Sour Cream Topping
> Hot Sauce

Chili Sauce

30 oz. tomato sauce
½ cup cooked wheat (simmered in water 45 minutes)
1 tsp. chili powder
1 4 oz. can green chilis, chopped
¼ tsp. sweet basil
½ tsp. seasoning salt
1 tbsp. honey, optional
1 clove garlic, crushed
¼ tsp. oregano
¼ tsp. thyme

Yield: 6-8 servings

Spinach Lasagna with Tofu Cheese
Serve with romaine salad and French bread (recipe in Breads)

8 spinach lasagna noodles
Fresh spinach leaves
Italian tomato sauce or 20 oz. jar of your favorite Spaghetti
 Sauce plus 1 cup of water to thin
Tofu cheese topping (below)

Yield: 6-8 servings

- Layer sauce, uncooked noodles, Tofu Cheese Sauce (below), and fresh spinach, ending with tomato sauce
- Cover with foil and bake 1 hour at 350° until bubbling hot
- Remove foil and bake 5-10 more minutes

Tofu Cheese Topping
A great substitute for ricotta cheese in lasagna. This makes a delicious dip for raw vegetables, is great on baked potatoes, and adds a new taste sensation to pizza.

½ cup raw cashews, washed
½ cup water
2 tsp. salt

   1 tbsp. food yeast flakes
   2 tbsp. lemon juice
     Pinch of garlic powder
   1 lb. tofu, rinsed and drained

Yield: approximately 3 cups

- Combine all ingredients and blend until creamy and smooth

Sweet & Sour Tofu

A terrific "light" meal, full to the brim with crunchy textures and garden freshness. And so easy!

   1 lb. tofu, cut in ¾" cubes
     Soy sauce
   1 large onion
   2 celery stalks, sliced diagonally
   1 large bell pepper, large slices
 6-8 fresh mushrooms, sliced
   1 large carrot, diagonally sliced
   1 tsp. salt
   ¼ cup tomato sauce
   1 tbsp. honey
   1 16 oz. can unsweetened pineapple chunks, undrained
   2 tbsp. cornstarch added to ½ cup water
   2 tbsp. lemon juice
   1 large tomato, sliced into wedges

Yield: 4-6 servings

- Tofu should be drained 15 minutes or more in strainer or on folded towels. For mashed, squeeze by hand or press against the side of a dish lined with towels.
- Place cubed tofu on Pam sprayed cookie sheet that has been sprinkled with soy sauce
- Sprinkle with soy sauce and toss
- Broil until crispy, turning often
- Cut vegetables into bite-size pieces and sauté until tender in large skillet or wok

- May use broccoli, water chestnuts, sugar peas, etc.
- Add drained pineapple to skillet or wok
- Cover and let vegetables steam while mixing remaining ingredients, including pineapple juice
- Add remaining ingredients and stir until thickened
- Serve over steamed brown rice and top with broiled tofu
- Use whatever vegetables you have, omitting or adding one or two just to give a little variety

Mizidra

Hearty fare for those blustery fall and winter days, yet, light enough for spring and summer appetites

    1 onion, chopped
    1 tbsp. olive oil
    2 cups lentils
    5 cups water
    1 tbsp. soy sauce
    1 tsp. marjoram
    ½ tsp. thyme
    1 bay leaf

Yield: 6-8 servings

- Brown onion in olive oil
- Simmer lentils and remaining ingredients 1 to 1½ hours or until done
- Serve over cooked brown rice; add cubed avocado and tomato, sliced olives and fresh lemon juice. Top with a sprinkle of garlic salt.

Meatless Entrées

Tofu Meat Balls

Great with spaghetti; a quick, excellent protein source

Mix:

   ¾ lb. tofu, broken up
   ½ cup flour, bread crumbs, rolled oats or corn flakes
   1½ tbsp. peanut butter
   3 tbsp. soy sauce
   ¼ cup parsley (or 2 tbsp. dried)
   1 small onion, chopped fine (use blender with ¾ cup water; drain
         off water in colander)
   ¼ tsp. cumin
   ¼ tsp. thyme
   ¼ tsp. basil

- Roll into 1½" balls, coat with flour and bake at 375° until
   browned
- For entrée, cover with tomato sauce and reheat

Tofu Oat Burgers

Very easy, very tasty, and extremely filling. Good with Barbecue
Sauce in hamburger buns. Also good covered with tomato gravy
and served as main dish.

   2 cups oats, finely cut in blender
   1 cup walnuts or pecans, ground, or chopped in blender
   1 onion, chopped
   1 lb. tofu, mashed
   ¼ cup gluten
   1 tbsp. Savorex or Vegex
   1 tsp. salt
   1 tsp. paprika
   1 tsp. Italian herbs or your choice

Yield: 8-10 large patties

- Mix all ingredients
- Form into patties and brown in skillet sprayed with Pam
- Use medium heat and cook 10-12 minutes on each side

Macaroni and Cashew Nut Cheese

One of the easiest and "most favorite" dishes we prepare. Great with dinner rolls and steamed broccoli. (freezes well)

Macaroni:

- Add 2½ cups macaroni or spirals to boiling salted (1 tsp.) water
- Bring to boil again, cover, and set aside for 10 minutes.
- Drain

Cheese Sauce:

> 1 cup raw cashew nuts
> 4 oz. pimentos
> ¼ cup lemon juice
> 6 tbsp. Brewer's yeast flakes
> 1½ tsp. salt
> ½ tsp. onion powder
> ½ tsp. garlic powder
> 3 cups water

Yield: 6-8 servings

Crumbs:

In blender:

> 4 slices whole grain bread
> 2 tbsp. Brewer's yeast
>   Few drops butter flavoring
> 1 tbsp. oil (optional)

- While macaroni is cooking, blend Cheese Sauce, saving 2 cups water to add last
- Mix macaroni and sauce in 9 × 12 pyrex dish
- Bake covered 30 minutes at 350°
- Remove foil, add crumbs, bake another 15 minutes uncovered

We always chop one onion and ½ a bell pepper, steam them in water in the microwave for 5 minutes, then stir into ingredients. They add nice texture and flavor.

Hawaiian Chestnut Balls and Mushroom Gravy

Mix ahead and chill if time permits. This enhances flavor and makes forming the balls easier.

1 lb. fresh tofu,* well drained
1 cup cooked brown rice
1 cup shredded carrots
1 cup thinly sliced green onions
1 cup (4-oz.) water chestnuts, grated
¼ cup Tamari or soy sauce
2 tbsp. food yeast flakes
1 tsp. garlic powder (optional)

Yield: 6 servings

*Tofu should be drained 15 minutes or more in strainer or on folded towels. To mash, squeeze by hand or press against the side of a dish lined with towels.

- Mash tofu; combine all ingredients; mix well; knead 2-3 minutes
- Form into small balls and bake in nonstick or sprayed baking dish at 350° for about 30 minutes
- Serve with Musroom Gravy (below)

Mushroom Gravy

Serve with potatoes, roasts, patties, etc.

Blend all ingredients but mushrooms with just enough water to turn blender:

⅓ cup cashews
1 cup cooked brown rice
2 tbsp. dried onions or ¼ chopped onion
1 tbsp. McKay's chicken-style seasoning
1 tsp. Savorex
½ tsp. garlic powder
¼ tsp. paprika
    water as needed
½ lb. fresh mushrooms, sliced and sautéed — stir in last

Yield: 2 cups

- When mixture is smooth and creamy, add enough water to blender to equal 4 cups total ingredients; pour into skillet
- Bring to boil, stirring constantly
- Stir in sautéed mushrooms

Garbanzo Loaf with Cashew Gravy

If there's any left over, mash with mayo and chopped celery, pickles, and olives for a terrific sandwich spread. Don't forget to add the sprouts!

    1 onion, chopped
    ½ green pepper, chopped

In blender:

    2 cups cooked garbanzos, mashed or pureed
    ½ cup peanut butter
    1 cup cooked Spanish-style tomatoes
    3 tbsp. flour
    1 tsp. sage
    ½ tsp. garlic salt
    ½ to 1 tsp. salt, or to taste
    1 cup dry bread crumbs or crushed cornflakes

Yield: 4-6 servings

- Sauté onion and pepper in small amount of water
- Combine remaining ingredients and blend until smooth
- Mix well and pour into sprayed loaf pan
- Bake at 350° for 1½ hours
- Serve with Cashew Gravy (after Kathy's Curry and Rice) and cranberry sauce
- Garnish with fresh parsley

Millet Patties

We had a "carnivorous" friend who used to tell us these patties were the vegetarian version of "chicken-fried steak." Try them on your family, smothered in mushroom gravy.

    3 cups cooked millet (1 part millet : 3 parts water)
    1 cup raw cashews (washed)
  1½ cups water (use small amount first)
    1 med. onion, chopped
    1 cup rolled oats
    ½ tsp. salt
    2 cups bread crumbs
    ½ tsp. garlic powder
    1 tbsp. soy sauce or Tamari

Yield: 6-8 servings of 2 patties each

- Cook millet in water for 1 hour
- Blend cashews with minimum water
- Pour into mixing bowl and add remaining ingredients; use remaining water to clean blender and to chop onion
- Mix well
- Form into patties with a large spoon and place on non-stick cookie sheet
- Bake at 350° for 35 minutes, turning at 20 minutes
- Serve with Mushroom Gravy or in a sandwich with all the fixings.

Sunflower Seed Patties or Loaf

This patty is exceptional served hot or cold for sandwiches. Freezes well to have on had for those unexpected sack lunches or picnics.

    3 cups cooked brown rice
  1½ cups ground raw sunflower seeds
    1 can mushroom soup or 1 cup Mushroom Gravy
  1½ cups finely chopped onion
  1-2 tbsp. Tamari or soy sauce

1 tbsp. chickenlike seasoning
1 clove garlic, minced
1 tbsp. whole wheat pastry flour

Yield: 6-8 servings of 2 patties each

- Combine all ingredients
- Form into patties (16 ¼-cup size); put on sprayed cookie sheet
- Bake at 375° for 20 minutes; turn and bake another 10-15 minutes
- Serve hot, plain or with Mushroom or Cashew Gravy

Alternate Method: Shape in round balls and roll in cornflake crumbs, baking as directed above, or place in loaf pan and bake 45 minutes at 350°

Breads

The art of bread making is returning, finally, with the help of machines designed to mill flour from grain and knead 4-6 large loaves of bread in 10-15 minutes. We recommend a Bosch Mixer and Magic Mill Flour Mill for your kitchen tools. The investment on this equipment is regained in less than two years' time by just making six loaves of bread a week as opposed to buying expensive, whole grain breads at the store. And your actual time investment for six hearty loaves of 100 percent whole grain goodness is less than a half hour weekly. Plus, you can't beat the accompanying blender and food processor for mixing, puréeing, and processing all your food needs. Nor can you find in store bought breads the vitamins and minerals found in freshly milled grains.

The bread recipes following are designed to be made with the Bosch/Magic Mill system. Our experience in teaching cooking classes has shown us that very few, if any, people have the time to make homemade, hand-kneaded bread on a consistent basis. Information about these machines is available by writing to the address given on page 249.

1½ Hour Honey-Wheat Bread

Add to the mixer in following order:

    5½ cups HOT water
    ⅓ - ½ cup *each* oil and honey
    1 tbsp. salt (scant)
    3 tbsp. Magic Mill Dough Enhancer
    13-15 cups freshly ground flour
    2¼ tbsp. Instant Yeast
    4 tbsp. vital gluten (optional)

¼ tsp. (1000 mg.) Vitamin C (if dough enhancer is not available)

- Mix 9 cups flour and all ingredients but yeast till moist; test dough; it should be warm, not hot

- Add yeast
- Continue to add flour until dough cleans bowl
- Knead until dough is smooth and elastic, usually 10-15 minutes
- Place in 4 standard bread pans or 6 junior loaf pans and let rise 2″ above pans in 150° oven
- Increase temperature to 350° and continue baking 30-40 minutes. Turn out immediately onto wire racks

For Sugarless Oilless Bread
If you don't tell, no one will know . . .

- Omit oil and honey; add

  ½ cup unsweetened applesauce or apple juice
  ⅓ cup cashews, sunflower or sesame seeds blended with part of the water
  ⅓ cup vital gluten flour

- Follow standard recipe above *except* preheat oven to 450° and when ready, bake 10 minutes then reduce to 350° and bake 35 minutes

For Multi-Grain Bread:
A nice variation for a change of taste.

- Add up to 2 cups freshly ground flours (rice, barley, triticale, oats, corn, millet, buckwheat, etc.)
- Add ⅓ cup gluten flour
- Decrease whole wheat flour by approximately 2 cups

For Raisin Nut Bread:
A great dessert. Attractive baked in heart, star, and flower-shaped tube pans and spread with Tofu cream cheese.

- Use standard recipe above, or sugarless Oilless recipe

- Plump 6 cups of raisins by pouring 5½ cups boiling water over them in Bosch bowl: cover and let sit 20 minutes
- Add 3 cups chopped nuts
- Use raisin water for 5½ cups water in recipe
- Proceed with directions for making bread, but make a very stiff dough as mixer will continue to squeeze water out of plumped raisins during kneading

For Sprouted Wheat Bread:
Absolutely and undeniably scrumptious.

- Soak 3 cups of wheat 24 hours in water to cover (included in the 3 cups you may add ¼ cup each lentils, soybeans, millet, barley, oat groats, etc.)
- Drain and discard water
- Grind through Meat and Food Grinder and place in mixer
- Add ¼ cup gluten flour
- Follow standard recipe, above; reduce flour by 2-3 cups
- This recipe is great for making hamburger buns and dinner rolls. Top with poppy or sesame seeds

For Three-Seed Bread:
This is undoubtedly one of our all-time favorite recipes to share with friends and loved ones.

- Follow standard recipe
- Before last addition of flour, add:

    1 cup sunflower seeds
    ¾ cup unhulled sesame seeds
    ⅓ cup poppy seeds

- Proceed with directions above
- This recipe makes attractive miniature loaves for individuals served on small bread boards with steak knives

For Rye Bread:

This is the only recipe we've seen for 100 percent whole grain rye bread. It's delicious as well as nutritious

4½ cups hot water
½ cup oil
1 cup Blackstrap Molasses
1 tbsp. salt
¼ cup gluten flour
3 tbsp. Dough Enhancer or 1,000 mg. Vitamin C
4-6 cups freshly ground flour
½ cup dry milk
2 tbsp. Pero. Postum or Carob powder
3 tbsp. caraway seeds
6 cups freshly ground rye flour (on fine)
2¼ tbsp. instant yeast

- Follow directions for bread, above

For Pizza:

A Peel and a Stone: two major investments in home pizza production for home bakeries, but one taste of the pizza and you'll have to have a set. Just skip a couple of trips to the "Pizza Place" and you'll have paid for them.

- roll out ½ lb. of dough on greased pizza pan
- Turn upside down onto Pizza Peel (a large, paddle-shaped wooden board with a handle) that has been covered with corn meal
- Cover with sauce, vegetables and toppings
- Slide carefully onto Stone preheated to 450°
- Bake 10-12 minutes until underside is brown
- Use Peel as trivet, setting hot Stone with pizza directly onto Peel to serve and keep hot.

For Sugarless Fruit Rolls:

- Roll out 2 lbs. of dough and spread with blended fruit mixture: 1 banana, 40 dates and enough juice to turn blender
- Sprinkle fruit mixture with chopped nuts and a dash of cinnamon
- Roll up, pinch seam and cut with dental floss
- Place in 9 x 14 pan that has been sprayed with Pam.
- Let double: bake at 350° until light brown, about 40-45 minutes
- Turn out immediately and frost with one cup apple juice thickened with 1½ tablespoon cornstarch. Sprinkle poppy seeds or nuts over top.

For Bread Sticks

- Reserve one lb. of dough. Cut off piece of dough about the size of your thumb and roll out to 12″. Use Pam if surface gets sticky.
- Sprinkle poppy or sesame seeds (about ½ tsp) over dough; roll to pick up all seeds
- Place crosswise (dough will shrink slightly) on two sprayed cookie sheets, dough should make approximately 24 sticks
- Let rise in 150° oven with loaves; bake at 350° for 10 minutes, then turn over and bake another 10 minutes until brown
- Double bag for freezing. To reheat, put in 400° oven for 7-10 minutes, watching closely. Absolutely the most with soups and salads. Better enlist the whole family's help in making these; they disappear so fast.

Soups

Black Bean Soup

Be sure to make the extra effort to serve this delicious soup with one of the suggested toppings. The contrast in colors is a good distraction for picky eaters!

In large, heavy kettle:

1 lb. black beans, cooked
1 onion, chopped
3 carrots, sliced
2 cloves garlic, minced
1 8 oz. can tomatoes with juice
½ tsp. oregano
2½ cups water (use bean broth)
1½ tbsp. Beef-like seasoning
1 tsp. sweet basil, or fresh, if available

Yield: 3 quarts

- Simmer all ingredients 20-30 minutes, until vegetables are just done
- Serve with lemon slices and minced scallions or a dollop of tofu sour cream sprinkle with lemon herb seasoning. Pass the bread sticks.

"Souper" Seashell Soup

A colorful, savory favorite. Nice complementary textures to keep the conversation interesting.

1 lg. onion
1 clove garlic
¼ cup fresh parsley
1 lg. bell pepper, sliced
2 stalks celery, sliced
1 lg. carrot, sliced
1½ cups vegaroni or shell macaroni
2½ cups cooked garbanzos
1 16 oz. can tomatoes

2-3 cubes onion bouillon
  2 tsp. salt
  ½ tsp. basil and oregano
3½ cups water
  1 large zucchini, cut in wedges

Yield: 2-3 Quarts

- Chop onion, garlic and parsley in blender with water, reserving water for soup
- Slice pepper, celery and carrot in food processor
- Sauté vegetables in skillet rubbed with olive oil (or in water, if desired)
- Simmer all ingredients 25-30 minutes, reserving zucchini for last 15 minutes
- Try substituting garbanzos with pintos or other legumes
- This is a very satisfying soup; served with bread, the combination of legumes plus the grain equals a complete protein diet

Boston Style Potato Soup

A very quick soup if you own a pressure cooker. Try using the cashews blended with water in place of 2 percent milk; you'll love the creamy taste!

6 cups cubed, raw, unpeeled potatoes (about 4 large potatoes)
2 cups chopped green onions
4 cups water
2 cups fresh or frozen green peas*
¼ cup chopped fresh parsley or 2 tbsp. dried flakes
2 tsp. celery seed
3 tsp. salt
4 cups milk, cashew is best

*Once in lieu of the peas, I used frozen corn. The combination was delicious.

Yield: 4-6 servings

- Pressure cook onion, potatoes and water 4 minutes

- Add remaining ingredients except milk and simmer until peas are done
- Turn to low heat and stir in cashew milk
- Serve with a tossed green salad and bread—Gourmet Fare!!

Cashew Milk:

- Blend 1 cup washed cashews with just enough of the water to turn blender, letting blender run until cashews are completely blended. May add some soy milk powder if desired. Rinse blender with the remaining 3 cups of water.

Curry Zucchini Soup

Your guests will wonder what gives this soup its rich, mellow and slightly sweet taste. You'll be surprised too.

    1 tbsp. margarine, or water to sauté
    2 lg. onions, chopped in blender
    2 apples, peeled, cored and chopped with onion
    8 cups water (use portion for blender and save)
    2 tbsp. chicken-style seasoning
    2 cups cooked brown rice
    4 cups diced, unpeeled zucchini (4-6 medium)
    2 cups milk (cashew is best for creamy taste)
      Slivered almonds, lightly toasted

Yield: 3 quarts

- In large kettle sauté onions and apples until soft
- Sprinkle with curry powder, then pour in water with chicken-style seasoning
- Simmer remaining ingredients until tender
- Pour into blender (in batches) and blend until smooth. Return to pan and add milk.
- Heat until flavors blend; adjust seasonings
- Top each serving with almond slices

Cream of Tomato Rice Soup

Like nothing you've ever eaten out of a can. Freezes well, and is a great way to get brown rice down the kids.

      1 stalk celery
      ½ large onion
      4 cups tomatoes, canned or fresh
      ½ cup water
      ½ cup cashews
      1 tsp. honey
      1 tsp. onion salt
      1 tbsp. flour
   1 ½ cup cooked brown rice

Yield: 4-6 servings

- Use blender to chop onion and celery
- Simmer in small amount of water while preparing remaining ingredients
- Blend tomatoes and water; reserve small amount to use for blending cashews and flour
- Add remaining ingredients
- Simmer 5-10 minutes while setting table
- Excellent with fresh spinach salad and bread sticks

Fruit Soup

Very wonderful spooned piping hot over crunchy toast topped with freshly-made peanut butter for breakfast. But also doubles as a light dessert served chilled to cool down a hot summer evening. Garnish with a dollop of cashew cream and pass the zwieback. Use scissors to cut up the dried fruit.

      1 can apricot nectar (Heinke has no sugar)
      1 cup dried prunes
      1 cup dried peaches
      ¼ cup raisins
      ¼ cup dried pears
      ¼ cup dried apples
      ¼ cup dried apricots

    pinch of salt
 2 tbsp. cornstarch or ¼ cup tapioca
 ¼ cup water or cold juice
    pinch of garlic powder, cumin, thyme, and sage

Yield: 6-8 servings or 3 quarts

- Bring juice to simmer while cutting dried fruit.
- Simmer fruit until soft (or turn off burner and let soak overnight)
- Stir cornstarch or tapioca into water, then pour into soup.
- Add dash of salt
- Simmer, stirring until thickened
- Store remaining fruit mixture in jars and use as a topping (like jam and jelly) for toast

Sandwich Ideas

Pita Bread

- Using dough from basic "Honey Whole Wheat" recipe (or from any recipe — although nuts and/or seeds in dough will not work), divide dough into 4 oz. balls (size of golf balls) and roll each out into 5″ diameter circle.
- Let circles rest, covered, 30 minutes to 1 hour on top of heavy dishtowel.
- Preheat pizza stone in 450° oven for 15 minutes before baking.
- Place circles on hot stone. Do not grease anything
- Bake 3-4 minutes, watching carefully
- Let cool slightly, place in plastic bag to cool completely, then cut in half and stuff pocket with Falafels or any other sandwich filling.

Falafels in Pita Bread

This is such a pleaser that you'll want to keep extra on hand in the freezer. This recipe feeds four starved or six hungry people.

    2½ cups soaked, uncooked Garbanzo beans (begin with 1 cup dry)
      3 green onions
    2-3 cloves garlic
      1 tsp. salt
      2 tbsp. sesame seeds
      ⅓ cup parsley sprigs, packed
      2 tbsp. milk
      1 tbsp. olive oil, opt.

- Run soaked beans through meat grinder with onions, parsley and garlic
- Spray skillet with Pam and toss ingredients about 15 minutes until lightly browned
- May need additional water (1-2 tbsp.) to moisten
- Serve in pocket bread with chopped tomatoes, sprouts, avocados and Ranch Style Dressing
- Plan on 3-4 pitas per person

Ranch Style Dressing

Blend following ingredients, letting stand 15 minutes to develop flavors.

    1 cup buttermilk
    ¼ cup freshly squeezed lemon juice
    1 cup mayonnaise (to make your own, see "Sauces, Seasonings & Miscellaneous" section
    1 tsp. onion salt
    ½ tsp. garlic salt
    1 tbsp. food yeast flakes
    1 tsp. sweet basil
    1 tsp. dill weed
       Other herbs as desired to season

Yield: 2 cups

Country Kitchen Salad Dressing (Dairy Free)

Blend following ingredients

    8 oz. tofu, rinsed and drained
    ¾ cup water
    ¼ cup raw cashews
    ½ tsp. garlic powder
    1 tsp. salt
    1 tsp. dill weed
    2 tsp. onion powder
    1 tsp. food yeast flakes
    1 tsp. sweet basil
    ¼ cup lemon juice. freshly squeezed

Yield: 2 cups

The "Big Mac"
Here it is; have it "your way" the right way

    1 cup chopped walnuts
    1 medium onion, chopped
    ½ cup of soaked, raw Garbanzo beans

½ cup water
1 cup rolled oats
4 tbsp. rich milk
½ tsp. salt
1 tsp. sage
1 tbsp. soy sauce

Yield: 6 large patties

- Chop walnuts in blender using spring switch
- Empty walnuts; put peeled, halved onion in blender; cover with water and chop; drain
- in same blender, whiz garbanzos and water
- Mix all ingredients in bowl
- Drop from spoon or ice-cream scoop to form patties on sprayed skillet
- Brown on both sides over medium heat
- Serve in burger buns with all the trimmings.
- Try serving "Skillet Fries" as an accompaniment. You'll think you've been to the drive in (but your body will know better).

Option: Place in casserole dish, cover with gravy, bake ½ hour at 350°

"Liver" à la Lentil Paté
Very rich, but satisfying. Extra freezes well.

- Mill ¾ cup lentils in flour mill or process in blender until powder fine
- In medium sauce pan stir:

2 cups V-8 juice
lentil flour, (above)
1 tbsp. Brewer's yeast flakes
1 tbsp. soy sauce
½ tbsp. onion powder
pinch of garlic powder, cumin, thyme, and sage

Yield: 4-5 cups

- Cook, over medium heat, stirring constantly, until mixture thickens
- Reduce to low, let cook 20-30 minutes, stirring often
- Refrigerate until set
- Add sliced olives, chopped pickles, celery, pimiento, onion and mayonnaise for a wonderful sandwich surprise.
- Serve on whole grain toast with lettuce and sprouts

"Egg Salad" à la Tofu
A 5-minute sandwich filling bound to please

- Mash a well-drained brick of tofu with

> 1 scallion, finely chopped
> 1 stalk celery, finely chopped
> ½ tbsp. Brewer's yeast
> Spike Seasoning to taste
> Dash of dill and cayenne
> Mayonnaise to moisten

- Serve with sprouts and tomato slices

Tofu Cream Cheese, Cukes and Sprouts

- Spread bread with mayonnaise, then Tofu Cream Cheese
- Add sliced cucumbers; sprinkle with Spike Seasoning
- Top with sprouts and another slice of bread
- Enjoy!

Enjoy recipes given in "Sauces, Seasonings and Miscellaneous"

Delectable Desserts

Carob Cream Pudding or Pie
with Absolutely Almond Pie Crust

2½ cups milk (cashew milk is very good)
¼ cup flour
2 tbsp. cornstarch or arrowroot
6 tbsp. toasted carob powder
¼ cup honey
3-4 pitted dates
¼ tsp. salt
2 tsp. vanilla
1 tbsp. oil

Yield: one 8″ pie filling or enough for six dessert dishes.

- In blender, combine small amount of milk and remaining ingredients except oil
- Spring-switch to blend dates, then process until mixture is smooth
- Pour into pan, rinse blender with remaining milk, bring all ingredients but oil to low boil. Stir in oil
- Pour into prepared, prebaked pie crust
- Let set up. Garnish with whipped topping, and carob curls
- Good with bananas under filling as well as for garnish with whipped topping

Absolutely Almond Pie Crust

Makes a lovely light crust. It's hard to believe this elegant dessert combination is "health" food.

1½ cups blanched, ground almonds*
3 tbsp. flour
¼ tsp. salt
2-4 tbsp. cold water

Yield: one 8″ crust

*To grind, run through meat grinder with small disc, or process in blender

- Mix flour, ground almonds and salt with wire whips in Bosch bowl or food processor
- Add water and mix until ball of dough can be formed in hand.
- Roll out between waxed paper, place in pan and shape
- Bake at 350° for 20-25 minutes, pricking crust with fork first

Nature's Confection

An attractive dessert piled on a cake stand and sprinkled with coconut. Garnish with fresh strawberries and mint sprigs.

    1 cup pitted dates
    ¼ cup dried apricots
    ¼ cup dried figs
    ½ cup macaroon coconut
    ¼ cup sunflower seeds, raw
    ⅓ cup pecans or nuts

Yield: approximately 2 dozen confections

- Grind fruit and seeds in meat grinder
- Grind pecans in meat grinder, making meal, and cleaning out fruit in process
- Make balls and roll in coconut or pecan meal or shape into log, roll in coconut or nuts and refrigerate. Cut in ½" slices

Banana Date Logs

The kids aren't the only ones who'll love these.

- Peel and halve bananas; put popsicle stick or plastic fork in banana
- Simmer ½ cup dates blended with ½ cup water (stir with fork); ¼ - ½ cup carob powder may be added to mixture, optional.
- Mix ingredients together and add 1 cup dry cereal crumbs until dough is pliable enough to flatten like tortilla between hands and wrap around banana
- Roll in coconut and/or nuts
- Place on cookie sheet and freeze
- Serve frozen

Yield: 4 servings

Carob Chip Cookies

The rice flour makes a terrific cookie if you have a flour mill.

⅓ cup oil
⅓ cup honey
⅓ - ½ cup apple juice
¾ tsp. vanilla
¾ tsp. salt
1⅔ cups brown rice flour or whole wheat flour
⅔ cup unsweetened macaroon coconut
1¼ cups rolled oats
¾ cup date sweetened carob chips
⅔ cup chopped nuts (even almonds are good)

- Mix oil and honey, adding juice, then flour
- Add remaining ingredients and mix
- Place on sprayed cookie sheet and bake at 350° for 15 minutes or so until lightly brown
- Remove immediately and place on racks to cool
- Easy to make and a real treat for that cookie craver in your home!

Strawberry Smoothie

A great substitute for those year 'round ice cream fans.

1 cup slightly thawed strawberries
2 frozen bananas (peel before freezing)
¼ cup dates simmered in ¼ cup water
Pineapple juice to turn blender

Yield: 3-4 servings

- Mix in blender, using as much juice as necessary to turn blender
- Serve immediately
- Try mixing several kinds of fruit and juices; bananas, however, are a good base

Granola Bars

Pack these in lunches for school, work or travels; they're always a favorite

    2 cups whole wheat flour
    2 cups rolled oats
    ¼ cup honey
    1 tsp. salt
    ⅔ cup walnuts or other nuts, ground
    ⅓ cup unsweetened coconut
    ¼ cup oil or ¼ cup cashews blended with water, below
    ¼ - ⅓ cup water
    2 cups chopped dates
       dash of cinnamon (optional)

Yield: about 2 dozen bars

- Mix dry ingredients
- Add oil; mix lightly until texture of fine crumbs
- Stir in dates
- Sprinkle enough water to moisten
- Press into cookie sheet sprayed with Pam
- Score into 3" × 1" strips
- Bake at 350° until delicate brown (15-20 minutes)
- Serve while still warm

Haystack Cookies

The shape and the coconut make these treats resemble miniature haystacks.

    4 cups coconut, unsweetened
    1 tsp. salt
    ⅓ cup oatmeal
    ½ cup peanut butter
    ¼ cup water
    1 cup chopped walnuts
    2¼ cups dates, chopped
    ⅔ cup whole wheat pastry flour
    ⅓ cup honey (or less)

Yield: about 2 dozen

- Mix together and scoop onto cookie sheet with ice-cream scoop, packing well
- Bake at 350° on sprayed cookie sheet for 20-30 minutes
- Remove when light brown

Frosty Fruit Sorbét
An easy yet elegant dessert (and nutritious too).

- Using any frozen fruit (unsweetened pineapple, cherries, bananas, raspberries, blueberries), push through Meat and Food Grinder, keeping fruit colors separate.
- Layer in compote dish and top with mint sprigs and a sprinkle of unsweetened coconut. Or serve layered in dessert dishes and sprinkle granola over top. A good strong blender will also purée the frozen fruit.

Nature's Apple Pie
This fruit pie is so unbelievably good few people can tell it's made without any refined table sugar.

   6-7 tart apples, or 3 cups sliced, dried apples
    12 oz. frozen pineapple or apple juice concentrate
     1 tbsp. lemon juice
     3 tbsp. arrowroot powder, cornstarch or flour
      pinch of salt
      dash of cinnamon or cardamon and coriander

Yield: one 9″ pie

- Thaw concentrate and slice apples directly into juice to prevent browning. Not necessary to peel apples. Add rest of ingredients and mix.
- Simmer mix until apples begin to look transparent
- Pour into a 9″ unbaked pie crust; top with second crust and bake at 375° for 45 minutes; edges may need covering last 20 minutes
- Cool on wire rack to prevent sogginess

Carob Candy Balls

Extremely rich; eat sparingly.

> 1 cup macaroon coconut, unsweetened
> ½ cup carob powder
> 2 tbsp. margarine or almond nut butter
> 1 cup soymilk powder
> ⅓ cup honey
>   pinch of salt
> 1 tsp vanilla, opt.

Yield: approximately 2½ dozen confections

- Combine, mix and roll into balls
- Roll in coconut and/or pecan meal

Sauces, Seasonings, & Miscellaneous

Instant Mayonnaise

> 1 cup water, preferably purified or distilled
> ½ cup soy milk powder
> ½ tsp. salt
> 2-3 tbsp. fresh lemon juice
> 1½ tbsp. instant Clear Jel*
> 1-2 tbsp. oil, opt or . . .
> 3 tbsp. raw cashews, thoroughly blended with the water

Yield: 1½ cups

- Whiz all ingredients in blender, adding Clear Jel last
- Blend until smooth
- Store in refrigerator 1½ -2 weeks
- Purified water is bacteria-free, therefore mayonnaise will keep longer

Instant Clear Jel is a precooked cornstarch product available from bakery wholesalers. It is great for making instant jams and pie fillings with fruit juices and for thickening salad dressings without oil.

Tofu Mayo, Cream Cheese, Salad Dressing, or Sour Cream

In blender:

> ½ tsp. onion powder
> 1 16 oz. brick tofu, rinsed
> ½ cup raw cashews
> ⅓ cup water
> 2 tsp. salt
> 1 tbsp. Brewer's yeast flakes
> 3 tbsp. lemon juice
> pinch garlic powder

Yield: approximately 3 cups

- Blend all ingredients thoroughly
- This must chill to set up
- Reduce water to ¼ cup for "Cream Cheese"
- Increase water to ¾ cup for "Salad Dressing" base; may add cucumber, avocado, tomato paste to this base. Try different herbs for seasoning.
- Use 1 tbsp. more lemon juice for "Sour Cream" and decrease water to ¼ cup

Alpine Cheese

This dairy-free, sliceable cheese has a pleasing texture and taste, plus it's very easy to make.

    1 cup water
    ⅓ cup plus 1 rounded tbsp. Emes unflavored gelatin
    1½ cups boiling water
    2 cups cashews
    ½ cup yeast flakes
    1 tbsp. salt
    2 tsp. onion powder or fresh onion
    ½ tsp. garlic powder
    ½ cup fresh lemon juice
    ½ small carrot, cut in pieces
    5-6 drops butter flavoring, (optional)

Yield: 1 quart

*Do not substitute sugar for Emes gelatin

- Soak gelatin in the 1 cup water in blender while assembling remaining ingredients
- Pour boiling water over soaked gelatin; add remaining ingredients and blend until mixture is the consistency of a creamy sauce with no bits of carrot visible.
- Pour into 1 quart mold; cool slightly
- Cover and refrigerate overnight before turning out and slicing

Walnut Wheat Grumbles

A "hamburger" like substitute that can be used in seasoned tomato sauce for tacos, in spaghetti sauce, lasagne, cream sauce for stroganoff or any place that burger is called for. The wheat and the nuts round out the protein.

> 1 cup walnuts
> 2 cups water
> 2 cups water (rinse blender)
> ½ cup onion flakes, dried
> ½ tsp. garlic powder
> 1 tsp. Spike seasoning
> 1 tsp. salt
> ½ tsp. thyme
> 2 cups bulgar wheat or cracked wheat (crack in blender)

Yield: approximately 2 quarts

- Blend walnuts and 2 cups water until smooth; pour into electric skillet; rinse blender with remaining 2 cups of water
- Add the remaining ingredients
- Simmer 20 minutes, covered, stirring several times
- Spread out on cookie sheet and dry out overnight at 160°
- Store in jars in refrigerator
- To use, soften in any sauce to rehydrate. Excellent meat-like texture and taste.

Seasoning Salt

> 1 cup salt
> 1 tsp. oregano
> 1 bay leaf
> 1 tsp. rosemary
> 2 tsp. onion powder
> 2 tsp. garlic powder
> 4 tsp. celery seed
> 1 tsp. thyme
> ¼ cup chicken-style seasoning
> 2 tsp. marjoram

Yield: Approximately 1½ cups

- Blend all ingredients
- Store in jar

Nature's Milk (#1)
Good for use in cooking

> ⅓ cup soyagen milk powder
> ⅓ cup raw cashews
> 1 cup water

- Pour all ingredients into blender
- Blend thoroughly
- Add 8-10 ice cubes and water to turn blender; blend
- Pour into container. Add water to make 1½ qts.

Nature's Milk (#2)
Great on cereals and desserts; for use in cooking, just blend 1 part cashews with 4 parts water.

> ½ cup cashews
> ¼ cup blanched almonds
> 1½ cups water
> 4 tsp. honey
> 2 tsp. vanilla
> ¼ tsp. salt

- Blend all ingredients
- Add 8-10 ice cubes and water to turn blender; blend
- Pour into container. Add water to make 1½ -2 qts.

For use in cooking, blend one part cashews with four parts water, and omit other ingredients.

SOME FACTS ABOUT CHOLESTEROL

Approximate Amount of Cholesterol in Various Foods

FOOD	CHOLESTEROL mg
Fruits any amount	0
Grains any amount	0
Legumes (peas, beans) any amount	0
Nuts any amount	0
Vegetables any amount	0
Beef, lamb, pork, veal (retail cuts, cooked, w/o skin) 3 oz.	80
Butter, regular ½ oz. 1 tbsp.	35
Buttermilk, non-fat cult. 8 oz. 1 cup	8
Cake, yellow/chocolate 2½ oz. 1/12 – 9″	36
Cheese, cheddar 1 oz. 1″ cube	28
Cheese, processed 1 oz.	20
Chicken, 1 drumstick w/o skin	47
Chicken, 1 drumstick w/skin 2 oz.	39
Chicken, breast w/o skin 3 oz.	63
Chicken, breast w/skin 3 oz.	74
Clams 1 cup, 19 large	114
Cottage cheese, creamed 8 oz. 1 cup pkg.	48
Cottage cheese, uncreamed 8 oz. 1 cup pkg.	13
Crab 1 cup, canned, packed	161
Cream cheese ½ oz. 1 tbsp.	16
Custard, baked 8 oz. 1 cup	278
Egg, whole 1 large	252

FOOD	CHOLESTEROL mg
Egg, yolk from 1 large	252
Fruit Pie 18 — 9″ diam.	0
Halibut, broiled 3 oz.	50
Heavy cream, whipping ½ oz. 1 tbsp.	20
Ice cream, regular 2½ oz. ½ cup	20
Ice milk, hardened 2½ oz. ½ cup	13
Kidneys, 3 oz.	675
Liver, 3 oz.	370
Lobster 1 cup ½″ cubes	123
Mayonnaise, commercial ½ oz. 1 tbsp.	10
Milk, low-fat 8 oz. 1 cup	22
Milk, non-fat	5
Milk, whole 8 oz. 1 cup	34
Oysters 1 cup, 19 — 31 medium	120
Pie, Custard ⅛ — 9″ diam.	120
Pie, Lemon Meringue ⅛ — 9″ diam.	98
Pumpkin ⅛ — 9″ diam.	70
Pudding, cooked 8 oz. 1 cup	32
Ricotta cheese (part skim) 1 oz.	9
Salmon, broiled 3 oz.	35
Sardines, drained	129
Shrimp 1 cup 22 large/76 small	192
Sour cream ½ oz. 1 tbsp.	8
Sponge Cake 2½ oz. 1/12 — 10″ diam.	162
Turkey, dark meat w/o skin 3 oz.	86
Turkey, light meat w/o skin 3 oz.	65
Yogurt, low-fat 1 cup	17

SOME FACTS ABOUT SUGAR

Some Hidden Sources of Sugar

"Food"	Size of Portion	Approximate Tsp. Sugar
Beverages		
Cola drinks	12 oz.	9
Ginger ale	12 oz.	7
Orangeade	8 oz.	5
Root beer	10 oz.	4½
Seven-Up	12 oz.	9
Soda pop	8 oz.	5
Sweet cider	8 oz.	5
Tang	1 cup	6
Kool Aid	1 cup	6
Jams and Jellies		
Apple butter	1 tbsp.	1
Jelly	1 tbsp.	4-6
Orange marmalade	1 tbsp.	4-6
Jam	1 tbsp.	5
Candies		
Chewing gum	1 stick	½
Chocolate mints	piece	2

Adapted from a list developed at University of Iowa. 1974

"Food"	*Size of Portion*	*Approximate Tsp. Sugar*
Fudge	1 oz.	4½
Hard candy	4 oz.	20
Lifesavers	1 pkg.	7
Peanut brittle	1 oz.	3½
Hostess Twinkies	2	18
Gum drop	1	2
Licorice	long rope	6
Pop Tart	1	6
Space-Food Stick	1 stick	2

Fruits and Canned Juices

Fruit cocktail	½ cup	5
Rhubarb, stewed	½ cup	8
Canned apricots	4 halves plus 1 tbsp. syrup	3½
Applesauce	½ cup	2
Canned peaches	2 halves plus 1 tbsp. syrup	3½
Canned fruit juice	½ cup	2
Fruit yogurt	1 cup	6

Sugar and Syrups

Corn syrup	1 tbsp.	3
Karo syrup	1 tbsp.	3
Honey	1 tbsp.	3
Maple syrup	2 tbsp.	5

Cakes, Cookies, and Condiments

Angel Food cake	1 (4 oz.)	7
Applesauce cake	4 oz.	5½
Cheesecake	4 oz.	2
Chocolate cake, iced	4 oz.	10
Coffeecake	4 oz.	4½

"Food"	*Size of Portion*	*Approximate Tsp. Sugar*
Cupcake, iced	1	6
Fruitcake	4 oz.	5
Pound cake	4 oz.	5
Sponge cake	1/10 of cake	6
Chocolate cookies	1	1½
Fig Newtons	1	5
Macaroons	1	6
Oatmeal Cookies	1	2
Chocolate eclair	1	7
Donut, glazed	1	6
Chocolate sauce	2 tbsp.	9
Ketchup	2 tbsp.	1½

Dairy Products

Ice cream	3½ oz.	3½
Ice cream cone	1	3½
Eggnog, all milk	1 cup	4½
Ice cream sundae	1	7
Chocolate milk	1 cup	6
Malted milk shake	10 oz.	5
Sherbet	½ cup	9

Desserts

Apple Cobbler	½ cup	3
Custard	½ cup	2
French pastry	1 (4 oz.)	5
Jello	1 cup	9
Apple pie	1 slice	7
Berry pie	1 slice	10
Cherry pie	1 slice	10
Cream pie	1 slice	4
Custard pie	1 slice	10
Lemon pie	1 slice	7

"Food"	Size of Portion	Approximate Tsp. Sugar
Fruit pie	1 slice	6
Raisin pie	1 slice	13
Bread pudding	½ cup	1½
Chocolate pudding	½ cup	4
Rice pudding	½ cup	5
Brown Betty	½ cup	3
Plain pastry	1 (4 oz.)	3

*Measured in teaspoon equivalents of granulated sugar.

**Exact amounts vary according to commercial product.

Sugar: What's In a Name?

Brown Sugar:	Sucrose crystals covered with a film of syrup.
Confectioner's Sugar:	Powdery sucrose.
Corn Sugar:	Sugar made from cornstarch.
Corn Sweetener:	A liquid sugar made from the breakdown of cornstarch.
Corn Syrup:	A syrup made by the partial breakdown of cornstarch.
Dextrose:	Another name for glucose.
Fructose:	The sugar found in fruit, juices and honey.
Glucose:	A monosaccharide (simple sugar) found in the blood, either derived from digested food or made by the body from other carbohydrates and from protein.
Granulated Sugar:	Sucrose.
Honey:	A syrup made up mostly of fructose.
Invert Sugar:	A combination of sugars found in fruits.
Lactose:	The sugar found in milk.
Maltose:	A sugar formed by the breakdown of starch.
Mannitol:	A sugar alcohol that is broken down in the body the same way as other sugars but absorbed more slowly.
Maple Syrup:	A syrup made from the sap of the sugar maple tree.
Molasses:	Syrup that is separated from raw sugar during processing.
Sorbitol:	A sugar alcohol produced by hydrogenation of glucose and invert sugar and absorbed more slowly than ordinary dietary sugar.
Sorghum:	Syrup made from sorghum grain.
Sucrose:	Table sugar.

Sucrose Content of Commercially
Available Breakfast Cereals

Name	Percent Sucrose by Weight
Less than 10 percent Sugar:	
Shredded Wheat (large biscuit)	1.0
Shredded Wheat (spoon size biscuit)	1.3
Cheerios	2.2
Puffed Rice	2.4
Uncle Sam Cereal	2.6
Wheat Chex	2.6
Grape Nut Flakes	3.3
Puffed Wheat	3.5
Alpen	3.8
Post Toasties	4.1
Product 19	4.1
Corn Total	4.4
Special K	4.4
Wheaties	4.7
Corn Flakes (Kroger)	5.1
Peanut Butter	5.2
Grape Nuts	5.6
Corn Flakes (Food Club)	7.0
Crispy Rice	7.3
Corn Chex	7.5
Corn Flakes (Kellogg)	7.8
Total	8.1
Rice Chex	8.5
Crispy Rice	8.8
Raisin Bran (Skinner)	9.0
Concentrate	9.9

Name	Percent Sucrose by Weight

10-19 Percent Sugar

Rice Crispies (Kellogg)	10.0
Raisin Bran (Kellogg)	10.6
Heartland (with raisins)	13.5
Buckwheat	13.6
Life	14.5
Granola (with dates)	14.5
Franola (with raisins)	14.5
Sugar Frosted Corn Flakes	15.6
40% Bran Flakes (Post)	15.3
Team	15.9
Brown Sugar-Cinnamon Frosted Mini Wheats	16.0
40% Bran Flakes (Kellogg)	16.2
Granola	16.6
100% Bran	16.4

20-29 Percent Sugar

All Bran	20.0
Granola (with Almonds)	21.6
Fortified Oat Flakes	22.2
Heartland	23.1
Super Sugar Chex	24.5
Sugar Frosted Flakes	29.0

30-39 Percent Sugar

Bran Buds	30.2
Sugar Sparkled Cornflakes	32.2
Frosted Mini Wheats	33.6
Sugar Pops	37.3

Name	*Percent Sucrose by Weight*
40-49 Percent Sugar	
Alpha Bits	40.3
Sir Grapefellow	40.7
Super Sugar Crisp	40.7
Cocoa Puffs	43.0
Cap'n Crunch	43.3
Crunch Berries	43.4
Kaboom	43.8
Frankenberry	44.0
Frosted Flakes	44.0
Count Chocula	44.2
Orange Quangaroos	44.7
Quisp	44.9
Boo Berry	45.7
Vanilla Crunch	45.8
Baron Von Redberry	45.8
Cocoa Krispies	45.9
Trix	46.5
Fruit Loops	47.4
Honeycomb	48.8
Pink Panther	49.2
50-59 Percent Sugar	
Cinnamon Crunch	50.3
Lucky Charms	50.4
Cocoa Pebbles	53.5
Apple Jacks	55.0
Fruity Pebbles	55.1
King Vitamin	56.5
More Than 60 Percent Sugar	
Sugar Smacks	61.3
Super Orange Crisp	63.0

APPENDIX C

SOME FACTS ABOUT SALT

The Hidden Salts in Various Foods

"Food"	*Size of Portion*	*Average* mg. of Salt*
Potato/Corn Chips	ind. bag	440
Popcorn, buttered	1 cup	875
Pizza, combination	1 piece	1,725
Peanuts, salted	1 oz.	330
Dill Pickle	1 large	930
Pretzel	5 pieces	625
Green Olives	3	1,250
Pork & Beans	1 cup	2,750
Fried Chicken TV Dinner	1	2,850
Canned Soup (all kinds)	1 cup	2,500
Canned Chili	1 cup	3,385
Macaroni & Cheese (box)	1 cup	1,415
Canned Ravioli	1 cup	3,375
Process Cheese	1 slice	600
Fast-Food Hamburger	1 average	4,250
Hot Dog	1 average	315
Canned Vegatables	½ cup	500
Sauerkraut	½ cup	2,185
Catsup	1 tbsp.	385
Mustard	1 tbsp.	475
Soy Sauce	1 tbsp.	1,870
MSG Seasoned Salts	1 tsp.	1,870

"Food"	Size of Portion	Average* mg. of Salt
Steak Sauce	1 tbsp.	690
Baking Soda	1 tsp.	2,500
Alka Seltzer	2 Tablets	2,500
Bisodol	1 packet	6,750
Bromo Seltzer	1 dose	2,135

*Salt consumption per average American: 18,000 mgms.

U.S. Dietary Goal Recommendation for consumption: about 1 tsp. or 5,000 mgms.

END NOTES

Chapter 2 — The Real Big Mac Attack

1. *Heart Facts* (Dallas: American Heart Association, 1987), 2.
2. Gayle Wilson, M.D. *Atherosclerosis* (Rapidan, VA: Hartland Health Center, 1986). Audio Cassette
3. Ibid.
4. Ibid.
5. *The Story of America* (Pleasantville, NY: The Readers Digest Association, Inc., 1975), 444-458.
6. *Heart Facts*, 2.
7. Ibid., 1.
8. R. B. Birrer et al, "The Mechanism Behind Atherosclerosis," *Modern Medicine* (December-January 1981): 137-138.
9. Wilson.
10. H. Gaspar, "New Aspects of the Pathogenesis of Atherosclerosis," *Current Medical Research and Opinion* (1981) 7:142-155.
11. Wilson.
12. Ibid.
13. "Nutrition for the Fitness Challenge" (Dallas, TX: American Heart Association, 1983), 11.
14. Wilson.
15. Ibid.
16. Ibid.
17. Ibid.
18. Ibid.
19. Ibid.
20. Birrer, 137-138.
21. Wilson.
22. Ibid.
23. P. Puska et al, "Controlled Randomized Trial of the Effect of Dietary Fat on Blood Pressure," *The Lancet* (18 January 83): 1-5.
24. Wilson.
25. D. H. Blankenship, "Will Atheroma Regress With Diet and Exercise?," *The American Journal of Surgery* (June 1981) 141:644-645.
26. Wilson.
27. Ibid.
28. P. T. Williams et al, "Coffee Intake and Elevated Cholesterol and Apoliopoprotein B Levels in Men," *JAMA* (8 March 85), 253:1407-1411.
29. Stella Stavish, "Thomas Preston: Cardiology's Ralph Nader," *Cardio* (February 85): 41-45.

30. Wilson.
31. Ibid.
32. Ibid.
33. Consensus Conference: "Lowering Blood Cholesterol to Prevent Heart Disease," *JAMA* (12 April 85), 253:2080-2097.
34. Ibid.

Chapter 3 — The Big Slowdown to Colon Cancer

1. *Diet, Nutrition, and Cancer* (Washington D.C.: National Academy Press, 1982), 1-3.
2. *Cancer Facts and Figures—1987* (New York: American Cancer Society, 1987), 20.
3. Ibid., 9.
4. Ibid.
5. D. Burkitt, "Some Diseases Characteristic of Modern Civilizations," *British Medical Journal* 1 (1973), 274; and idem., "Dietary Fiber and Disease," *JAMA* (1974) 229:1068.
6. *Diet, Nutrition, and Cancer*, 73.
7. *Dietary Guidelines for Healthy American Adults,* (Dallas, TX: American Heart Association, 1986) 1.
8. Nathan Pritikin, *The Pritikin Program for Diet and Exercise* (New York: Bantam Books, 1979), 9.
9. J. C. Bailer, and E. M. Smith, "Progress Against Cancer" *New England Journal of Medicine* (1986) 314:1226-32.
10. John A. McDougall, *McDougall's Medicine: A Challenging Second Opinion* (Piscataway, NJ: New Century Publications, 1985), 48.
11. Cruse, J. Pet, et al, "Dietary Cholesterol Deprivation Improves Survival and Reduces Incidence of Metastic Colon Cancer in Dimethylhydrazine-Pretreated Rats," *Gut* (1982) 23:594-599.
12. Pritikin, 16-17.
13. *Facts on Colorectal Cancer* (New York: American Cancer Society, 1978), 6.
14. "Why Sugar Continues to Concern Nutritionists," *Tufts U Diet and Nutrition Letter,* Vol. 3, No. 3 (May 1985): 3-6.
15. Ibid., 3.
16. A. M. Thrash and C. L. Thrash, "Nutrition for Vegetarians" (Seale, AL: Thrash Publications, 1982), 63.
17. John Bagdade, "The Effect of Hyperglycemia on Host Defense Mechanism," *Pfizer Laboratories Division* industry publication (January 1972): 28-33.
18. *Diet, Nutrition, and Cancer,* 332.
19. Ibid.
20. "Wrap-Up Fiber," *University of California, Berkeley, Wellness Letter*, Vol. 1, Issue 11 (August 1985): 4-5.
21. Ibid.
22. Ibid.
23. Ibid.
24. K. H. Duncan et al, "The Effects of High and Low Energy Density Diets on Satiety, Energy Intake and Eating Time of Obese and Non-Obese Subjects," *The American Journal of Clinical Nutrition* (May 83), 37:763-767.
25. A. N. Smith et al, "The Effect of Coarse and Fine Canadian Red Spring Wheat and French Soft Wheat Bran on Colonic Motility in Patients with Diverticular Disease," *The American Journal of Clinical Nutrition* (November 1981) 34:2460-2463; and *University of California, Berkeley, Wellness Letter,* p. 4.

26. D. P. Burkitt et al, "Effect of Dietary Fiber on Stools and Transit-Times and its Role in the Causation of Disease," *Lancet* (December 1972), 792:1408-1412.
27. Genesis 1-2.
28. "Eating to Resist Disease," *Healthyourself Seminar* (Dayton, MD: Total Health International, Inc, 1984), 90-91.

Chapter 4 — The Rush to Diabetes

1. Dorothea F. Sims, *Diabetes: Reach for Health and Freedom* (St. Louis: C. V. Mosby Co., 1984), 86.
2. S. H. Kahn and R. Coughlin, "Diabetes in America: Where Do You Fit In?" *Diabetes Forecast Reprint* (1986), DF:361.
3. Ibid.
4. Ibid.
5. *An Introduction: What You Need to Know About Diabetes* (Nashville: American Diabetic Association, 1984), 1-2.
6. L. J. Hirsch and M. E. Molitch, "Diagnosis: Diabetes" *Diabetes Forecast* Reprint (1986), DF:315A.
7. "Report Examines Status of Diabetes in U.S." *Diabetes Dateline,* Vol. 6, No. 5 (September-October 1985): 1-2.
8. Sims, 59; and Giles Monif, "Can Diabetes Mellitis Result from an Infectious Disease?," *Hospital Practice* (March 1973): 124-130.
9. Coughlin.
10. Jesse Roth, "Insulin Receptors in Diabetes," *Hospital Practice* (May 1980): 98-103.
11. Coughlin.
12. Charles and Dudley Kilo, J.D., "Peripheral Arterial Disease," *Diabetes Forecast* (July 1987): 42-47.
13. Ibid.
14. Frederick C. Goety and Thomas H. Hostetter, "Kidney Treatment Today," *Diabetes Forecast Reprint* (1984), DF:317A.
15. Hirsch.
16. Roth.
17. Ibid.
18. Phyllis Crapo and Margaret A. Powers, "Alias: Sugar," *Diabetes Forecast* Reprint (1985), DF:327.
19. Thrash, 41.
20. G. Collier and K. O'Dea, "Effect of Physical Form of Carbohydrate on the Postprandial Glucose, Insulin and Gastric Inhibitory Polypeptide Responses in Type 2 Diabetes," *The American Journal of Clinical Nutrition* (July 1982), 36:10-14.
21. J. S. Skyler, "Diabetes and Exercise: Clinical Implications." *Diabetic Care* (May-June 79), Vol. 2, No. 3; 307-311.
22. Ellen G. White, *The Ministry of Healing* (Nampa, ID: Pacific Press, 1905), 293.
23. Kilo.
24. Ibid.
25. Ibid.
26. Ibid.
27. Ibid.
28. Ibid.
29. Coughlin.
30. D. M. Nathan, et al, "Ice Cream in the Diet of the Insulin-Dependent Diabetic Patients," *JAMA* (1 June 84), Vol. 251, No. 21, 2825-2827.

31. Thrash, 108.
32. Ibid., 26.
33. Peter Banks, "Diabetes at Home on 'Our House,'" *Diabetes Forecast* (May 1987), 40:24.
34. Ibid., 26.

Chapter 5 — One in a Hundred and Your Immune System

1. Jean-François Bach, *Immunology* (New York: John Wiley and Sons, 1979), 797-812.
2. Ibid., 814-819 and 934-936.
3. C. Everett Koop, "Surgeon General's Report on Acquired Immune Deficiency Syndrome," *JAMA* (28 November 86) Vol. 2546, No. 20, 2784-89.
4. *Cancer Facts and Figures* (New York: American Cancer Society, 1987), 3.
5. Peter Jaret, "Our Immune System: The War Within," *National Geographic*, Vol. 169, No. 6 (June 1986): 702-734.
6. Ibid.
7. Ibid.
8. Ibid.
9. Ibid.
10. Ibid.
11. Ibid.
12. Jaret; and Bach, 713.
13. Jaret.
14. Ibid.
15. J. S. Oliver, "AIDS Management: The Federal Role," *Journal of Medical Technology* Vol. 3, No. 3 (1986): 159-164.
16. Gene Antonio, *The AIDS Cover-up?* (San Francisco: Ignatius Press, 1987), 134.
17. "Conference Report, Second International Conference on the Acquired Immune Deficiency Syndrome" *Medical Journal of Australia* (17 November 86): 529.
18. Antonio, 240.
19. Medical News *JAMA* (November 1985), 22:2866.
20. Antonio, 108.
21. Ibid., 98.
22. Ibid., 244-245.
23. Ibid., 24.
24. P. A. Palsson, "Slow Virus Diseases of Animals and Man," ed. by R. H. Kimberlin, (Amsterdam: N. Holland Pub. Co., 1976), 37.
25. J.I. Slaff and J. K. Brubaker, *The AIDS Epidemic: How You Can Protect Yourself and Your Family — Why You Must* (New York: Warner Books, 1985), 173.
26. Ibid., 140.
27. Antonio, 10-11.
28. "Two Get AIDS Virus for Donor's Organ's Which First Tested Safe *The Tennessean*, Nashville, TN (29 May 1987).
29. M. H. Heckler, "The Challenge of the Acquired Immunodeficiency Syndrome," *Annuals of Internal Medicine* (1985), 103:655-656.
30. D. Gleman et al, "AIDS," *Newsweek* (12 August 1984), 22.
31. Antonio, 13.
32. Ibid., 15.
33. Ibid., 16-20.
34. Koop.

35. J. Oleske et al, "Immune Deficiency Syndrome in Children" *JAMA,* Vol. 249, No. 17 (6 May 1983): 2345-2349.
36. A. S. Fauci, "The Acquired Immune Deficiency Syndrome: The Ever-Broadening Clinical Spectrum," *JAMA,* Vol. 249, No. 17 (16 May 1983): 237-238.
37. Koop.
38. "Summary: Recommendations for Preventing Transmission of Infection with HTLV-III/LAV in the Workplace, Leads from the MMWR" *JAMA* (1985), 254:3023-3026.
39. Antonio, 107.
40. R. Rosner, "Is Chemotherapy Carcinogenic?" *Cancer* (1978), 28:57.
41. Jaret.
42. S. J. Schleifer et al, "Suppression of Lymphocyte Stimulation Following Bereavement," *JAMA,* Vol. 250, No. 3 (15 July 1983): 374-377.
43. D.C. McClelland et al, "Stressed Power Motivation, Sympathetic Activation, Immune Function, and Illness," *Journal of Human Stress* (June 1980), 11-18.
44. G. Fernandes, "Nutritional Factors: Modulating Effects on Immune Function and Aging," *Pharmacological Review,* (1984), 36:1235,1295.
45. Ibid.
46. Zane Kime, *Sunlight* (Penryn, CA: World Health Pub, 1980), 102-103; see also Sidney S. Mirvish, "Effects of Vitamin C and E on N-Nitroso Compound Formation, Carcinogenesis and Cancer," *Cancer* (October 15, 1986) 58:1842-1850; and Scott Grundy, "Nutrition" *The Daily Progress* Charlottesville, Virginia (March 18, 1987).
47. M. Sestilli, "Possible Adverse Health Effects of Vitamin C and Ascorbic Acid," *Seminars in Oncology,* Vol. X, No. 3, (September 1983): 299-304; and Kime, 83, 87.
48. D. N. Buell, "Potential Hazards of Selenium as Chemopreventive Agent," *Seminars in Oncology,* Vol. X, No. 3 (September 1983): 311-321.
49. H. B. Simon, "The Immunology of Exercise," *JAMA* (1984), 252:2735-2738.

Chapter 6 — Mything Out on Life or "Do You Have Another Diet Plan for Me to Try?"

1. "Living Without Diet Books," *University of Caifornia, Berkeley, Wellness Letter,* Vol. 1, No. 12 (September. 1985), 1.
2. George Bray, "The Energetics of Obesity," *Medicine and Science in Sports and Exercise* (1983) 15:32-40.
3. Thrash, 27.
4. "Living Without Diet Books."
5. "Guess How Much You Eat? Guess Again?" *Tufts University Diet and Nutrition Letter,* Vol. 3, No.2 (April 1985), 1.

Chapter 7 — Cool, Clear, and Restful: Water and Rest

1. "In the Heat, Drink Up," *University of California, Berkeley, Wellness Letter* Vol. 1, No. 11 (August 1985), 1.
2. Richard Pearce, "Body Fluids," *Runner's World* (April 82): 45-48.
3. S. M. Brooks, *The Sea Inside Us: Water in the Life Processes* (New York: Meredith Press, 1968), 4.

4. Ibid.
5. C. A. Keel and E. Samson Neil, *Wright's Applied Physiology* (New York: Oxford University Press, 1965), 16, 18, 126.
6. "More Energy, Less Fatigue" *Healthyourself Seminar* (Dayton, MD: Total Health International, Inc, 1984), 37-38.
7. "In the Heat, Drink Up."
8. "More Energy, Less Fatigue."
9. Ibid., 42.
10. Ibid., 69-70.
11. Ibid., 44-46.
12. G. C. Pitts et al, "Factors Affecting Work Output in Hot Environments," *American Journal Physiology* (1944), 142:254.
13. Pearce.
14. Ibid.
15. "More Energy, Less Fatigue," 76.
16. "U.S. Food and Nutrition Board. Water Deprivation and Performance of Athletes," *American Journal Clinical Nutrition* (1974) 27:1096-7.
17. "More Energy, Less Fatigue," 40-41.
18. Ibid., 53-54.
19. Thrash, 88.
20. Ibid., 115.
21. "More Energy, Less Fatigue," 60.
22. Thrash, 132.
23. Ibid., 71.
24. "More Energy, Less Fatigue," 69-70.
25. Ibid., 83-84.
26. Pearce.
27. K. Saketkhoo et al, "Effects of Drinking Hot Water, Cold Water, and Chicken Soup on Nasal Mucus Velocity and Nasal Airflow Resistance," *Chest* (October 78) 1074:408-410.
28. "Coffee-Not Guilty," *University of California, Berkeley, Wellness Letter* Vol. 3, No. 6 (March 1987): 2.
29. John A. McDougall, *McDougall's Medicine: A Challenging Second Opinion* (Piscataway, NJ: New Century Pub., Inc., 1984), 113-114.
30. "Coffee-Not Guilty."
31. Raymond and Dorothy Moore, *Homemade Health* (Waco, TX: Word Books, 1986), 112-113; and Thrash, 112.
32. "More Energy, Less Fatigue," 80-83.
33. Ibid.
34. Ibid., 83-84.
35. Ibid., 86-87.
36. Ibid., 84.
37. Thrash, 113.
38. "More Energy, Less Fatigue," 87-89.
39. Ibid.
40. "Wrap Up: Drinking Water," *University of California, Berkeley, Wellness Letter*, Vol. 2, No. 2 (November 1985): 4-5.
41. "Wrap Up: Sleep," *University of California, Berkeley, Wellness Letter* Vol. 1, No. 7 (April 1985): 4-5.
42. Shakespeare, *MacBeth.*
43. Kirstine Adam and January Oswald, "Protein Synthesis, Bodily Renewal and the Sleep-Wake Cycle," *Clinical Science,* 65:561-567.

44. Ibid.
45. Kirstine Adam and January Oswald, "Sleep Helps Healing," *British Medical Journal* (24 November 1984), 289:1400-1401.
46. R. P. Elliot, *Get a Good Night's Sleep* (Englewood Cliff, NJ: Prentice Hall, Inc., 1983), 180.
47. Ibid., 4.
48. P. Goldberg and D. Kaufman, *Natural Sleep* (Emmaus, PA: Rodale Press, 1978), 32.
49. Richard C. Friedman et al, "The Intern and Sleep Loss" *New England Journal of Medicine* Vol. 285, No. 4, (22 July 1971) 201-203.
50. Phil Gunby, "A Drink at Night Keeps Good Slumber at Bay," *JAMA* (7 August 1981), 246:589.
51. John R. Sulton, "Sleep Disturbances at High Altitude," *The Physician and Sports Medicine* (June 1982) 10:79-84.
52. Ibid.
53. Ian Oswald, "Aberrant Sleep: Too Much—Too Little," *Drug Therapy* (July 1976): 28-37.

Chapter 8—Outward Bound: Fresh Air, Sunshine, and Exercise

1. M. Korcok, "Summer Olympics to be Under Ozone Cloud," *JAMA* (17 July 1981): 246:202.
2. Ibid.
3. Ibid.
4. R. Mitchel, "Health Effects of Urban Air Pollution," *JAMA* (14 September 1979) 242:1163-1168.
5. Ibid.
6. Ibid.
7. Ibid.
8. Ibid.
9. Wilson.
10. William G. Cahn, "Sins of Smoking Parents Against Embryos, Infants and Children," *Medical Tribune* (April 1985) 26:1,15.
11. R. B. Birrer, 137-138.
12. Jody Zylke, "Studying Oxygen Life and Death Roles If Taken from or Reintroduced into Tissue," *JAMA* (February 1988) 259:960-965.
13. Kime, 193-194.
14. W. H. Eddy, et. al., "The Effect of Negative Ionization on Transplanted Tumors," *Journal of Cancer Research* (1951), 245.
15. *Why You Should Know About Melanoma* (New York: The American Cancer Society, 1985), 1-2.
16. Kime, 27.
17. *Why You Should Know About Melanoma,* 3.
18. Kime, 92-93.
19. Ibid., 93-110.
20. Ibid., 94-101.
21. Ibid., 75-89.
22. S. A. Levine and P. M. Kidd, "Beyond Antioxidant Adaptation: A Free Radical-Hypoxia Colonal Thesis of Cancer Causation," *Journal of Orthomolecular Psychiatry* (1985) Vol. 14, No. 3; and Kime, 75-114.
23. *Why You Should Know About Melanoma,* 2.

24. Kime, 81-88.
25. Ibid.
26. C. Garland et al, "Dietary Vitamin D and Calcium and Risk of Colorectal Cancer," *Lancet* (February 1984), 1:307; and C. F. Garland and F. C. Garland, "Do Sunlight and Vitamin D Reduce the Likelihood of Colon Cancer?" *International Journal of Epidemiology* (1980) 9:227-231.
27. R. M. Allen and T. K. Cureton, "Effect of Ultraviolet Radiation on Physical Fitness," *Archives of Physical Medicine* (October 1945), 640-644.
28. Kime, 38.
29. Ibid., 39.
30. R. Altschul, "Ultraviolet Irradiation and Cholesterol Metabolism" *Arch. Phys. Med.* (1955) 36:394.
31. A. Ohkawara et al, "Glycogen Metabolism Following Ultraviolet Irradiation," *The Journal of Investigative Dermatology* (1972) 59:264-268.
32. Kime, 112-115.
33. Ibid., 41-42.
34. Ibid., 89.
35. M. Moggio et al, "Wound Infections in Patients Undergoing Total Hip Arthroplasty," *Archives of Surgery* (July 79) 114:815-823.
36. Kime, 221.
37. Garland and Garland, 227-231.
38. Allen and Cureton, 640-644.
39. Ohkawara, 264-268.
40. Kime, 172-183.
41. Ibid., 172-185.
42. Zylke, 960-965.
43. Kime, 38.
44. Ibid., 38, 89.
45. Ibid., 75-89.
46. M. Moggio, 815-823.
47. F. Ellinger, "The Influence of Ultraviolet Rays on the Body Weight," *Radiology* (1939) 32:157-160; and Kime, 22.
48. Roth Matthew et al, "A Clinical Trial of the Effects of Oral Beta-Carotene on the Response of Human Skin to Solar Radiation," *The Journal of Investigative Dermatology* (1972) 59:349-353.
49. Kime, 148-150.
50. Ibid., 152.
51. Thrash, 113.
52. Skyler, 307-311.
53. Ibid.
54. Mike Moore, "Endorphins and Exercise: A Puzzling Relationship" *The Physician and Sports Medicine* Vol. 10, No. 2 (February 1982), 111-114; and M. A. Short et al, "Effects of Physical Conditioning on Self-Concept of Adult Obese Males" *Physical Therapy* Vol. 64, No. 2 (February 1984), 194-198.
55. M. Gerhardsson et al, "Sedentary Jobs and Colon Cancer" *American Journal of Epidemiology* Vol. 123, No. 5 (1986), 775-780.
56. Philip Hage, "Diet and Exercise Program for Coronary Heart Disease: Better Late Than Never" *The Physician and Sports Medicine,* Vol. 10, No. 9 (September 1982), 121-126.
57. H. B. Simon, "The Immunology of Exercise," *JAMA* (1984), 252:2735-2738.

58. H. A. deVries, "Tranquilizer Effect of Exercise: A Critical Review," *The Physician and Sports Medician,* Vol. 9, No. 11 (November 81), 47-55.
59. Ibid.

Chapter 9 — Eat to Live: Nutrition and Self-Control

1. Peter Jenkins, *Across China* (Spring Hill, TN and New York: Sweet Springs/Morrow, 1986), 89.
2. George Bray, "Management Options in Obesity," *Hospital Practice* (April 1982), 104A.
3. Ibid.
4. Ibid.
5. "Survey of Physical Activity," Centers for Disease Control, Atlanta, GA (1985).
6. Bray.
7. A. C. Guyton, *Textbook of Medical Physiology* (Philadelphia: W. B. Saunders, Co., 1976), 761.
8. "Clues to Better Digestion," *Healthyourself Seminar* (Dayton, MD: Total Health International, Inc, 1984), 44-46.
9. Ibid., 47.
10. Duncan et al, 763-767.
11. Thrash, 20.
12. "Clues to Better Digestion," 57-65.
13. Guyton, 882.
14. Thrash, 88.
15. "Clues to Better Digestion," 64-65, 72.
16. Ibid., 33-38.
17. Thrash, 13, 22, 35.
18. G. Fernandes, "Nutritional Factors: Modulating Effects on Immune Function and Aging," *Pharmacological Review,* Vol. 36 (1984): 1235-1295.
19. Thrash, 111, 115.
20. "Living with Circadian Rhythms," *Healthyourself Seminar* (Dayton, MD: Total Health International, Inc, 1984), 41-50.
21. Ibid.
22. "Clues to Better Digestion," 96-98.
23. Barbara J. Rolls, "Experimental Analyses of the Effects of Variety in a Meal on Human Feeding," *The American Journal of Clinical Nutrition,* Vol. 42 (November 84): 932-939.
24. Ibid.

Chapter 10 — Inside Nutritional Myths: More on Food

1. Thrash, 3.
2. Ibid., 51.
3. Ibid., 98.
4. Ibid., 52.
5. Ibid.
6. Sang Lee, M.D., *Protein* (Weimar, CA: Weimar Institute, 1985). Audio Cassette.
7. Ibid.; and Thrash, 55-56.
8. Ibid., 37.

9. Lee.
10. Thrash, 51-59.
11. Ibid.
12. Naomi Levin et al, "Energy Intake and Body Weight in Ovo-lacto Vegetarians," *Journal of Clinical Gastroenterology,* Vo. 8, No. 4 (1986), 451-453; P. M. Dodson et al, "High Fibre and Lowfat Diets in Diabetic Mellitis," *British Journal of Nutrition* (1981) 46:289-94; Duncan et al, 763-767; Collier and O'Deo, 10-14.
13. Thrash, 98.
14. Gary E. Fraser et al, "The Effect of Various Vegetable Supplements on Serum Cholesterol," *The American Journal of Clinical Nutrition* (July 1981), 34:1272-1277.
15. Thrash, 33.
16. Ibid.
17. Moore, 10.
18. Collier and O'Deo.
19. Ibid.
20. John Bogdade, *The Effect of Hyperglycemia on Host Defense Mechanism,* Pfizer Laboratories Division (January 1972), 28-33.
21. Thrash, 34.
22. David Reuben, "The Save Your Life Diet," (New York: Ballentine Books, 1975), 81.
23. Burkitt., 1408-1412.
24. "Wrap-Up: Fiber," *University of California, Berkeley, Wellness Letter,* Vol. 1, Issue 11 (August 85): 4-5.
25. Ibid.
26. Ibid.
27. I. H. Ullrich and M. J. Albrick, "Lack of Effect of Dietary Fiber on Serum Lipids, Glucose and Insulin in Healthy Young Men Fed High Starch Diets," *The American Journal of Clinical Nutrition* (July 82), 36:1-9.
28. K. H. Duncan et al, "The Effects of High and Low Energy Density Diets on Satiety, Energy Intake and Eating Time of Obese and Non-Obese Subjects," *The American Journal of Clinical Nutrition* (May 1983); 37:763-767.
29. Thrash, 44-47.
30. Ibid., 48.
31. Ibid., 46.
32. Ibid.
33. John A. and Mary A. McDougall, *The McDougall Plan* (Piscataway, NJ: New Century Pub., 1983), 6.
34. Moore, 53.
35. Kime, 126-130.
36. Thrash, 37.
37. Ibid., 3.
38. McDougall, 2.
39. Thrash, 71-72.
40. Lee.
41. Thrash, 132.
42. Warren Peters and Gayle Wilson, *Hartland Heartsavers* (Rapidan, VA: Hartland Institute, 1984), 40-41.
43. Ibid.
44. Ibid.
45. Ibid.
46. Thrash, 74-75.

47. D. N. Buell, "Potential Hazards of Selenium as a Chemopreventative Agent," *Seminars in Oncology,* Vol. 10, No. 3: (September 1983), 311-321.

48. Thrash, 76.

49. Ibid., 76-77.

50. Reported to Author by Dr. Warren Peters who had personal conversation with Dr. Victor Herbert.

51. McDougall, 39-40 and Thrash, 66-69.

52. Ibid.

53. Victor Herbert, "Biology of Disease: Megaloblastic Anemias," *Laboratory Investigation* (1985), 52:3-19.

54. T. Kummet and F. L. Meykens, "Vitamin A: A Potential Inhibitor of Human Cancer," *Seminars in Oncology,* Vol. 10, No. 3 (September 83): 281-289.

55. Thrash, 68.

56. Ibid., 68, 132.

57. Herbert.

58. Thrash, 68-69.

59. M. J. Albert et al, "Vit B-12 Synthesis by Human Small Intestinal Bacteria," *Nature* (21 February 1980), 283:781-782.

60. "Some Diseases of Cattle Transmitted to Man Through Milk," *Journal of American Veterinary Medical Association* (1931), 78:500-505.

61. "The Jungle of Meat Technology," *Tufts University Diet and Nutrition Letter,* Vol. 3, No. 2 (April 1985), 3.

62. Ibid.

63. Ibid.

64. Ibid.

65. D. A. Snowdon et al, "Meat Consumption and Fatal Ischemic Heart Disease," *Preventive Medicine* (1984) 13:490-500.

66. Frank M. Sacks et al, "Effects of Ingestion of Meat on Plasma Cholesterol of Vegetarians," *JAMA* (7 August 1981), 246:640-644.

67. Agatha and Calvin Thrash, *The Animal Connection: Cancer and Other Disease from Animals and Foods of Animal Origin* (Seale, AL: Thrash Pub., 1983), 109-112.

68. "Food Poisoning and Poisonous Foods," *Emergency Medicine,* (October 1977), 195; see also "Diphyllobothriasis," *American Family Physician* (September 1979), 20(3):127-128.

69. Ibid.

70. Keaven M. Anderson et al, "Cholesterol and Mortality: Thirty Years of Follow-up from the Framingham Study," *JAMA,* Vol. 257, No. 16 (24 April 1987), 2176-2180.

71. Frank M. Sacks et al, "Plasma Lipoprotein Levels in Vegetarians: The Effect of Ingestion of Fats from Dairy Products," *JAMA,* Vol. 254, No. 10 (13 September 1985), 1337-1341.

Chapter 12 — Basic Food Facts

1. *Hartland Health Center Manual,* (Rapidan, VA: Hartland Institute, 1984), 65.

2. Ibid., 67.

3. Ibid., 39.

RESOURCES

If you would like information about any of the following:

- Living Well Seminars, highlighting the principles and the program outlined in this book;
- Centers in your area offering live-in "health-conditioning" lifestyle programs;
- Bosch Kitchen Machines or Magic Mill flour mills; or
- Water Purification Systems for the home . . .

. . . please contact the Martins in writing at:

Living Well Enterprises
P.O. Box 3584
Frederick, MD 21701

COLOPHON

The typeface for the text of this book is *Baskerville*. Its creator, John Baskerville (1706-1775), broke with tradition to reflect in his type the rounder, yet more sharply cut lettering of eighteenth-century stone inscriptions and copy books. The type foreshadows modern design in such novel characteristics as the increase in contrast between thick and thin strokes and the shifting of stress from the diagonal to the vertical strokes. Realizing that this new style of letter would be most effective if cleanly printed on smooth paper with genuinely black ink, he built his own presses, developed a method of hot-pressing the printed sheet to a smooth, glossy finish, and experimented with special inks. However, Baskerville did not enter into general commercial use in England until 1923.

Substantive editing by George Grant and Steven Samson
Copy editing by Grace Herron and Lynn Hawley
Cover design by Kent Puckett Associates, Atlanta, Georgia
Typography by Thoburn Press, Tyler, Texas
Printed and bound by Maple-Vail Book Manufacturing Group
Manchester, Pennsylvania
Cover Printing by Weber Graphics, Chicago, Illinois